WALKING - - - - - →
PHILADELPHIA

30 Tours of Art, Architecture, History, and Little-Known Gems

Natalie Pompilio and Tricia Pompilio

 WILDERNESS PRESS . . . *on the trail since 1967*

Walking Philadelphia: 30 Tours of Art, Architecture, History, and Little-Known Gems
First edition, first printing

Copyright © 2017 by Natalie Pompilio and Tricia Pompilio

Distributed by Publishers Group West
Manufactured in the United States of America

Cartography and cover design: Scott McGrew; map data: OpenStreetMap
Interior design: Lora Westberg; typesetting: Annie Long
Cover and interior photos: Tricia Pompilio; photo on p. 160 by Scott Biales
Project editor: Holly Cross
Copy editor: Kate Johnson
Proofreader: Rebecca Henderson
Indexer: Rich Carlson

Library of Congress Cataloging-in-Publication Data

Names: Pompilio, Natalie, author. | Pompilio, Tricia, 1975- author.
Title: Walking Philadelphia : 30 tours of art, architecture, history, and
    little-known gems / Natalie and Tricia Pompilio.
Other titles: Walking Philadelphia, thirty tours of art, architecture,
    history, and little-known gems
Description: First edition. | Birmingham, AL : Wilderness Press, [2017]
Identifiers: LCCN 2016053508 | ISBN 9780899977287 (pbk.)
Subjects: LCSH: Philadelphia (Pa.)—Tours. | Philadelphia (Pa.)—Guidebooks.
    | Walking—Pennsylvania—Philadelphia—Guidebooks. | Historic
    buildings—Pennsylvania—Philadelphia—Guidebooks. | Historic
    sites—Pennsylvania—Philadelphia—Guidebooks.
Classification: LCC F158.18 .P66 2017 | DDC 917.48/1104—dc23
LC record available at https://lccn.loc.gov/2016053508

Published by: **WILDERNESS PRESS**
              An imprint of AdventureKEEN
              2204 First Ave. S., Suite 102
              Birmingham, AL 35233
              800-443-7227, fax 205-326-1012

Visit wildernesspress.com for a complete list of our books and for ordering information. Contact us at our website, at facebook.com/wildernesspress1967, or at twitter.com/wilderness1967 with questions or comments. To find out more about who we are and what we're doing, visit blog .wildernesspress.com.

Cover photo: Swann Memorial Fountain in Logan Square (see Walk 4, page 22)

SAFETY NOTICE: Although Wilderness Press and the authors have made every attempt to ensure that the information in this book is accurate at press time, they are not responsible for any loss, damage, injury, or inconvenience that may occur to anyone while using this book. You are responsible for your own safety and health while following the walking trips described here.

Dedication

For Mom
Patricia Pompilio
January 24, 1944–July 18, 2014

When next we meet, we'll walk together.

Acknowledgments

From Natalie: One advantage of writing about Philadelphia is the wealth of information easily found online and in the library. Writing this guide would have been much less enjoyable if I hadn't had Hidden City Philadelphia, Naked Philly, and the Association of Public Art. *The Philadelphia Inquirer* and *The Philadelphia Daily News,* both found at philly. com, were also essential. I found some lovely snark published in *Philadelphia* magazine. The Free Library of Philadelphia was a great resource/makeshift office. Please see the bibliography at the end for further reading. I apologize if I forgot anyone.

Thanks to everyone at AdventureKEEN—Tim Jackson, Holly Cross, Kate Johnson, Amber Henderson, Scott McGrew, Annie Long, Lora Westberg, and Tanya Sylvan—for editorial, production, and marketing support and for understanding when the book was temporarily derailed. Barri Bronston, author of *Walking New Orleans,* provided encouragement.

Some of the city's best shared two already-organized walks, with much appreciation to Jane Golden of the Philadelphia Mural Arts Program, Cari Feiler Bender of Relief Communications, and Cara Schneider of Visit Philadelphia. Cari and Cara never responded to e-mails—as they could have —with, "That's a dumb question" or "Please stop e-mailing me."

I very much appreciate the friends who took time away from their busy lives and families to show me around their neighborhoods. Dante Zappala's tour of Mount Airy was made even more fabulous by his childhood insights. Paint Nite bestie Christy Speer LeJeune made Fairmount manageable and fun. Fon Wang provided her architecture insights and Chinatown history while letting LeiLei be my friend.

My father, Lou Pompilio, promised to buy multiple copies of the book, but he did so when he thought photos of him were included. Look, Dad! I got your name in! I'm thrilled my sister, Tricia Pompilio, could use this outlet for her fabulous photos. I hope this leads to endless opportunities. Thanks to Fred and Lynn for the cell phone thingy that meant I didn't drop mine while riding around town. I had the support of Team Barnett/Fletcher, Katie's kettlebell class, and too many others to list. Rocky and Spike, you were faithful companions/obstructions throughout the writing process. Lisa Wathen, always my biggest cheerleader, read the finished tours and called them brilliant when they weren't. That's a friend.

A big shout-out to my faves: Fiona, Luna, and Poppy Savarese and Will, Maddie, and Nora Paxson. It's hard to be stressed when talking about Noisette and the No Nut Shop, playing Mr. Bowl, or making up another story about the Chewys.

Finally, I want to thank my husband, Jordan Barnett. During the mad push to finish, he made maps, made dinner, and made me laugh. Jordo, our relationship's truly special.

From Tricia: First, thank you to my talented older sister, Natalie, for making this happen. Although you were less than thrilled at my arrival 40 years ago, you have never wavered in your support. Thank you to Rochelle Litman, my friend and neighbor. You listened patiently when I was overwhelmed, drove me around the city for hours, and have been a constant cheerleader as I start my new career.

My kids: Fi, Lu, and Poppy. You inspire me every day. I love you more than all the stars in the sky. And lastly, thank you to my husband, Vince. Your unwavering support, love, and patience is astounding. You never complain when I disappear into my office for hours, run off on weekends for sessions, or throw my heavy camera bag on your back. I'll back you up always.

Author's Note

There are a lot of great things about living in Philadelphia. Being able to walk almost everywhere I need to go is one of them. The gym, the post office, the doctor and dentist, the grocery store, the open-air market, the pharmacy, my sister's house, my nieces' school, and more restaurants and bars than I can quickly count—none of those places is more than 1 mile from my home.

This city has hosted some of my life's biggest milestones. I thought I knew a lot about it, too, having worked here as a professional journalist and lived here as a nonprofessional nosy person since November 2002. I was so wrong.

Researching different neighborhoods and buildings, and the people behind them, I often found myself falling down the rabbit hole, digging deeper and deeper because it was all so interesting and new. More than once, I'd emerge from reading an original historic-designation nomination form or news clippings from the 1920s to find I'd spent more than an hour on a single stop on a single tour. I couldn't stop myself: I love tidbits and odd facts, and I'd get so excited by each one.

I was also constantly distracted because I kept thinking how tour 31—"Natalie Pompilio"—might read. One of the tours will take you within a block of my home. Another passes the hotel where my husband and I married. A third brings you to my nieces' school, and a fourth passes in front of my sister's house. I should probably include her address in case you need a bathroom.

I tried to write a walking guide that I would like to read, one that's fun and funny but also educational with a lot of "Wow. I didn't know that" moments. I like to imagine readers stopping in their tracks, in the middle of Rittenhouse Square or in Fishtown, and calling a friend to say, "I have to tell you about the cool thing I just read."

This book is not the definitive Philadelphia walking guide. It's a good one, yes, and a great introduction to the city. But to be definitive, it would need to include more of the city's famed neighborhoods. I started plotting my tours at the city's center and never reached the edges. Perhaps in a second edition? Until then, enjoy.

—*Natalie*

Table of Contents

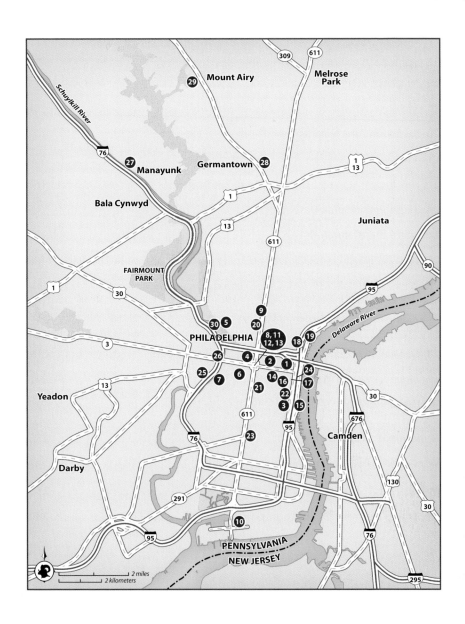

Introduction

Philadelphia is having a moment. That's not completely true. It's been having moments for the last 250 years, but people outside the city are only now catching on.

Philly wins at early American history. It just does. The Declaration of Independence and the US Constitution? Written here. The first seat of national government? Here. In other cities, Benjamin Franklin is just that guy on the $100 bill. Here, he's a local.

More recently, Pope Francis dropped by for a visit. Soon after, the city made history again, when, for the first time, a major political party chose a woman as its presidential nominee during a convention here. The first UNESCO World Heritage site in the United States? We'll take that, too.

For too long, many saw Philadelphia as New York's sad little sister. But consider this: travel authority Lonely Planet ranked Philadelphia the best place to visit in the United States in 2016, citing the city's ability to retain "its historic roots and gritty flavor, as well as its affordability—a pleasant surprise for a city so cosmopolitan and accessible." *Condé Nast Traveler* put Philadelphia second on its list of "The Best Shopping Cities in the World" in 2015 (Barcelona, Spain, was No. 1.) Philadelphia's Fairmount Park is almost five times as large as Manhattan's Central Park.

Little sister's all grown up. Come see what you're missing.

Independence Hall is where the Declaration of Independence was signed and the US Constitution was ratified.

1 Independence National Park:
America's Most Historic Square Mile

BOUNDARIES: Chestnut St., Race St., N. Sixth St., N. Second St.
DISTANCE: 1.2 miles
DIFFICULTY: Easy
PARKING: There are multiple pay lots in the area.
PUBLIC TRANSIT: The subway has a stop at Fifth and Market Sts.

Philadelphia is where the Founding Fathers signed the Declaration of Independence and ratified the US Constitution, Benjamin Franklin operated a printing press and ran the local post office while experimenting with electricity, and George Washington lived and worked for much of his presidency. The city is proud of its role in the shaping of America.

Walk Description

Begin at the ❶ **Free Quaker Meeting House** at the corner of Arch and Fifth Streets. Philadelphia founder William Penn, who lent his family name to the

Commonwealth of Pennsylvania, was a Quaker. Also referred to as Friends, Quakers believe in living simply and serving others. They are pacifists. Persecuted for Quaker practices in England, Penn intended his new city to welcome all religions.

During the Revolutionary War, some Quakers went against their faith and fought. They were later asked to leave their congregations, so they renamed themselves the Free Quakers and built this Georgian brick gathering place in 1783. The interior has two original benches.

Continue on Arch Street to the ❷ **National Constitution Center,** the only museum dedicated to the US Constitution. Visitors are first treated to a live theatrical performance known as "Freedom Rising," which looks at US history and the country's development since the Constitution's ratification in 1787. Many exhibits are interactive, allowing guests to vote on Supreme Court cases or swear the presidential oath of office. The main exhibition area ends in Signers' Hall, which has 42 life-size statues of the men who signed the Constitution, including James Madison and Alexander Hamilton. While towering in thought, they were short in life.

Cross Arch Street to ❸ **Christ Church Burial Ground,** the final resting place of prominent Colonial and Revolution-era leaders, including five Declaration of Independence signatories and the founders of the United States Navy. Benjamin Franklin's grave is easily viewed through the iron fence. Many people toss pennies onto Franklin's flat stone, a nod to the proverb he made famous: "A penny saved is a penny earned." About 75,000 coins are tossed each year.

Cross Arch Street again. The historic marker in front of the United States Mint marks the former headquarters of the Female Anti-Slavery Society, cofounded by Lucretia Mott and others in 1833. "We deem it our duty as professing Christians to manifest our abhorrence of the flagrant injustice and deep sin of slavery by united and vigorous exertions" read the organization's constitution. The society disbanded in 1870 after ratification of the 15th amendment, which granted African American men the right to vote.

At 239 Arch St., the ❹ **Betsy Ross House** features a costumed Betsy reenactor who works in the upholstery shop and recounts the adventures of the entrepreneur who made the nation's first flag. Nicknamed the Little Rebel, Ross also produced munitions here. Questions about the veracity of the flag claim were quashed in 2014, when curators at Washington's Mount Vernon estate found a receipt showing Ross's shop made beddings for Washington's Virginia home. Legend has it that a few months later Washington asked Ross to create a flag with six-pointed stars. Ross folded a piece of paper and, in one snip, created the five-pointed star seen on today's flag.

Continue to ❺ **Elfreth's Alley,** between Race and Arch Streets, the oldest continuously inhabited residential block in the country. The 32 buildings on this narrow cobblestone street were built between 1720 and 1830. The Elfreth's Alley Museum prides itself on being "one of the few landmarks dedicated to the every day American," as the city's tourism board notes. Residents open their homes to the public twice a year, in December and June.

Return to North Second Street and turn right. ❻ **Christ Church** was founded in 1695 and is called the nation's church, with notable early worshippers including George Washington. Still an active church, the pastor boasts there's been a Sunday service here every weekend for more than 300 years. The children's book *Ben and Me,* published in 1938 and then made into a film, tells the story of a church mouse named Amos who contributed to Ben Franklin's career. Visiting children still ask to see the prayer book Amos allegedly nibbled.

Elfreth's Alley is the oldest continuously inhabited street in the country.

Continue on North Second Street, which changes to South Second Street as you cross Market Street. Turn right on Market Street. Spend a little time in Philadelphia and it's clear the city is freaky for Franklin. The ❼ **Benjamin Franklin Museum and Franklin Court** stand at the site of Franklin's home, which he called his niche. None of that original structure remains, but outlines on the ground show where it stood. Franklin, founder of the United States Postal

Christ Church is sometimes called the nation's church.

Service, was appointed the first Postmaster General in 1775. Cards and letters mailed here are hand-stamped with the B. Free Franklin seal.

Exit via Chestnut Street and cross the road to **8 Carpenters' Hall,** where the First Continental Congress was held in 1774, or as local history buffs call the gathering, "the one that didn't get anything done." (The Declaration of Independence was adopted a year later during the Second Continental Congress.)

Take a look at the tourism placards around the Georgian building. One shows men talking in small groups as a cat walks into the frame in the bottom right-hand corner. Is this the First Continental Cat?

Leave Carpenters' Hall and turn left onto Chestnut Street. The **9 Second Bank of the United States,** one of the first Greek Revival buildings in the country, was completed in the 1820s. It houses a free portrait gallery. (The First Bank of the United States is a few blocks away at 120 S. Third St.)

Continue on Chestnut Street to **10 Independence Hall,** site of the Second Constitutional Congress. The Declaration of Independence and the US Constitution were both signed here. Today, the hall is a centerpiece of the city's July Fourth celebrations and a tourism hub. When Pope Francis visited Philadelphia in 2015, he gave a speech about immigration on its steps. There are free tours that require timed tickets, available at the Independence Visitor Center. Go early to get one.

Continue to South Sixth Street and turn right. **11 Liberty Bell Center** is at the corner. Designed in 1751, the bell was cast in London and arrived to take its place atop the Pennsylvania State House—now Independence Hall—in 1753. It weighs more than 2,000 pounds, the clapper alone topping 40 pounds. The infamous crack first developed in the 1840s. No tickets are required to enter the Liberty Bell's pavilion, but lines are long during the summer.

Walk along South Sixth Street to The President's House, at Sixth and Market Streets. The brick mansion that once stood here housed George Washington for seven years and John Adams for three before the capital moved to Washington, DC. In 2007, a major excavation uncovered the foundations of the back buildings, including slave quarters. Exhibits in this open-air pavilion feature these enslaved workers. The tour ends here, across from Independence Visitor Center, where you can get maps, tickets, and other information.

The National Constitution Center is the only museum dedicated to this founding document.

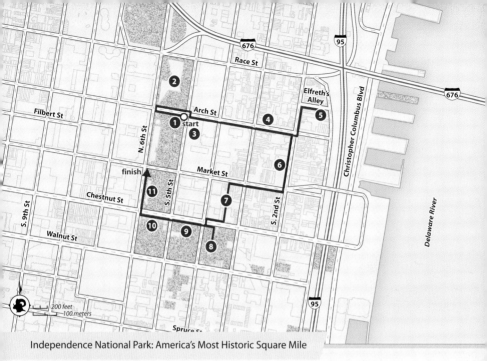

Independence National Park: America's Most Historic Square Mile

Points of Interest

1 Free Quaker Meeting House 500 Arch St., 215-629-5801, nps.gov/inde

2 National Constitution Center 525 Arch St., 215-409-6600, constitutioncenter.org

3 Christ Church Burial Ground Arch and N. Fifth Sts.

4 Betsy Ross House 239 Arch St., 215-686-1252, historicphiladelphia.org/betsy-ross-house/what-to-see

5 Elfreth's Alley N. Second St. between Race and Arch Sts.

6 Christ Church 20 N. American St., 215-922-1695, christchurchphila.org

7 Benjamin Franklin Museum and Franklin Court 317 Chestnut St., 267-514-1522, nps.gov/inde

8 Carpenters' Hall 320 Chestnut St., 215-925-0167, carpentershall.org

9 Second Bank of the United States 420 Chestnut St.

10 Independence Hall 520 Chestnut St., 215-965-2305, nps.gov/inde

11 Liberty Bell Center S. Sixth and Market Sts., 215-965-2305, nps.gov/inde

Eric Okdeh's *How We Fish* was designed to spur workforce development and job creation.

2 Chinatown:
A Bustling Yet Tight-Knit Community

BOUNDARIES: Vine St., Arch St., N. 11th St., N. Eighth St.
DISTANCE: 1.1 miles
DIFFICULTY: Easy
PARKING: Street parking in this area is difficult. There are pay lots nearby.
PUBLIC TRANSIT: SEPTA bus lines that stop in Chinatown include the 23, 47, 48, and 61. The SEPTA Chinatown subway stop is also nearby.

Philadelphia's Chinatown was established in the 1870s when Chinese immigrants from the West Coast moved east to escape growing anti-Chinese sentiment and violence, a migration known as The Driving Out.

Today this is the third-largest Chinatown on the East Coast. Residents have battled multiple government attempts to upend it and have largely avoided the gentrification that has occurred in the Chinatowns of New York and Boston. About 3,000 people live here, the vast majority of Asian descent, including those of Korean, Vietnamese, Burmese, Japanese, and Malaysian origin. It's a tight-knit group. They say if you bring any 20 neighbors together, 5 of them will be related—or at least as close as family.

Walk Description

Start at ① **Chinatown Friendship Gate,** which rises four stories then curves over North 10th Street at Arch Street. This 40-foot-tall authentic Chinese gate, dedicated in 1984, was a gift from Philadelphia's sister city, Tianjin, China. The multicolored carvings include dragons and a phoenix, and the four Chinese characters spell out "Philadelphia Chinatown." In 2008, artisans from Tianjin spent four months restoring the gate. They used traditional Chinese methods, including gallons of fresh pigs' blood as paint primer.

Walk north on North 10th Street. Note the sidewalk panels with the Chinese symbol for prosperity in red outlined in black. These can also be seen on the low wall separating Chinatown from the Vine Street Expressway.

The building at 125 N. 10th St. was originally built in 1831 and housed the Chinatown YMCA. It was owned by Chinese-born T. T. Chang, known as "the mayor of Chinatown" for his work improving residents' lives. Changes to the original building include a jade-colored glazed tile awning on the first floor, red balconies, a gabled roof, and red entry doors with lion's-head door knockers. Inscribed to the door's right is "1970" and the corresponding Chinese calendar year of "4668." That's when the building exterior was given Mandarin Palace accents by C. C. Yang, an influential 20th-century architect.

Turn left onto Cherry Street. ② **Fo Shou Temple** is the city's newest Buddhist temple, featuring red columns of coiling dragons and flying eaves. Open daily, the first floor features three golden Buddhas, while the top has an ancestral shrine, a nod to the Chinese practice of combining ancestor worship and Confucianism. (You'll see similar ancestral altars in local businesses.)

Return to North 10th Street. For a beverage, stop at ③ **Tea Dó,** a contemporary teahouse offering bubble teas and snacks. Across the street, the Philadelphia Fire Department's Engine 20/Ladder 23 is known as the House of Dragons. Why would a flame-spewing animal be the official symbol of an organization dedicated to fighting fires? Because in Chinese mythology, dragons control water, including rain and the flow of water from a hose. Dragons bring life-giving water to the people who honor and respect them while punishing enemies with hurricanes and floods.

Continue on North 10th Street, turning left on Race Street. Note the Chinese characters spelling out the road's name. ❹ **David's Mai Lai Wah** is one of the neighborhood's original late-night dining spots, open most days until 4 a.m. The owner recently admitted he sometimes leaves work before dawn and heads to South Philly to grab a cheesesteak.

Continue on Race Street. The building at 1010–1014 formerly housed the Heywood Chair Factory, which began operation in 1892. The factory, known for its high-quality products, currently houses condominiums and is an example of how buildings from the city's manufacturing days have been repurposed.

❺ **Dim Sum Garden** specializes in *xiao long bao,* or soup dumplings from Shanghai. Owner Shizhou Da says she is descended from the first chef to make soup dumplings and hers is an original recipe passed down through five generations. Da worked in restaurants in China for 30 years and has made dumplings at this location since 2013. Fans recommend the Shanghai crab or the pork soup dumplings.

Turn right on North 11th Street. Pass ❻ **Yakitori Boy,** an *izakaya* (a Japanese pub serving small plates and alcohol) and upscale karaoke lounge with private rooms. Cross Spring Street, passing two Vietnamese restaurants, another nod to the neighborhood's diversity.

The mural on the side of the 6th Police District, North 11th and Winter Streets, is dedicated to officer Daniel Faulkner, who was killed on the job in 1981.

Turn left onto Vine St. ❼ *Colors of Light: Gateway to Chinatown* uses images of a dragon, scroll, and woman's face to portray Chinatown's past, present, and future. Note that the dragon extends beyond the wall. The mural's location is significant as this area was part of the site of a proposed Major League Baseball stadium in 2000.

Turn right, crossing the Vine Street Expressway. On the opposite corner, look left to see the Asian Arts Initiative, a multidisciplinary arts center and community gathering space. When local officials proposed razing parts of the neighborhood for a baseball stadium, a casino, and a prison over the last two decades, this organization helped rally resistance.

Turn right on Vine Street, and continue past North 10th Street. Dedicated in 1941, ❽ **Holy Redeemer Chinese Catholic Church and School** was the first in the Western Hemisphere built specifically for Chinese Catholics. Today about 200 people attend Sunday services, and Masses are offered in English, Cantonese, and Mandarin.

Take 10th Street south across the westbound lanes of the Vine Street Expressway to 10th Street Plaza, where two seven-ton Chinese foo dogs stand guard. When the plaza was dedicated in 2011, a Buddhist monk dabbed red ink on the lions' faces and backs to awaken them as neighborhood protectors.

The statue of Lin Zebu honors the scholar known for his opposition to opium smuggling. In 1838, he supervised the confiscation of 20,000 chests of opium marked for Britain, destroying the drug. This action sparked the first opium war between Britain and China.

Chinatown's Friendship Gate was a gift from Philadelphia's sister city of Tianjin, China.

Cross the expressway's eastbound lanes. Note the low wall decorated with prosperity symbols. ❾ *History of Chinatown,* at North 10th and Winter Streets, was commissioned to mark Chinatown's 125th anniversary in 1995. Its placement is defiant, a staking of territory made when officials built the neighboring expressway. At top is a laundry worker—the first Chinese settler here in the 1800s opened a laundry business at 913 Race Street—and the drops of water flow to show families, a highway, and protesters carrying signs that say HOMES NOT HIGHWAYS in front of bulldozers.

Continuing on North 10th Street, look at the bronze sidewalk medallions representing the animals of the Chinese zodiac. The ➓ **Chinese Christian Church** sits at the corner with Mitzi Mackenzie Place. Maribelle "Mitzi" Mackenzie, who died in 2009 at age 88, was an American Baptist Home missionary. In 1941, she founded a center to help Chinese immigrants and is credited with helping thousands of immigrants find their way. This church grew from that ministry.

Continue to Race Street and turn left. The building at 941 is an example of Late Victorian Eclectic architecture, featuring terra-cotta brick, large medallions, and arched windows. Built in 1900 as a private home, it later became a commercial building. In the 1940s, it housed the Merry-Go-Round Cafe, similar to an Automat.

Turn right onto North Ninth Street, then left onto Arch Street, where four dragons twist in the air on the left. These 1,500-pound bronze beasts were installed in 2009.

Continue to Francis House of Peace, 810 Arch St., opened in 2015 and named for Pope Francis. The building has 94 affordable housing units and offers social services in English, Mandarin, and Cantonese. The words "None of us are home until all of us are home" are written in English and Chinese. That's the motto of local nonprofit Project HOME.

Turn left onto North Eighth Street. ➓ *How We Fish,* at 125 N. Eighth St., honors the history of work in Philadelphia. The placement is significant: this building was originally constructed for children of workers of the International Ladies Garment Workers Union and the Amalgamated Men's Clothing Union. The garment industry is highlighted in the mural, as is denim, considered the fabric of the working class. The title comes from the proverb, "Give a man a fish, he eats for a day. Teach a man to fish, he eats for a lifetime." The eye-catching work spans 3,156 feet and includes 400 square feet of glass mosaics and the words "Work unites us."

One of four dancing dragon statues that float in the air on Arch Street

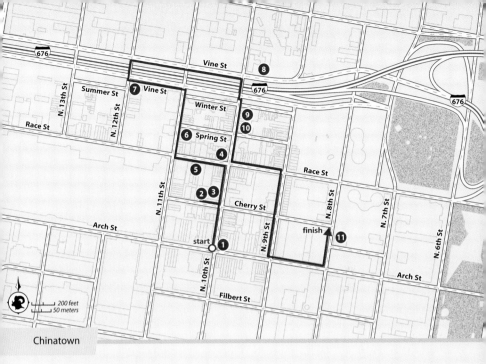

Chinatown

Points of Interest

1 **Chinatown Friendship Gate** N. 10th and Arch Sts. For more information, contact the Chinatown Development Corporation 215-922-2156, chinatown-pcdc.org.

2 **Fo Shou Temple** 1015 Cherry St., 215-928-0592, phillytemple.tripod.com/index.html

3 **Tea Dó** 132 N. 10th St., 215-923-8088, tea-do.com

4 **David's Mai Lai Wah** 1001 Race St., 215-627-2610

5 **Dim Sum Garden** 1020 Race St., 215-873-0258, dimsumgardenphilly.com

6 **Yakitori Boy** 211 N. 11th St., 215-923-8088, yakitoriboy.com

7 *Colors of Light: Gateway to Chinatown* 247 N. 12th St. For more information, contact Philadelphia Mural Arts, 215-685-0750, muralarts.org.

8 **Philadelphia Holy Redeemer Chinese Catholic Church and School** 915 Vine St., 215-922-0999, holyredeemer.cc

9 *History of Chinatown* N. 10th and Winter Sts.

10 **Chinese Christian Church** 225 N. 10th St., 215-627-2360, cccnc.org

11 *How We Fish* 125 N. Eighth St. For more information, contact Philadelphia Mural Arts, 215-685-0750, muralarts.org.

The Liberty Bell is an icon of independence and freedom, which is why abolitionists adopted it as a symbol.

3 African American Philadelphia:
A Long and Complex Relationship

BOUNDARIES: Arch St., South St., Front St., Seventh St.
DISTANCE: 2.4 miles
DIFFICULTY: Easy
PARKING: Metered parking is available along both South and Front Sts.
PUBLIC TRANSIT: SEPTA's 40 bus stops about three blocks away.

The first Africans who came to Philadelphia did so in chains. Records show Dutch and Swedish settlers in the Delaware Valley imported enslaved Africans as early as 1639. The founder of the commonwealth of Pennsylvania, William Penn, believed in equal rights for people of different religions, an anomaly for his time, but he owned slaves until his death.

But it was here in Philadelphia and in Pennsylvania that the earliest movements to break those chains began. The Germantown Quaker Petition Against Slavery, published in the city in 1688, is the first antislavery protest in the colonies. The commonwealth was the first state to pass a law ordering the emancipation of all slaves within its borders.

This tour showcases people and places integral to African American history, beginning where Mason and Dixon began their land survey and including sites where abolitionists worked, slaves took shelter, and freed African Americans began to make their mark.

Walk Description

Start at Front and South Streets, near a pedestrian walkway crossing I-95. Here in 1763, Charles Mason and Jeremiah Dixon began their surveying work to end a land dispute between Pennsylvania founder William Penn and Baltimore's Calvert family. Mason and Dixon spent four years evaluating 244 miles of land and then created their "line," which is actually four segments. Less than a century later, this imaginary marker would divide free states from slave-holding states.

Turn left and walk four blocks north along Front Street, paralleling the Delaware River. A marker here acknowledges where Thomas Paine founded the Society for the Relief of Free Negroes Unlawfully Held in Bondage in 1775. In the 1780s, this organization became the Pennsylvania Abolition Society, and its president, Benjamin Franklin, petitioned the new US Congress to ban slavery. After the Civil War, the organization was a model for other groups seeking equal opportunities for African Americans.

Cross Spruce Street. The ❶ **Philadelphia Korean War Memorial** at Penn's Landing is rich with details about the United States' role in the conflict between 1950 and 1953.

To the right is a small memorial featuring a spread-winged eagle atop a globe, the anchor of a ship cutting through the world. This honors the Philadelphia men who died on October 23, 1983, in Beirut, Lebanon.

Continue three long blocks to the intersection of Front and Market Streets and the statue of Tamanend, chief of the native Lenni Lenape nation. His name is synonymous with affable, and he was considered the colonies' patron saint by its settlers. The statue dedication quotes Tamanend, saying the Lenni Lenape and the settlers would "live in peace as the waters run in the rivers and creeks and as long as the stars and moon endure."

Franklin Fountain's signature flavor is Franklin Mint Chip.

Turn left on Market Street. Here, near where the London Coffee House once stood, captured Africans were unloaded and sold. Census data from the 1760s shows one out of every six households had at least one slave. Thomas Paine rented a room across from the auction site and published one of the first editorials condemning the practice.

The London Coffee House, opened in 1754, was a popular meeting place where Colonials enjoyed a light meal called an "ordinary" in a private booth. The Bradford brothers owned the restaurant and the neighboring printing shop where the "Proceedings of the First Continental Congress" was printed.

Walk west on Market Street into the Old City neighborhood. At ❷ **Franklin Fountain,** bow-tied staff serve homemade ice cream in a parlor fashioned to look like it dates to the 1800s. (It actually opened in 2004.) In 2015, the Food Network named the creamery's Mt. Vesuvius sundae one of the nation's best. Food Network host Alton Brown recommends one of the tangy vintage sodas.

Cross North Second Street and turn right, crossing Market Street. ❸ **Christ Church,** the nation's church, was founded in 1695. Notable early Americans, including George Washington, worshiped here. The church has a role in early African American church history: Absalom Jones, the first African American priest in the Episcopal church, was ordained here. Jones also cofounded the Free African Society with Richard Allen and Cyrus Bustill.

Continue on North Second Street to Arch Street. Turn left. The blue sign at 210 Arch St. marks the ❹ **former home of Cyrus Bustill,** mentioned above. Bustill, who was of white, black, and American Indian heritage, was born into slavery in 1732. He was sold to a baker, who taught him his trade then released him. Bustill baked bread for the troops during the Revolutionary War, becoming one of the 5,000 freed Africans and African Americans who aided the patriot cause. After the war, he settled here and opened a bakery. The Bustill family was active in the Underground Railroad. Bustill's great, great-grandson is Civil Rights activist Paul Robeson.

Continue on Arch Street to ❺ **Betsy Ross House,** where a reenactor plays Phillis, a freed African American who worked as a domestic in Colonial Philadelphia. It is likely Ross hired someone like Phillis, as she was too busy running her upholstery shop to take time out for domestic tasks.

Continue on Arch Street, crossing North Third Street. The hunk of concrete on the sidewalk to the left, in front of the Arch Street Meeting House, was once a trough that provided water for man and beast. Installed by the Philadelphia Fountain Society in 1867, the fountain's beneficiary is known only as "a lady." There were once more than 100 of these fountains. About 12 nonworking structures remain.

Members of ❻ **Arch Street Meeting House** were called on at their 1775 Yearly Meeting to free their slaves, according to their website. By 1778, most of the area Quakers had done so. The name *Quaker* was originally meant to be an insult, referring to the way some members would quake with emotion during services.

Continue to North Fifth and Arch Streets, with Ben Franklin's grave on the left. Cross Arch Street to the United States Mint, where the headquarters of the ❼ **Philadelphia Female Anti-Slavery Society** once stood. Founded in 1833 by female leaders such as Lucretia Mott, the society was interracial, enraging the pro-slavery crowd. Society members sold baked goods, needlework, and pottery to raise money for their causes, including the Underground Railroad and the Pennsylvania Abolition Society. The society also opened a school for children of African descent and called for a boycott of products made with slave labor.

Continue on Arch Street, passing the Constitution Center and the Free Quaker Meeting House. Turn right on North Sixth Street. Cross North Sixth Street, and then turn right. The large glass structure on the left, the current headquarters of WHYY, was the site of ❽ **Pennsylvania Hall.** Financed by abolitionists looking for a safe meeting space, the hall was formally opened on May 14, 1838. A letter from former president John Quincy Adams, read at the building's dedication, said, "I learnt with great satisfaction . . . that the Pennsylvania Hall Association have erected a large building in your city, wherein liberty and equality of civil rights can be freely discussed, and the evils of slavery fearlessly portrayed. . . . I rejoice that, in the city of Philadelphia, the friends of free discussion have erected a Hall for its unrestrained exercise." A mob burned the hall to the ground four days after it opened.

Turn around and walk back to Arch Street. Turn right. The ❾ **African American Museum** was founded in 1976. Its permanent collection includes more than 500,000 photos by Jack T. Franklin, who did work for *The Philadelphia Tribune,* the nation's oldest African American newspaper, and captured images during the 1963 March on Washington, the 1965 Selma to Montgomery March, and the first major Black Power rally in 1966. A sculpture outside honors Crispus Attucks, an escaped slave killed during 1770's Boston Massacre, the first casualty of the War for Independence.

Cross Arch Street and continue on North Seventh Street. The ❿ **Philadelphia History Museum at the Atwater Kent** explores more than 300 years of city history, including the local African American Experience. Its collection includes slave manifests from the 1800s, photographs of notable locals like singer Marian Anderson, and a 1910 handbill titled "Should Negroes Come North?" A section on modern politics documents how the growth of the African American population has influenced city leadership: Philadelphia elected its first African American mayor in 1983. African Americans hold offices on the local, state, and national level.

Return to Market Street. Turn right. ⓫ **The President's House** was the nation's first executive mansion, home to Presidents George Washington and John Quincy Adams. A section of the exhibit remembers the nine slaves Washington kept here. (His letters show he went to great lengths to get around a Pennsylvania law that would have freed slaves who lived in the city for an unbroken six-month stretch by sending them to neighboring New Jersey for day trips.) Among the enslaved was Oney Judge, a gifted seamstress who was a teenager when she became Martha Washington's personal maid. Judge escaped. Washington twice sent mercenaries to recapture her, and twice they failed. She was still considered a fugitive slave when she died more than 50 years later.

Walk south on South Sixth Street, passing the pavilion housing the ⓬ **Liberty Bell.** The bell, commissioned in 1751, is inscribed with the Biblical quote, "Proclaim Liberty throughout all the land unto all the inhabitants thereof." Prior to the 1830s, Philadelphians called it the old bell. Then abolitionists adopted it as a symbol of their movement, and New York Anti-Slavery Society called it the liberty bell, telling their Philadelphia counterparts, "the bell has not obeyed the inscription and its peals have been a mockery, when one sixth of 'all inhabitants' are in abject slavery."

Continue on South Sixth Street, passing Independence Hall. In the 1800s, enslaved people who escaped and were recaptured were brought to trial here. A newspaper article from 1851 details the case of "two alleged fugitives, Helen and Dick." One man testified that, "Helen had been his slave; his father had owned her mother Charity, whose mother he had bought . . . they were made a present about six months after the marriage."

At South Sixth and Chestnut Streets, note the historical marker for the Walnut Street Jail, here between 1775 and 1835. In 1793, as the first air balloon prepared to launch from the prison yard, President Washington gave the French aeronaut a "passport" he could present if the balloon landed in a foreign place. The balloon floated over the Delaware River and landed in New Jersey.

Continue on South Sixth Street to ⓭ **Washington Square,** one of the city's five original park spaces. In early days, this was a graveyard for slaves and the very poor. It was also a popular gathering place for enslaved Africans, earning the name Congo Square. During the Revolutionary War, soldiers from both sides of the conflict were interred here, prompting John Adams in 1777 to say the graves "are enough to make the heart of stone melt away." The square also holds the bodies of those who died in disease outbreaks, such as the yellow fever epidemic of 1793. The tomb of the Unknown Revolutionary War soldier is marked by a statue of George Washington and an eternal flame.

The Korean War memorial at Penn's Landing

The ⓮ **Athenaeum of Philadelphia,** a member-supported museum and library, aims to document US history and is the go-to resource for information about architecture and interior design from 1800 to 1945.

⓯ Mother Bethel African Methodist Episcopal Church, founded by former slave turned minister Richard Allen in 1794, is the first A.M.E. church in the world sitting on the oldest parcel of land continuously owned by African Americans in the nation. Original congregants were African Americans who left their old church because of forced segregation during services. A devoted abolitionist, Allen began helping free slaves newly arrived in the city in the 1790s. Later, the church was a stop on the Underground Railroad.

The current church, built in the late 1800s, includes a museum with items that belonged to the 2,500 black soldiers Allen rallied to fight in the War of 1812. Allen, who died in 1831, is entombed here. One admirer called him "one of the greatest divines who has lived since the apostolic age."

Stop at the corner of South Sixth and Lombard Streets. A historical marker here refers to the Lombard Street riot of 1842. On August 1, about 1,000 members of an all-black abolitionist group paraded to commemorate the anniversary of slavery's end in the West Indies. They carried a banner reading "How grand in age, how fair in truth, are holy Friendship, Love and Truth."

Irish Catholics attacked the marchers near this corner. There had long been tension between the Irish and the freed African Americans as they competed for jobs and housing. The conflict continued for three days. A church was destroyed by fire, and several homes were looted.

Continue to South Street. Turn right. The mural painted on this fire station is *Mapping Courage: Honoring W. E. B. Du Bois and Engine #11.* Du Bois, a Harvard University PhD who conducted a door-to-door survey of African Americans, lived nearby while completing the study, called "The Philadelphia Negro." He asked the question, "Would America have been America without her Negro people?"

Points of Interest

❶ Philadelphia Korean War Memorial Penn's Landing, between Dock and Spruce Sts.

❷ Franklin Fountain 116 Market St., 215-627-1899, franklinfountain.com

❸ Christ Church 20 N. American St., 215-922-1695, christchurchphila.org

African American Philadelphia

4 Former home of Cyrus Bustill 210 Arch St. (not open to the public)

5 Betsy Ross House 239 Arch St., 215-629-5801, historicphiladelphia.org/what-to-see

6 Arch Street Meeting House 320 Arch St., 215-413-1804, archstreetmeetinghouse.org

7 Former headquarters of the Philadelphia Female Anti-Slavery Society (now the United States Mint) 151 N. Independence Mall E., 215-408-0112, usmint.com

8 Former site of Pennsylvania Hall (now the headquarters of WHYY) 150 N. Sixth St., 215-351-1200, whyy.org

9 African American Museum 701 Arch St., 215-574-0380, aampmuseum.org

10 Philadelphia History Museum at the Atwater Kent 15 S. Seventh St., 215-685-4830, philadelphiahistory.org

11 The President's House 524–30 Market St., 800-537-7676, phlvisitorcenter.com

12 Liberty Bell Center S. Sixth and Market Sts., 215-965-2305, nps.gov/inde

13 Washington Square Walnut St. between Sixth and Seventh Sts., 215-965-2305, nps.gov/inde

14 Athenaeum of Philadelphia 219 S. Sixth St., 215-925-2688, philaathenaeum.org

15 Mother Bethel African Methodist Episcopal Church 419 S. Sixth St., 215-925-0616, motherbethel.org

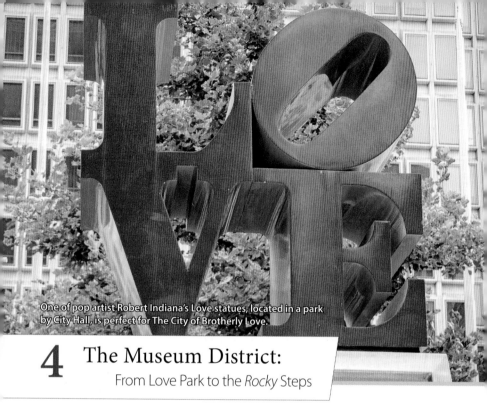

One of pop artist Robert Indiana's Love statues, located in a park by City Hall, is perfect for The City of Brotherly Love.

4 The Museum District:
From Love Park to the *Rocky* Steps

BOUNDARIES: N. 15th St., N. 24th St., Arch St., Kelly Dr.
DISTANCE: A direct walk from Love Park to The Philadelphia Museum of Art is 1 mile. Figure another 0.5 mile for your detours.
DIFFICULTY: Easy
PARKING: Street parking is very limited in this neighborhood, as are public parking lots. Public transportation is the best way to get here.
PUBLIC TRANSIT: Options include taking the SEPTA Market–Frankford or Broad Street Line, any regional rail line, or bus routes including 2, 17, 27, 31, 32, 33, 44, 124, and 125.

Benjamin Franklin Parkway is one of the earliest examples of urban renewal in the United States, breaking up William Penn's grid and bringing grandeur to the city. This 1-mile stretch has been called Philadelphia's Champs-Élysées, running through its cultural heart. In a downtown of narrow streets and alleys, some impassable by cars, the parkway stands out.

This walk takes you from one iconic location to another, from the park highlighting the city as a place of brotherly love to the phenomenal art museum that deserves a visit after you run up the stairs like a certain fictional boxer.

Walk Description

Start at John F. Kennedy Plaza, at 15th Street and John F. Kennedy Boulevard, better known as ❶ **Love Park** because of its iconic red sculpture by pop artist Robert Indiana. Versions of this 1950s sculpture are in urban centers worldwide, including New York, Indianapolis, and Tokyo.

The fountain behind the sculpture is named for Ellen Phillips Samuel, a great supporter of local cultural events. City leaders sometimes dye the fountain's water to mark specific events, such as pink for Breast Cancer Awareness Month. A less popular dye job: the water flowed blood red in 2007 to promote the Showtime series *Dexter,* about a serial killer who kills serial killers.

Love Park, opened in 1965, was the brainchild of city planner Edmund Bacon, whose influence can be seen throughout the city. In 2002, when city leaders first talked of banning skateboards from the park, the 92-year-old Bacon strapped on a helmet and, with the help of aides, rolled through the park. He later told one television station, "My whole damn life has been worth it, just for this."

Walk west on John F. Kennedy Boulevard toward the glass building that looks like a flying saucer. The ❷ **Fairmount Park Welcome Center** is one of the best examples of midcentury modern architecture in Center City. The building opened in 1960 as the Philadelphia Hospitality Center. Its future is in question, and a Save the Saucer campaign began in 2014.

Across from the saucer is the Art Deco Suburban Station, which opened in 1930. Cross 16th Street, and turn right. Cross Arch Street to *Monument to Six Million Jewish Martyrs.* The bronze sculpture, placed in 1964, was a gift to the city from a group whose families fled Europe during World War II.

Begin walking northwest along Benjamin Franklin Parkway. The flags, representing 90 nations, were placed in 1976 to mark the bicentennial and the city's diversity.

After crossing 17th Street, note the sculpture on the side of the Embassy Suites hotel tower, at 1776 Ben Franklin Parkway. This is Tuscan Girl, a no-longer-functioning fountain placed here in 1965 as part of a city ordinance requiring developers to spend 1% of their construction budget on public art. There are four figures here, and it's unclear which is a Tuscan girl.

Cross 18th Street, pausing at the statue of General Thaddeus Kosciuszko, a Polish-born engineer who joined the American patriot cause. Kosciuszko helped the rebels strengthen their positions, including along the Philadelphia waterfront. He also put his skills to work in West Point, New York, a fortification so daunting that it became known as the American Gibraltar.

Because of the parkway's width, crossing as a pedestrian can be a challenge. To reach ❸ **Sister Cities Park,** walk about half a block to the Swedish flag, and then use the crosswalk to reach the median and then the far side of the parkway.

Originally dedicated in 1976, Sister Cities was neglected for decades before being rehabilitated in 2012. The 1.75-acre park packs in a lot, with climbing rocks, a cafe, and a boat pond. The centerpiece is a ground-level fountain with Philadelphia surrounded by spouts representing its 10 sister cities. Robert Indiana's 6-foot-tall *AMOR*, which means "love" in Spanish and Latin, was acquired for Pope Francis's 2015 visit and placed here afterward.

Two statues honor European-born men who helped the American Revolutionary cause: Thomas Fitzsimons, an Irish immigrant, funded Washington's army and later served three terms in Congress. Don Diego de Gardoqui, later the first U.S. ambassador to Spain, helped transfer funds from Spanish banks.

Stepping away from the statues, follow the diagonal path northwest to the corner of Vine Street and the parkway, and turn left. Take the crosswalk under the Botswana flag to the median and then follow the next crosswalk to ❹ **Logan Square,** one of the city's five original green spaces. The park hosted public executions in the 1700s and public gatherings in the 1800s, including the Great Sanitary Fair in 1864. President Lincoln spoke at the event, a fundraiser for supplies for Union soldiers. The Swann Memorial Fountain, installed in 1924, was designed by Alexander Stirling Calder, whose father's William Penn statue tops City Hall and whose son crafted another nearby work. The three bronze American Indians represent the city's three main waterways: The Delaware and Schuylkill Rivers and

Academy of Natural Sciences scientist Ted Daeschler co-discovered *Tiktaalik roseae,* the fossil believed to show the link between fish and land animals.

Wissahickon Creek. The water-spouting swans are a pun on the fountain's name.

Circle the fountain about three-quarters of the way to use the crosswalk to cross the parkway to the ❺ **Academy of Natural Sciences of Drexel University.** Founded in 1812 by some of the country's leading naturalists, this is the oldest natural-sciences institution in the Western Hemisphere, housed here since 1876.

There are two statues near the entrance. The one closest to the door shows two small, meat-eating dinosaurs that will remind *Jurassic Park* fans of velociraptors. This is *Deinonychus,* which means "terrible claw." The one to the right depicts Joseph Leidy, who is considered the father of American vertebrate paleontology. He holds the jawbone of the Ice Age lion he identified.

Turn right onto Race Street. ❻ **Moore College of Art & Design** is the first and only all-female college of art and design in the country. The school is named in honor of a generous donor. At the front entrance is a whispering bench with twisting horns set apart for visitors to try. The gallery inside is public.

Continue on Race Street to 20th Street. Turn right and enter ❼ **Aviator Park.** Renovated in 2007, the park features the large gilded-bronze sculpture *Aero Memorial* by Paul Manship. It honors the pilots of World War I. The celestial sphere shows the constellations and the signs of the zodiac. The artist included a carving of himself with a star on his forehead; it's near the Pisces sign.

Turn left and walk around the low wall until you reach the sculpture closer to the corner of 20th and Winter Streets. This is the *All Wars Memorial to Colored Soldiers and Sailors,* which depicts real fighting men who posed for the artist. Completed in 1934, when the US military was still segregated, the statue was first placed in an obscure corner of Fairmount Park. It was moved here in 1994, almost 50 years after President Harry S. Truman issued an executive order integrating the military.

At the corner of 20th and Winter Streets, turn left and cross 20th Street. **❽ The Franklin Institute** was founded in 1824 and named for Ben Franklin. It is one of the nation's premier museums as well as a center for science education and research. The institute, at this location since 1934, was ahead of its time with scientific innovation and its views on equality among scientists. The first female was accepted for membership in 1833; the first member of African descent was accepted in 1870.

The Franklin Institute and its member scientists have long been highly respected, so citizens panicked in March 1940 when a local radio station reported the world was going to end the next day, April 1, as "confirmed by astronomers of the Franklin Institute, Philadelphia." The station had learned of Earth's imminent doom from a press release sent by the institute's press officer, who wrote that the release was *not* an April Fool's Day joke. It was.

Logan Square, a popular gathering place, features the Swann Fountain.

Among the museum's permanent exhibitions are the iconic *Giant Heart* and *Your Brain*. Inside is Franklin National Memorial, which features a 20-foot-tall, 30-ton statue of the Founding Father.

Continue walking on Winter Street to the corner of 21st Street. Turn right and follow the crosswalk over the Vine Street Expressway to return to Ben Franklin Parkway.

Turn left onto the parkway, crossing 22nd Street, and continue toward 24th Street. Look at the green space below you on the left. Remember

Edmund Bacon's skateboard ride through Love Park? This is Paine's Skateboard Park, created to provide an outlet for skateboard enthusiasts chased from there.

At 24th Street, cross to the median at right, and then cross again to reach the park opposite the art museum.

This is ➒ **Eakins Oval,** 8 acres of public space named for painter Thomas Eakins and called the Park on the Parkway. It has served as center stage for numerous events, including Masses led by Pope John Paul II in 1979 and Pope Francis in 2015, the Live 8 Concert in 2005, and the city's annual Fourth of July concerts.

The most notable art here is the fountains. The largest is the Washington Memorial Fountain, featuring a uniformed Washington mounted on a horse. The artist modeled the face on a mask made during Washington's lifetime.

Leave the oval via the walkway nearest the northernmost fountain, the corner of Kelly Drive and the parkway. Cross the street at the crosswalk.

Walk left to reach the steps leading to the ➓ **Philadelphia Museum of Art.** Built in 1928, the museum is not only one of the largest in the country—with works by Henri Matisse, Marcel Duchamp, Paul Cézanne, and John Singer Sargent—but also a well-known movie location; many visitors charge the steps, as is done in three of the *Rocky* films. In 2011, screenjunkies.com said the steps were the second-most famous movie location in the world. (Grand Central Terminal was first.) To the right (northwest) at the bottom of the steps is a statue of fictional boxer Rocky Balboa, originally a prop in the 1980 film *Rocky III.*

Continue to *Charioteer of Delphi,* a bronze cast of an original 5th century B.C. work given to the city by the Greek government in 1976. The final stop, the statue of *Young Meher,* is a memorial to the thousands of Armenians killed by the Ottoman Empire in 1915. Meher, a legendary Armenian folk hero from the Middle Ages, looks into the sky, holding a cross aloft as he prepares for battle. The local Armenian community gifted the statue to the city.

The second parkway tour (page 29) returns to Love Park.

The Museum District: From Love Park to the *Rocky* Steps

Points of Interest

1 **Love Park** 15th St. and John F. Kennedy Blvd.

2 **Fairmount Park Welcome Center** 1599 John F. Kennedy Blvd., 215-683-0246, tinyurl.com/fairmountwelcomecenter

3 **Sister Cities Park** 218 N. 18th St., 215-440-5500, ccdparks.org/sister-cities-park

4 **Logan Square** Vine Street Expressway and Benjamin Franklin Parkway, tinyurl.com/logansquarephilly

5 **Academy of Natural Sciences of Drexel University** 1900 Benjamin Franklin Parkway, 215-299-1000, ansp.org

6 **Moore College of Art & Design** 1916 Race St., 215-965-4000, moore.edu

7 **Aviator Park** Race and N. 20th Sts.

8 **The Franklin Institute** 222 N. 20th St., 215-448-1200, fi.edu

9 **Eakins Oval** 2451 Benjamin Franklin Parkway, 215-607-3477, theovalphl.org

10 **Philadelphia Museum of Art** 2600 Benjamin Franklin Parkway, 215-763-8100, philamuseum.org

The Philadelphia Museum of Art, with the Water Works below,
as it looks from across the Schuylkill River

5 The Museum District:
From the Art Museum to the Cathedral

BOUNDARIES: Fairmount Ave., Ben Franklin Pkwy., Pennsylvania Ave., N. 16th St.
DISTANCE: About 2 miles, depending on how many detours you take
DIFFICULTY: Easy. It's a flat walk.
PARKING: There is a parking garage behind the art museum that you can reach via
  Art Museum Drive or Waterworks Drive.
PUBLIC TRANSIT: SEPTA bus routes 2, 7, 32, 33, and 48, or take the PHLASH to Stop 13.

You ran up the Philadelphia Museum of Art's steps and did your best Rocky impression at
the end of the other Benjamin Franklin Parkway tour. Catch your breath, and prepare to
return to Love Park, stopping at one of the city's newest and most popular museums and
seeing some of the amazing statuary that makes Philadelphia an outdoor art gallery.

Walk Description

Begin at the art museum's ❶ **Ruth and Raymond G. Perelman Building,** at the
intersection of Fairmount and Pennsylvania Avenues. This landmark Art Deco

structure was built in 1926 as the headquarters for Fidelity Mutual Life Insurance Company. The carved facade is one of the 20th century's most elaborate. Look for Egyptian-style sculptures of animals representing the attributes of insurance: the opossum of protection, the owl of wisdom, the dog of fidelity, the pelican of charity, and the squirrel of frugality.

The words above the arched main entrance on Pennsylvania Avenue read: "In the honor and perpetuity of the family is founded the state. In the nobler life of the household is the nobler life of mankind."

Leaving the Perelman Building, walk southeast on Pennsylvania Avenue, turning right at 25th St. The life-sized golden statue of Joan of Arc, at Kelly Drive and 25th Street, shows the medieval French heroine astride a horse as she prepares to fight the English during the Hundred Years' War. There are two other casts of Emmanuel Frémiet's original 1874 statue in the United States, in Portland, Oregon, and New Orleans. Some locals call this "Joanie on a pony."

Turn left onto Kelly Drive. The 34-foot-tall shimmering silver sculpture called *Symbiosis,* at 24th Street and Kelly Drive, was installed here in 2014. Sculptor Roxy Paine hand-soldered thousands of pieces of stainless steel pipes, plates, and rods to create what could be a tree or a part of the vascular system. Nearby is *Iroquois,* on Benjamin Franklin Parkway at Eakins Oval and Spring Garden Street, a 40-foot-tall sculpture of red steel installed in 2007. Abstract impressionist sculptor Mark di Suvero described his works, made of steel I beams, as "paintings in three dimensions with the crane as my paintbrush."

Continue on the parkway, passing a large grassy area with a baseball field, playgrounds, and picnic tables. This is Von Colln Memorial Park, named in honor of Philadelphia Police Department Sergeant Frank Von Colln, killed in the line of duty in August 1970.

Some are confused to see a copy of Auguste Rodin's *The Thinker* here, but Philadelphia has the largest collection of the artist's works outside of Paris. The ❷ **Rodin Museum** was a gift from movie theater magnate Jules Mastbaum, a

Philadelphia native who began collecting Rodin's works in the 1920s but died before it opened in 1929.

The museum honors the artist's French roots with a formal French garden on site. Note how the building is a scaled-down version of a grand Beaux Arts structure. As noted in the first parkway tour (page 22), the original architects envisioned this as a grand boulevard much like Paris's Champs-Élysées.

Continue to the leafy grounds of the ❸ **Barnes Foundation,** housing the extensive art collection of self-made millionaire Dr. Albert Barnes. In 1922, Barnes opened his museum in the suburb of Lower Merion, personally placing each work of art—including pieces by Renoir, Matisse, Picasso, Cézanne, and Seurat—in exhibition rooms that highlighted its relationship to the objects around it, including metalworks and furniture.

Barnes died in 1951, and his will decreed the museum was to stay in the suburbs. The controversial move to downtown Philadelphia was completed in 2012. Supporters note more than 1 million people visited the Philadelphia location in one year, almost three times the number of visitors who went to the suburban location in five years.

The museum is a low-key, two-storied limestone structure critics have called sophisticated, simple, and soulful. Inside, the art is displayed in rooms that are almost exact replicas of the ones Barnes himself decorated. The museum also has concert and lecture halls and a gallery for temporary exhibitions.

Continue toward 20th Street. Walk straight, ignoring the parkway's bend. The road becomes Vine Street. The ❹ **Free Library of Philadelphia** opened in 1927 and is the cornerstone of the city's public library system. The outside is Beaux Arts beauty, and the interior houses an amazing array of art and sculpture.

As with so many Philly firsts, Ben Franklin created the first library system when he and 50 friends combined funds to buy books for the new Library Company. Years later, Franklin noted that foreign visitors were impressed by the sophistication of Philadelphians. He credited that in part to the locals' love of reading.

The neighboring building at 1801 Vine St. once housed the juvenile and domestic branches of the municipal court system. This New Deal–funded public works project was built in 1938. While not currently in use, the building exterior reveals its original intentions. Note the two triangular pediments on the upper front corners. On the left is *Juvenile Protection,* which includes a seated woman with an olive branch sitting near the scales of justice. On the right is *Family Unity,* which shows a reclining woman holding a baby and a reclining man holding a dog.

Continue on Vine Street to take in Philadelphia's newest site, the Philadelphia Pennsylvania temple of **5** **The Church of Jesus Christ of Latter-day Saints.** This eye-catching building, completed in 2016, is the local home for 41,000 members of

the Mormon faith. The 197-foot-tall white structure is topped with a gold-leafed Angel Moroni, who led founder Joseph Smith to the golden plates from which *The Book of Mormon* was derived. The temple, open only to Mormons, is used for special ceremonies. The redbrick building across the street is for regular worship.

Circle the building to fully appreciate its size and symmetry. Then return to 18th Street, and cross the road to reach **6** **Cathedral Basilica of Saints Peter & Paul,** at 18th and Race Streets. This is the principal church of the Catholic Archdiocese of Philadelphia, modeled after Rome's Church of Saint Charles and completed in 1864. The original structure here was built without street-level windows for fear of vandalism after the anti-Catholic riots that swept the city in the 1840s. To determine window placement, the architect tossed

The Philadelphia Museum of Art's Perelman Building once housed an insurance company.

rocks at the building, then placed the windows just above the highest rock strike. Lower windows were added during a 1950s renovation.

To the right of the entrance is *Jesus Breaking Bread,* depicting a young Christ holding a broken half of pita bread in each hand. This sculpture caused a stir in 1976, with critics saying that artist Walter Erlebacher's depiction of Christ was inaccurate. (The artist's response: How do you know? Do you have any photos?) Supporters said it seemed the statue is calling people to church.

Walk to the corner of Benjamin Franklin Parkway, and turn left. The abstract work *Three Disks, One Lacking* is by Alexander Calder of the great Calder family of artists. (His grandfather is perhaps best known for the William Penn statue atop City Hall, while his father designed the nearby Swann Memorial Fountain in Logan Square; both works are visible from here.) Take a knee and look through the cutout section toward City Hall. You'll find the William Penn statue perfectly framed within the loop.

Continue to *Three Way Piece Number One: Points* by Henry Moore between 16th and 17th Streets. Placed here in 1990, this bronze statue on a black-granite base changes as the viewer moves around it. The artist said sculpture "should always at first sign have some obscurities and further meanings." Note the tool marks on parts of the work, and admire how this great weight is balanced on three small points. Some people see a three-legged animal; others, a giant tooth.

Continue to 16th Street. *The Prophet* by Jacob Lipkin is at the corner. Ahead is Love Park. Consider a stop at ❼ **Capriccio at Café Cret,** the small coffee bar at left named to honor French-born architect Paul Philippe Cret, one of the parkway's principal planners.

This tour ends here. Continue to City Hall to pick up another tour (Walk 8, page 49) that begins there.

(continued on next page)

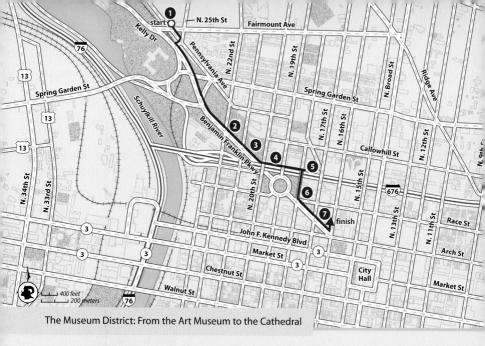

The Museum District: From the Art Museum to the Cathedral

Points of Interest

1 **Ruth and Raymond G. Perelman Building** Fairmount and Pennsylvania Aves., 215-763-8100, philamuseum.org

2 **Rodin Museum** 2151 Benjamin Franklin Parkway, 215-763-8100, rodinmuseum.org

3 **Barnes Foundation** 2025 Benjamin Franklin Parkway, 215-278-7000, barnesfoundation.org

4 **Free Library of Philadelphia** 1901 Vine St., 215-686-5322, freelibrary.org

5 **The Church of Jesus Christ of Latter-day Saints** 1739 Vine St., 801-240-1000, lds.org/church/temples

6 **Cathedral Basilica of Saints Peter & Paul** 1723 Race St., 215-561-1313, cathedralphila.org

7 **Capriccio at Café Cret** N. 16th St. and Benjamin Franklin Parkway 215-735-9797, capricciocafe.com

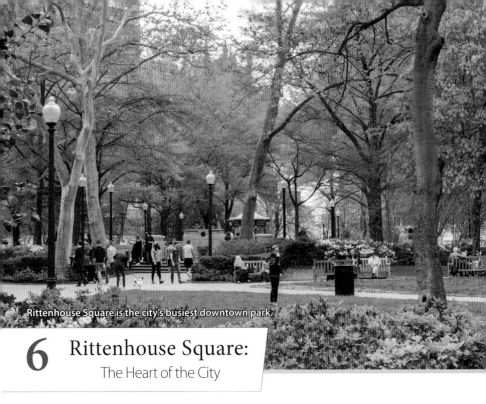

Rittenhouse Square is the city's busiest downtown park.

6 Rittenhouse Square:
The Heart of the City

BOUNDARIES: S. 17th St., S. 20th St., Delancey Pl., Walnut St.
DISTANCE: 1.1 miles
DIFFICULTY: Easy
PARKING: Street parking is a challenge near Rittenhouse, and the few paid lots are overpriced. Public transportation may be the best option.
PUBLIC TRANSIT: SEPTA buses 9, 12, 21, and 42 stopping on Walnut St. The SEPTA subway stop is at 19th and Market Sts., two blocks north of the square.

Rittenhouse Square is one of the city's five original squares, part of William Penn's plan for a "greene country town." It's a popular meeting place for locals, offering greenery and great people-watching, and is the site of an annual art fair, weekly farmers' markets, and occasional concerts. In 2010, the American Planning Association put Rittenhouse on its list of the top 10 Great Public Spaces in the United States.

That's ironic, as in the 1700s, Southwest Square was a popular pasture for livestock and for dumping "night soils." It was cleaned up and renamed in honor of astronomer David

Paul Manship's *Duck Girl*
in Rittenhouse Square

Rittenhouse in 1825. This walk highlights the square, its art, and the surrounding upscale residential neighborhood.

Walk Description

Begin at South 18th Street and Rittenhouse Square East. The nonprofit Philadelphia Art Alliance, at 251 S. 18th St., was founded in 1915 to present a variety of art forms in one venue. It presents up to 12 exhibitions a year.

Walk north on South 18th Street, with ❶ **Rittenhouse Square** to your left. The former Barclay Hotel, 237 S. 18th St., was considered the finest hotel in the city when it opened in 1929. It was converted to condominiums in 2005. Unit 14A—a 5,000-square-foot space with 5-plus bedrooms and 5.5 baths—was offered for sale in 2016 for $5.7 million. The monthly $4,000 fee covered extras such as doormen and a chauffeur-driven Mercedes S550.

Continue to the ❷ **Curtis Institute of Music,** which boasts that 30% of musicians playing with the country's "big five" orchestras are alums. Other notable graduates include Leonard Bernstein and Samuel Barber. Curtis provides full-tuition, merit-based scholarships to all students.

❸ **Parc** and ❹ **Rouge** are neighboring posh restaurants with prime park-side seating. Both have a Parisian air, which makes sense for Parc, a brasserie, but not Rouge, an American bistro known for its burger. Both restaurants draw visiting celebrities—such as Denzel Washington and Justin Timberlake—and aspiring ones.

At Walnut Street, turn left. Cross South 18th Street and enter the park via the path on the left. The Evelyn Taylor Price Memorial Sundial, installed in 1947, honors a past president of the park-improvement association. One art historian called the piece—which features two children holding up a sunflower—a "poetical reminder of the fleeting joys of sunshine."

Follow the diagonal path toward the park's center, passing a sculpture called *Giant Frog,* which is . . . a giant frog. The next statue shows a lion crushing a serpent. This is—you guessed it—*Lion Crushing Serpent.* A bronze cast of the original piece by Antoine-Louis Barye, which is in the Louvre, it is an allegory for the French Revolution, with the lion symbolizing the power of good and the serpent representing evil.

Turn right. Follow the path toward the fountain, passing a small guardhouse. Rising from the water is Paul Manship's *Duck Girl,* a local favorite.

Walk to the back of the fountain to read the tribute to a founding member of the Rittenhouse Square Improvement Association. While this drinking fountain no longer works, the shell-shaped spouts are still a nice touch.

Continue on the path, going down four stairs and turning right at the first opportunity. Follow the bench-lined walkway to a clearing. On the right is a goat sculpture, *Billy,* a landmark for locals. Legend has it that rubbing its horns brings good luck. His tail, too, has been rubbed to a shine, although there's no luck attached to that practice.

Follow the path to the right, walking toward Walnut Street. When four paths meet, go left toward the corner of Rittenhouse Square West and Walnut Street. Exit the square. The ❺ **Church of the Holy Trinity** dates to 1857 and is known for its stained glass, including five windows by Louis Comfort Tiffany. The bell tower rings on the hour. In the 1860s, the church's rector wrote the lyrics to the Christmas carol "O Little Town of Bethlehem."

Turn left on Rittenhouse Square West, with the park to your left. ❻ **The Rittenhouse** is a luxury hotel featuring La Croix restaurant, which hosts a weekly $60-per-person Sunday brunch that offers items such as whipped foie gras cannoli, carrot bread French toast, and Vietnamese beef broth with quail egg.

Continuing to the corner of the park, look left. These statues, *Rittenhouse Square Dogs,* are . . . dogs. They were donated in 1988 by friends of the late art collector

Henry McIlhenny, whom Andy Warhol once called "the only person in Philadelphia with glamour."

Cross Rittenhouse Square South and turn left, passing the Ethical Humanist Society, at 1906 Rittenhouse Square South. At South 19th Street turn right. ❼ **Metropolitan Bakery** is a local favorite known for its homemade granola and many bread varieties.

The Rafsnyder-Welsh House is a visual delight—or nightmare.

Turn left on Spruce Street. The Gothic Revival ❽ **Temple Beth Zion–Beth Israel Synagogue** was originally built to house a Methodist congregation but was repurposed in 1954. The renovations included installing new stained glass windows to represent important aspects of Jewish history and worship.

Continue to the now-commercial building at 1710 Spruce St., the former home of Harry K. Thaw. Thaw, an eccentric known to light his cigars with $5 bills, was heir to a Pittsburgh mine and railroad fortune. In 1906, he shot and killed architect Stanford White in New York. Thaw's wife, actress Evelyn Nesbit, had dated White before their marriage. Thaw felt White had tainted Nesbit. The court case that followed was the original trial of the century. Thaw was eventually found not guilty by reason of insanity. E. L. Doctorow included details of the case in his book *Ragtime*.

At South 17th Street, turn right. At Delancey Place (also called Delancey Street), one of the most beautiful streets

Evelyn Taylor Price
Memorial Sundial

in the city, turn right again. ❾ **Plays and Players** is one of the oldest professional theater companies in the country and is still active. Actor Kevin Bacon appeared onstage here as a child in 1974.

The private residence at 1827 Delancey Place, with a curved brick facade topped with an iron balcony, was built in 1861 and has a historic feel, but a 2016 real estate listing revealed it has some distinctly modern touches, including an elevator, a roof deck, and a working waterfall. It was listed for $2.8 million.

The house at 1836 Delancey Place was once occupied by Union General George Gordon Meade, who is best known for leading his troops to victory during 1863's Battle of Gettysburg. This home was his reward for his service, and his name is still engraved above the door. He died here in 1872.

Cross South 19th Street. The ❿ **Horace Jayne House** was designed by Frank Furness. As one critic noted, the Victorian architect "pushed ugliness to the point where it almost turned to beauty" with this project. The National Register of Historic Places says it is a landmark house with elements that both anticipate the work of Frank Lloyd Wright and recall Thomas Jefferson's Monticello.

Turn right (north) on South 19th Street. Turn left on Spruce Street. The ⓫ **Rafsnyder-Welsh House** is a visual delight—or nightmare, depending on your tastes. Built in 1855 as a flat-roofed, redbrick home like those surrounding it, the building was renovated in the late 1890s to add red sandstone and terra-cotta trim. Note the different window shapes and the off-center placement of both the entrance and the middle window on the third floor. The redesign inspired others on the block to remodel similarly.

Continue on Spruce Street. At South 20th Street turn left. Walk to Delancey Place and turn right. Unlike other area homes long ago converted to apartments, condos, or offices, the Civil War–era mansions here remain largely unchanged. The block, one of the city's most picturesque, is also its most filmed residential swath, featured in at least five movies or TV shows. In 1983's *Trading Places,* Dan Aykroyd's wealthy character is said to live at 2014 Delancey Place. In a scene from 1999's *The Sixth Sense,* the psychiatrist played by Bruce Willis stands before "his" house at 2006 Delancey Place.

The **⑫ Rosenbach Museum and Library** showcases the collections of Phillip and A. S. W. Rosenbach, dealers of rare books and manuscripts who lived here from 1926–1952. Among the 130,000 manuscripts, 30,000 rare books, and other items showcased are hundreds of letters written by Presidents George Washington and Abraham Lincoln, the only known surviving copy of the 1773 edition of Ben Franklin's *Poor Richard Almanac,* and Lewis Carroll's own copy of *Alice in Wonderland.* The museum also has James Joyce's handwritten manuscript of *Ulysses* and celebrates Joyce and his masterpiece each year on Bloomsday, June 16.

This tour ends here. The Fitler Square tour (page 42) picks up a few blocks away.

The Horace Jayne House was designed by noted architect Frank Furness.

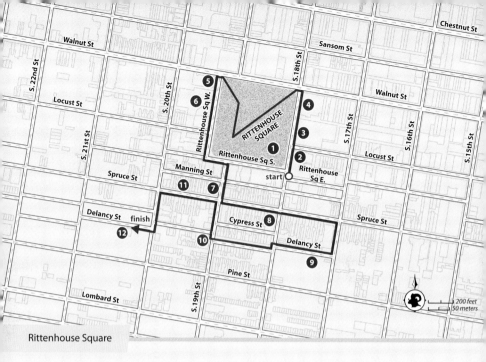

Rittenhouse Square

Points of Interest

① **Rittenhouse Square** S. 18th and Walnut Sts., 267-586-5675, friendsofrittenhouse.org

② **Curtis Institute of Music** 1726 Locust St., 215-893-5252, curtis.edu

③ **Parc** 227 S. 18th St., 215-545-2262, parc-restaurant.com

④ **Rouge** 205 S. 18th St., 215-732-6622, rouge98.com

⑤ **Church of the Holy Trinity** 1904 Walnut St., 215-567-1267, htrit.org

⑥ **The Rittenhouse** 201 W. Rittenhouse Square, 800-635-1042, rittenhousehotel.com

⑦ **Metropolitan Bakery** 262 S. 19th St., 215-545-6655, metropolitanbakery.com

⑧ **Temple Beth Zion–Beth Israel Synagogue** 1800–1804 Spruce St.

⑨ **Plays and Players** 1714 Delancey Place, 215-735-0630, playsandplayers.org

⑩ **Horace Jayne House** 320 S. 19th St.

⑪ **Rafsnyder-Welsh House** 1923 Spruce St.

⑫ **Rosenbach Museum and Library** 2008–2010 Delancey Place, 215-732-1600, rosenbach.org

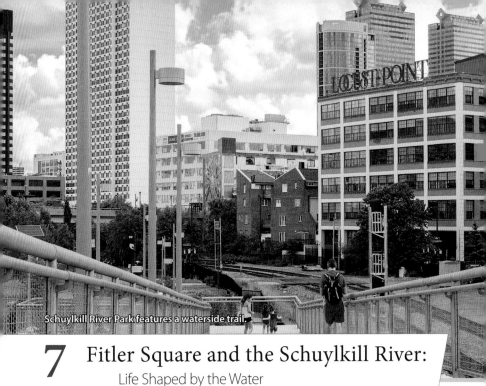

Schuylkill River Park features a waterside trail.

7 Fitler Square and the Schuylkill River:
Life Shaped by the Water

BOUNDARIES: Lombard St., Chestnut St., S. 22nd St., Schuylkill River
DISTANCE: 1.3 miles
DIFFICULTY: Easy
PARKING: There are no paid parking lots here; the only options are metered street parking or limited but free 2-hour street spots.
PUBLIC TRANSIT: If you're coming into the city by rail—including SEPTA and Amtrak—it's easy to exit at 30th Station and cross the Schuylkill River at South Street. By bus, the 40 or 42 will drop you a few blocks from your starting point.

The Schuylkill River wharves made this an industrial hub in the first half of the 1800s, with coal pouring in from northern Pennsylvania's mines. Irish immigrants who worked on the water and in nearby manufacturing plants lived here.

As ships grew and business moved to the deeper and wider Delaware River, the neighborhood's fortunes declined. In a book about urban progress and poverty, author Jeanne Lowe described Fitler Square in the 1950s as a "muddle inhabited by drunks and empty bottles."

Today this residential area of single-family homes dating from the mid-19th to the 20th century is in high demand. While real estate may not cost as much as that surrounding Rittenhouse Square, it's not far off. Some people have dubbed the area between the two parks Rit-Fit and Fittenhouse Square.

Walk Description

Start at **1** **The Philadelphia School,** on the corner of Lombard and South 25th Streets. This well-respected private school continues to creatively adapt existing buildings for modern uses. Part of the main school, established in 1976, was once the Philadelphia-based New York Pie Baking Company. Company founder William "The Pie Man" Thompson believed pies were good for you and convinced the public that his factory-made pies—made with pure ingredients in sterile conditions—were nutritious.

More recently, the school converted an asphalt-covered, fenced-in parking lot into a playground with green learning space. A former railroad company building became an early-childhood development center.

Walk north on South 25th Street to Pine Street. Turn right. In the late 1920s, city councilman Charles Hall returned from a trip to France determined to bring French flair to his hometown. He began by changing the stretch of Pine Street where he lived into Little Paris. University of Pennsylvania professor James Metheny liked Hall's idea, so he designed and built himself the house at 2420 Pine St.

Metheny also designed the Horn Mansion, 2410 Pine St., for Joseph Horn, who with partner Frank Hardart opened the chain of Automats that bore their names. The first was on Chestnut Street in Philadelphia, and you can still see "Horn & Hardart" engraved above the doors.

Automats were popular during the Depression and into the 1950s. Customers viewed prepared foods behind windows, then inserted coins to lift the glass. They ate standing at counters—there were no tables.

In 1922, a company ad boasted that one out of every 16 Philadelphians enjoyed a daily meal at an Automat. In the 1976 movie *Rocky,* Paulie invites Rocky to

Thanksgiving dinner. Rocky excitedly notes that "Last time I had a turkey, it was when they had a special at Horn & Hardart's about three years ago." In the book *Rosemary's Baby,* the company's pumpkin pie is mentioned as a great dessert.

Continue to ❷ **Fitler Square,** at 24th and Pine Streets, a half-acre park named for one-term Mayor Edwin Fitler, who owned a rope factory and supported the Union in the Civil War by providing uniforms for employees who served. At center is a working Victorian-era fountain. There are three animal sculptures: *Fitler Square Ram, Grizzly,* and *Family of Turtles,* all self-explanatory.

Continue on Pine Street, passing ❸ **Tria,** a comfortable wine bar and restaurant with outdoor seating.

Notice the fire mark between the third-floor windows at 2215 Pine St. Fire marks are medallions that people who purchased fire insurance attached to their homes to tell firemen they'd be paid if they responded to a blaze at that address.

At South 22nd Street, turn left, passing Good Karma Cafe, at 331 S. 22nd St., and an apartment building, at 327 S. 22nd St., that seems to be covered with hanging plants. (A recent count showed more than 50.)

The ❹ **Neill and Mauran Houses**—two residences under one roof—blend Colonial, Queen Anne, and medieval elements. Architect Wilson Eyre, the founder of *House and Garden* magazine, designed this house in 1890. Note the asymmetry augmented by the window size and arrangement and the large doors with tiny mail slots.

Continue to ❺ **Trinity Memorial Church,** on the left as you reach Spruce Street. Completed in the 1880s, it is an integral part of the neighborhood. As the church's website notes, "hordes of neighbors regard it as 'their church' but do not attend—some of them regard it as such even though they are Jewish." Many nonmembers volunteer for its community outreach programs. As one neighbor told a local newspaper in the 1990s, "Trinity is the glue that holds the neighborhood together."

Continue to Chandler Place, 251 S. 22nd St., built in 1904 as the private home for the bishop of Pennsylvania's Episcopal Church. Architect Theophilus Chandler, founder of the University of Pennsylvania's Department of Architecture, designed many religious properties, including the nearby Church of the New Jerusalem and its parish house.

At the intersection of South 22nd Street and St. James Place is ❻ **English Village.** These Tudor-style houses, each slightly different, were built in the 1920s around a leafy pedestrian courtyard. The homes originally sold for $27,000–$30,000. This is a coveted location, but properties here rarely turn over. In 2016, a house was on the market for $735,000.

Continue on South 22nd Street, crossing Walnut Street. The property at 133 S. 22nd St. once belonged to Dr. James Hutchinson, whose grandfather founded the Philadelphia College of Physicians. The elder Hutchinson, in France when the American Revolution began, returned to the colonies with a dispatch from Benjamin Franklin to the Continental Congress. He became one of the Continental Army's senior surgeons, inoculating more than 3,000 soldiers against smallpox at Valley Forge. He died after treating patients during the 1793 Yellow Fever epidemic.

The home at 125 S. 22nd St., with its ornate carvings and Juliet balcony, belonged to prominent lawyer and civic leader John Christian Bullitt. Bullitt drafted the Philadelphia City Charter in the 1870s, and his statue stands on the north side of City Hall.

Pass Chloe Grace Boutique, 115 S. 22nd St., and Albert M. Greenfield Public School, 2200 Chestnut St. At Chestnut Street, turn right. Church of the New Jerusalem, 2129 Chestnut St., is a Swedenborgian Church, built in 1881. It is now used for offices. The parish house is Stars & Stripes, a retail store showcasing American-made products.

The ❼ **First Unitarian Church of Philadelphia,** on the left, was designed by architect Frank Furness. His father, the Reverend William Henry Furness, was the church leader who hired him for the project. The Reverend Furness is credited with setting the church on its social justice path, arguing for an end to slavery and supporting the Underground Railroad decades before the Civil War.

Continue to Van Pelt Street, taking in the ❽ **Lutheran Church of the Holy Communion** on the right. The congregation moved to this building, a former

Protestant church, in the early 1900s, bringing parts of their original church, including a Frank Furness–designed pulpit, baptismal font, organ panel, and altar.

Turn left on Van Pelt Street. De la Salle in Towne, 25 Van Pelt St., is a nonprofit that aims to help boys and young men by using the trauma-informed care approach. This space has historically been used by charitable entities, beginning with the Evening Home for Boys, a charity focused on helping unsupervised, homeless, and uneducated boys and young men by providing food, study, fun, and guidance.

Continue to Ludlow Street. The mural on one wall of the parking lot is *Mapping Freire,* a mosaic of 6,000 photographs, mostly taken by students from Freire Charter School.

Turn left on Ludlow Street, and walk to South 22nd Street. Turn left. **9 Mütter Museum of the College of Physicians of Philadelphia** holds a collection of medical curiosities, antique medical equipment and lots of pickled things in jars. Featured items include a tumor removed from President Grover Cleveland, the liver of conjoined twins Chang and Eng, slides of Einstein's brain, and tissue from John Wilkes Booth's thorax. A glass case holds the 8-foot-long colon that was removed from a man who had complained of constipation for most of his life.

Continue to the museum's Benjamin Rush Medicinal Plant Garden. Rush—a signer of the Declaration of Independence, doctor, and founding member of the College of Physicians—wanted a garden his colleagues could use to replenish their medical supplies. The four beds feature more than 60 medicinal plants, including spiderwort, which is used in laxatives.

Walk to Ranstead Street, and look across South 22nd Street. The building on the right is Sidney Hillman Apartments, also known as Sidneyville, subsidized housing for seniors built in 1969 by the Philadelphia Men's Garment Workers Union and named for labor leader/FDR confidante Sidney Hillman.

On the left is Wilson Eyre Condominiums. Does it look creepy from here? Cross the street to get a closer look. Eyre originally designed this building in the 1880s for a University of Pennsylvania literary society. The first floor was a social club with living space on the top floors. Eyre adorned the exterior with what appears to be screaming or smirking doll heads. One website said the babies are singing.

Continue on Ranstead Street. A sign says this is private space, but that simply means loitering is not allowed. (Not that anyone would want to hang out with the baby heads.)

The **❿ 23rd Street Armory** is a granite fortress in the middle of the modern city, the home of the First Troop, Philadelphia City Cavalry, the oldest cavalry unit in continuous service. The unit was formed in 1774 by city leaders who acted as George Washington's personal bodyguards during the Revolutionary War while also fighting by his side. It is now part of the Pennsylvania National Guard.

Turn left onto South 23rd Street. **⓫ Bonner's Irish Pub** is known for its cheap drinks and relaxed atmosphere and is a reminder that Irish dock workers once lived nearby.

The mural on the side of Erawan Thai Cuisine, 123 S. 23rd St., is *Wild Tuscan Lilies,* a lovely painting even if the connection between Thailand and Tuscany is tenuous.

At Locust Street, turn right. Follow the road as it bears left. **⓬ Schuylkill River Park** was recently expanded to include a 15-foot walkway hovering above the water to the South Street Bridge. A pedestrian bridge over the active railroad tracks becomes a path leading to Fairmount Park and beyond.

This walk ends here. The starting points for the Rittenhouse Square (page 35) and West Philadelphia II (page 194) tours are nearby.

(continued on next page)

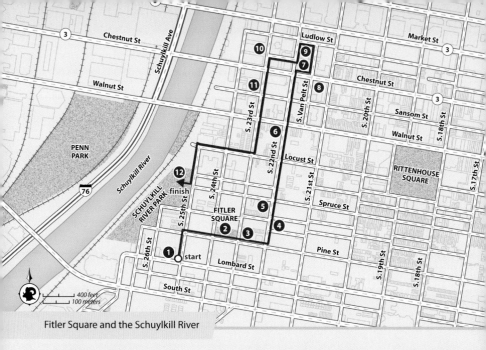

Fitler Square and the Schuylkill River

Points of Interest

1 The Philadelphia School 2503 Lombard St., 215-545-5323, tpschool.org

2 Fitler Square 23rd and Pine Sts., fitlersquare.org

3 Tria 2227 Pine St., 215-309-2245, triaphilly.com

4 Neill and Mauran Houses 315–17 S. 22nd St.

5 Trinity Memorial Church 2200 Spruce St., trinityphiladelphia.org

6 English Village S. 22nd St. and St. James Place

7 First Unitarian Church of Philadelphia 2125 Chestnut St., 215-563-3980, philauu.org

8 Lutheran Church of the Holy Communion 2110 Chestnut St., 215-567-3668, lc-hc.org

9 Mütter Museum of the College of Physicians of Philadelphia 19 S. 22nd St., 215-560-8564, muttermuseum.org

10 23rd Street Armory 22 S. 23rd St., 215-564-1488, 23rdstreetarmory.org

11 Bonner's Irish Pub 120 S. 23rd St., 215-567-5748

12 Schuylkill River Park 300 S. 25th St., fsrp.org

Philadelphia's ornate City Hall is topped with a statue of founder William Penn.

8 North Broad Street I: From City Hall to "Hummingbird Way"

BOUNDARIES: Broad St., John F. Kennedy Blvd., Poplar St.
DISTANCE: 1.3 miles
DIFFICULTY: Easy
PARKING: Public parking is limited, and private parking can be costly.
PUBLIC TRANSIT: Take SEPTA to the City Hall station via the Broad Street line or one of the numerous buses that circle the plaza.

At 12 miles long, Broad Street is the country's longest straight city street. This area developed more slowly than the southern stretch despite attempts by a handful of well-known residents—including department store magnate Ellis Gimbel and actor Edwin Forrest—to make it the next Millionaire's Row. Still, North Broad has some impressive architecture, highlighted in this tour, and, this being Philadelphia, it's impossible to escape tales of American and local history.

Note: Because of the width of the street, you may want to cross back and forth to take in the sites. Be mindful of traffic.

Walk Description

Begin on the north side of **❶ City Hall,** North Broad Street and John F. Kennedy Boulevard. Two statues of men atop horses frame North Broad Street. On the right is General John Fulton Reynolds, a decorated soldier killed on the first day of the Battle of Gettysburg. This was the city's first public monument to a Civil War soldier and its first equestrian statue.

On the left is Civil War General George McClellan, the "Hero of Antietam." An equestrian, he helped the army develop an improved saddle that became standard-issue. That's why people were angry that this statue showed a horse with an ill-fitting bridle.

Walk to the corner of North 15th Street and John F. Kennedy Boulevard, following the crosswalks across JFK to the **❷ Municipal Services Building** and the surrounding art-filled plaza. Start with the statue of a man with his arm raised as if hailing a taxi. This 9-foot-tall bronze sculpture is controversial Mayor Frank Rizzo, who sometimes threatened violence to get his way, once using the Italian phrase *spacco il capo* ("knock their heads") to describe what he wanted to do to opponents. This statue, a gift from Rizzo's family and friends, was modeled after a photo of Rizzo waving at supporters during a parade.

To the right is *Government of the People,* a 30-foot-tall totem pole–like sculpture the Rizzo administration commissioned for the bicentennial, only for the mayor to denounce it, saying it looked like someone had dumped a load of plaster. Other critics have said it looks like a pile of crushed people. The Association for Public Art saw more in the work, writing, "As a symbol of democracy, the sculpture suggests a process of continual struggle, mutual support and dedication, and eventual triumph."

Move around the plaza to see the game pieces—from Monopoly, Parcheesi, dominoes, chess, and checkers—that collectively make up *Your Move.* One of the three artists involved said the sculptures were meant to juxtapose carefree childhood memories with adult responsibilities, which city workers undoubtedly appreciate at 8 a.m. on a Monday.

Leave the plaza via the steps in front of the Rizzo statue. Turn left. Walk to North Broad Street, and turn left again. *Benjamin Franklin, Craftsman,* North Broad Street and John F. Kennedy Boulevard, was commissioned by the Masonic temple across the street. Fans say this sculpture is a welcome change, depicting Franklin as a young man instead of full bellied and balding. Others wonder why the proportions seem uneven. Rumor is the artist was blind in one eye and losing sight in the other when he took this commission.

The Masonic Temple with *Government of the People* in the foreground

The ❸ **Masonic Temple** is the headquarters of the Grand Lodge of Pennsylvania, Free and Accepted Masons. Freemasonry is the oldest continuously existing fraternal organization in the world. Many of the Founding Fathers, including George Washington, were Freemasons.

The Norman cathedral–like building was completed in 1873, but the elaborate interior—which includes seven lodge rooms, each designed in a different period style—took another 20 years to finish. Each room is reportedly designed with one flaw to signify man's imperfection.

Washington's Masonic apron, embroidered by the wife of the Marquis de Lafayette, is on display in the library. In 1902, the Masonic Temple became one of the city's first fully electrified buildings.

Next door is ❹ **Arch Street United Methodist Church,** built in 1870 on the site of a coal yard. The Gothic marble structure has always housed a forward-thinking congregation. In the mid-1800s, Bishop Matthew Simpson was a close friend and supporter of Abraham Lincoln; he later delivered the president's eulogy. Today, the church is a hub of social activism with a welcoming congregation.

Continue on North Broad Street. ❺ **Pennsylvania Academy of the Fine Arts** is headquartered in an 1806 building that combines impressive Second Empire, creative Renaissance, and elegant Gothic architectural styles. Standing above the door is a headless statue of Ceres, Greek goddess of the harvest.

Next to it is the 51-foot-high *Paint Torch,* leaning at a daring 60-degree angle. This gravity-defying work by artist Claes Oldenburg, installed in 2011, includes the 6-foot-tall orange paint blob at its base. Oldenburg also created the *Clothespin* sculpture near City Hall. A 2015 *Philadelphia* magazine article listing the city's 12 worst pieces of public art criticized the artist, wondering if Philadelphia was the only city to "get suckered in" by Oldenburg. "Right now, he's likely over in Stockholm rubbing his palms together and wondering what new eyesore he can pawn off on our oh-so-gullible citizenry. We really have got to learn to say no to giant household items."

Continue north. ❻ *How to Turn Anything into Something Else* is a fantastical mural designed by students who were challenged to consider "obstacle as opportunity," one artist said. A lemon transforms into a bird, and a boat becomes a whale. The young artists named the girl in the top right Kira, the strongest woman in the world, with flashlight eyes that can see through the dark.

On the side of Hahnemann University Hospital is ❼ *Independence Starts Here.* Covering 12,000 square feet and rising seven stories, this mural features locals with disabilities who receive services here. Note the American Sign Language finger alphabet spelling out the word *independence.* Students from the Pennsylvania School for the Deaf posed their hands for the artist.

Stop at Vine Street. The goal of ❽ *The Evolving Face of Nursing* was to encourage its viewers to see nurses in different ways, artist Meg Saligman said. She interviewed more than 100 nurses and included their faces and words in the mural. The mural is the first in the city to use LED lighting technology and special paint that seemingly animate it at night.

Roman Catholic High School, 301 N. Broad St., was the first in the country to offer a free parochial education. The massive Victorian Gothic building opened in 1890.

A few blocks away is the Packard Motor Corporation Building, 317–32 N. Broad St., which originally housed a showroom and offices for the Packard company but is now condos. Built in 1911, the seven-story structure was one of the first in the nation made using reinforced concrete in a steel frame.

This stretch was once known as Automobile Row. A photo from 1910 shows multiple auto dealerships, including Ford, Oldsmobile, Hudson, and Buick.

Continue on North Broad Street. The 18-story white building on the northwest corner of Broad and Callowhill Streets is ❾ The Inquirer Building, which housed the city's two daily newspapers, *The Philadelphia Inquirer* and *The Philadelphia Daily News*. Friends—and enemies—sometimes referred to the building as The Tower of Truth.

In a city of few tall structures, this one made a major impact when it was completed in 1924, with a gold dome and the four-faced clock that could be seen for miles. With the decline of the newspaper industry, the building was sold in 2011. The media entities moved to Market Street.

Continue to Spring Garden Street. Another Saligman mural, ❿ *Common Threads,* towers on the east side of the street, featuring students from two nearby high schools and dolls that belonged to the artist's grandmother.

Opposite the mural, on two sides of Benjamin Franklin High School, 550 N. Broad St., is *All Join Hands: Visions of Peace*. The design was inspired by a yearlong, citywide antiviolence initiative.

In the 1800s, this intersection was a hub of industrial activity, site of the sprawling 17-acre Baldwin Locomotive Works. Company founder Matthias Baldwin designed *Old Ironsides,* a 6-ton locomotive that was one of the first successful models made in the United States. Assembling the train was so involved that, when it was finished, Baldwin declared, "This is the last locomotive that we'll ever build." He was wrong. His company became the largest locomotive maker in the world. At its peak, it churned out 2,500 a year, shipping them as far as Siberia.

⓫ Congregation Rodeph Shalom is the oldest Ashkenazi Jewish congregation in the Western Hemisphere, founded by worshippers from Germany, Holland, and

Poland in 1795. The 1975 book *The History of the Jews of Philadelphia from Colonial Times Until the Age of Jackson* notes the congregation offered free membership to the poor and rabbis gave money to those in need, with the expectation that the recipients would attend weekly services. There are two museums within the Moorish synagogue: The Philadelphia Museum of Jewish Art and the Obermayer Collection of Jewish Ritual Art.

Continue on North Broad Street, passing Old Zion Lutheran Church, 628 N. Broad St. ⑫ **Divine Lorraine Hotel** is named for charismatic Father Major Jealous Divine, called The Messenger. His church, Universal Peace Mission Movement, purchased

this building, the Lorraine Hotel, in 1948. The Gilded Age beauty, built in 1894 as an upscale rental property, became the first hotel in the country to be fully racially integrated. Visitors were expected to follow church rules, which included no smoking, drinking, or profanity. Women and men had rooms on separate floors, and modesty—in part meaning women had to wear skirts—was enforced.

The Salvation Army headquarters, 701 N. Broad St., has a mural on its side that features a smiling bell ringer. Across the street, the ⑬ **Greater Exodus Baptist Church** was built in 1877 for a Presbyterian congregation, served as a Roman Catholic church, and has been a Baptist ministry since the 1970s. The church was failing when, in

The Divine Lorraine Hotel, abandoned and empty for decades, is currently being converted to condos.

1982, former professional football player Herbert H. Lusk II became minister. Under Lusk, who played for the Philadelphia Eagles, the church has thrived, with more than 2,000 members serving the community in a variety of ministries. The historic building features a vestibule mural showing the history of African American Baptists.

Continue north on Broad Street. Pass Parrish Street. The **14** **Philadelphia Metro-politan Opera House** was built by Oscar Hammerstein, grandfather of the famous lyricist, to challenge the popular Academy of Music on South Broad Street. Local newspapers predicted wealthy locals would never travel to North Broad Street to see a show. The rivalry was put to the test on opening night, November 18, 1908, when The Met offered a production of *Carmen* with a 700-member cast and the Academy presented beloved opera singer Enrico Caruso. According to reports, spectators at the Academy listened to Caruso until intermission, then headed uptown to watch the second half of *Carmen*. Both venues sold out that night.

The Met closed after two sold-out seasons. Since then, the building has housed a movie theater, a church, and a sporting arena. In late 2016, a development group said The Met would reopen as a music venue with a restaurant. The building was in the film *Twelve Monkeys*.

This stretch of Poplar Street through North 21st Street is also known as Dixie Hummingbirds Way after the Grammy-winning gospel quartet, formed in the 1920s, that inspired soul musicians such as James Brown. In 1983, Philadelphia's 76ers basketball team was heading to the NBA finals. Someone at ABC asked if the band could perform a song at half time about Moses—in this case 76ers star Moses Malone—leading his people to a better place, also known as victory. The band wrote the song, "Moses is Going to Take Us to the Promised Land," within hours and performed it live on television. The 76ers won the championship.

This walk ends here. The second North Broad Street walk (page 57) begins in the 1200 block of North Broad Street.

(continued on next page)

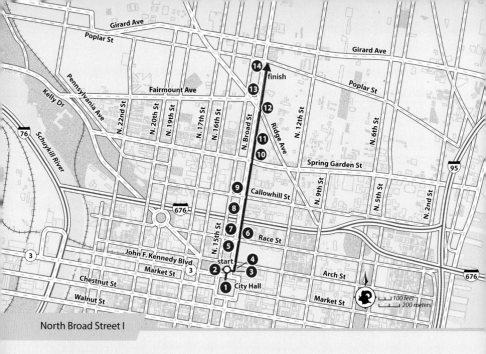

Points of Interest

1 City Hall 1401 John F. Kennedy Blvd., 215-686-1776, phila.gov

2 Municipal Services Building 1401 John F. Kennedy Blvd., 215-686-8686, phila.gov

3 Masonic Temple 1 N. Broad St., 215-968-1917, pamasonictemple.org

4 Arch Street United Methodist Church 55 N. Broad St., 215-568-6250, archstreetumc.org

5 Pennsylvania Academy of the Fine Arts 118–128 N. Broad St., 215-972-7600, pafa.org

6 *How to Turn Anything into Something Else* 207 N. Broad St. For more information, contact Philadelphia Mural Arts, 215-685-0750, muralarts.org.

7 *Independence Starts Here* 216 N. Broad St. For more information, contact Philadelphia Mural Arts, 215-685-0750, muralarts.org.

8 *The Evolving Face of Nursing* N. Broad and Vine Sts. For more information, contact Philadelphia Mural Arts, 215-685-0750, muralarts.org.

9 The Inquirer Building 400 N. Broad St.

10 *Common Threads* N. Broad and Spring Garden Sts. For more information, contact Philadelphia Mural Arts, 215-685-0750, muralarts.org.

11 Congregation Rodeph Shalom 615 N. Broad St., 215-627-6747, rodephshalom.org

12 Divine Lorraine Hotel 699 N. Broad St., thedivinelorrainehotel.com

13 Greater Exodus Baptist Church 714 N. Broad St., 215-235-1394, gebch.com

14 Philadelphia Metropolitan Opera House 858 N. Broad St.

Jackie Robinson successfully slides into home in this mural.

9 North Broad Street II: Temple University and Urban Renewal

BOUNDARIES: Girard Ave., Glenwood Ave., N. Broad St.
DISTANCE: 1.8 miles
DIFFICULTY: Easy
PARKING: There are two public parking garages on the Temple University campus.
PUBLIC TRANSIT: SEPTA's Broad Street Line stops near Temple University at N. 10th and Berks Streets. Bus stops within 0.5 mile include the C bus, 3 and 23.

Broad Street is the longest straight urban road in America, part of the original city plan. There is no 14th Street in the street grid between the Delaware and the Schuylkill Rivers; Broad Street has taken its place. Someone who gives directions to a location on 14th Street is a prankster.

This stretch of North Broad Street has been heavily influenced by the growth of Temple University. This walk looks at some architectural gems as well as some of that new development and public art pieces that honor history and look forward. Because of the width of the street, some walkers may want to cross back and forth to take in sites on both sides. Be mindful of traffic.

Walk Description

Start at North Broad Street and Girard Avenue. *North Philadelphia Heroes,* 1214 N. Broad St., honors seven locals who made a difference, including Dr. Ethel Allen, the city's first African American councilwoman and physician, and Lillia "Mom" Crippen, whose 1999 obituary called her "a one-woman social-service agency." She founded a community center and is believed to have had a hand in the raising of as many as 40 children, many of them handicapped and unwanted. In 1988, she told *The Philadelphia Inquirer,* "All you have to do is say you don't want them and I'll take them."

Memories and Mementos, 1221 N. Broad St., is by David McShane, a lifelong baseball fan also responsible for a mural honoring Jackie Robinson in this walk. McShane also created *The Legendary Blue Horizon,* 1314 N. Broad St., a tribute to the 1,500-seat boxing venue that stood here. Made up of three circa 1865 four-story houses, the Horizon became a sporting hot spot in the 1960s and closed in 2010. *Rocky V* was filmed there. The mural features Muhammad Ali, Joe Frazier, Larry "The Easton Assassin" Holmes, and George Foreman.

Temple University's continued growth means ongoing change on N. Broad St.

The Italianate building housing ❶ **New Freedom Theatre** was the home of actor Edwin Forrest, after whom the Forrest Theatre downtown is named. Born in Philadelphia, Forrest was a teenager when he volunteered to take part in an experiment on the effects of nitrous oxide (laughing gas) and delivered a Shakespearean soliloquy under its influence. A lawyer who witnessed the performance introduced Forrest to a local acting troop, thus launching his career.

In May 1849, Forrest's fans clashed with supporters of rival actor William Macready in New York's Astor Place Riot, in which 22 people were killed.

The building is now Pennsylvania's oldest African American theater company, offering an award-winning performing arts training program. Alums include Tony Award winner Leslie Odom Jr., honored for his performance as Aaron Burr in Broadway's *Hamilton*.

Charles Ellis House, 1430 N. Broad St., now belongs to a religious group, but the 1890s mansion was built by Ellis, who made his fortune operating a horse-drawn trolley company and died here in 1909. His $4 million estate established the Charles E. Ellis College for Fatherless Girls in Delaware County. The college closed in 1977, but the trust fund continues to help young women, awarding more than $1 million in education grants annually.

Alfred E. Burk House, 1500 N. Broad St., is a hulking Beaux Arts building dating to 1909 that historian and author Robert Morris Skaler called "the last great mansion built on North Broad Street." Burk and his brothers owned a leather-goods factory located about 2 miles from here.

The bustling commercial hub that is ❷ **Sullivan Progress Plaza,** the oldest African American–developed and –owned shopping center in the country, has a rich history. In the 1960s, Baptist minister Leon Sullivan—the so-called Lion of Zion—led efforts to develop a shopping center for this underserved African American neighborhood. In 2009, a $22 million renovation brought a new grocery store anchor and new energy. Sullivan, awarded the Presidential Medal of Freedom in 1999, is featured on a mural panel on the center.

Cross Oxford Street. This is part of the 105-acre main campus of Temple University, a state-related institution with about 28,000 undergraduate and 10,000 graduate students. The red-and-white T logo is predominant.

Cecil B. Moore Avenue honors the lawyer and civil rights activist who worked with both Martin Luther King Jr. and Malcolm X. He also served on the Philadelphia City Council and as president of the Philadelphia chapter of the NAACP. A 1987 article in *The Philadelphia Inquirer* described Moore as a "loud, cigar-chomping man who demanded—and got— respect."

Temple University's Liacouras Center, 1776 N. Broad St., was renamed in 2000 for the late Peter J. Liacouras, university president from 1981 to 2000. His 2016 obituary noted that Liacouras is credited with transforming the university from a "commuter school on North Broad Street to . . . a world-class institution." He promoted the school with the marketing campaign, "We could have gone anywhere. We chose Temple."

Continue past Conwell Hall, built in 1929 and named for university founder Russell Conwell. The ❸ **Temple Performing Arts Center** is housed in the former Grace Baptist Church, which Conwell once led. In 1882, a young man in Conwell's congregation who couldn't afford college asked the minister to tutor him. Soon Conwell was teaching a group of men in the evenings. They were dubbed the Night Owls, inadvertently naming the university's future sports teams. A few years later, the charter for Temple College was issued, with Conwell as its president.

A popular speaker, Conwell gave his "Acres of Diamonds" lecture more than 6,000 times between 1869 and 1925. The speech, later printed as a book, proposed that people don't need to travel far to find success because all they need is within their home community. The title comes from an opening anecdote about a man who sold his property to search for riches, only to have the property's new owner discover a diamond mine there.

The center also has a Chapel of the Four Chaplains, dedicated by President Harry Truman in 1951 and named for four men of different religious faiths who gave up their life jackets to other sailors when the SS *Dorchester* was torpedoed by a German U-boat on February 3, 1942.

Continue on North Broad Street, crossing Berks Street. The low stone wall on the west side of North Broad Street is one of the only remaining signs that Monument Cemetery, a Victorian garden–style resting place modeled after Paris's Père Lachaise, once covered four square blocks here. In the 1950s, Temple University received permission to expand and convert the cemetery into sports fields and parking lots.

Of the 28,000 people buried there, family members claimed about 8,000 bodies. The rest were moved to another city cemetery. Many of the headstones were used to construct the base of the Betsy Ross Bridge. Writer Luke Barley wrote on citylab. com that "at low tide, some of the headstones are still visible, no longer a testament to a person beneath, but to the uniquely American habit of turning anything, paradise or cemetery, into a parking lot."

Continue on North Broad Street. The 1895 former residence of real estate developer John Stafford and his family, 2000 N. Broad St., is now the Alpha Epsilon Pi fraternity house. For those who wonder how the Staffords feel about this, a 2009 article in the daily *Temple News* detailed paranormal activity in the home, including doors opening and closing, items disappearing, and the sound of footsteps climbing to the third floor.

At the intersection of North Broad and Diamond Streets is a mural of Grover Washington Jr., the American jazz/funk/soul saxophonist who is often credited—or blamed—with creating the smooth jazz genre. ❹ **Berean Presbyterian Church**

The now-closed Uptown Theater

has occupied this space since the 1950s. Founder Dr. Matthew Anderson used his platform to improve the lives of African Americans by encouraging home ownership—even establishing a loan company to finance purchases—and opening a trade school. Anderson and his work were supported by his wife, Caroline Still, the daughter of a leader in the Underground Railroad and one of the nation's first female African American doctors.

❺ **Uptown Theater,** on the left between Susquehanna Avenue and Dauphin Street, was a major venue on the so-called chitlin circuit between 1951 and 1978, welcoming comedians such as Redd Foxx and Flip Wilson. Still a community gathering point, residents grouped outside to mourn the 2009 death of singer Michael Jackson.

DJ Georgie Woods began promoting shows here in the 1950s, using the AM radio airwaves to talk about civil rights. He was so influential that in 1964, when race riots broke out blocks from the theater, police asked him to speak to the crowds, which disbanded at his request. The NAACP later honored Woods. At the next corner, a red sign designates this stretch as Georgie Woods Boulevard.

The ❻ **Philadelphia Doll Museum,** on the right, collects dolls representing African Americans, tracking the general public's feelings about race through 500 dolls, handmade and machine manufactured, from the United States, Africa, and Europe.

Continue on North Broad Street, passing Official Unlimited, 2331 N. Broad St., a clothing store housed in the former Dropsie College for Hebrew and Cognate Learning, which closed in 1986. Faculty members included Benzion Netanyahu, whose son Benjamin would later become prime minister of Israel. A 2015 article about the younger Netanyahu in *The Washington Post* was headlined, "Why Benjamin Netanyahu is so tough: He's from Philadelphia." The family lived here for four years.

The Philadelphia and Reading Railroad's former North Broad Street Station, 2601 N. Broad St., was built in the 1920s and closed in the 1960s because of dwindling ridership. The building has been converted to low-income housing with space for people leaving homeless shelters.

The large empty lot across from the station was the Baker Bowl, home field for the Philadelphia Phillies. Officially called National League Park, the stadium cost $80,000 to build in 1887 and could comfortably seat 12,000. This is where Pittsburgh's Honus Wagner slammed his 3,000th career hit in June 1914; where President Woodrow Wilson became the first president to attend the World Series; and where Babe Ruth played his final major league game.

A colorful mural on the building at the corner of North Broad Street and Lehigh Avenue reads SHINE. Remember that.

The 10-story former Ford Motor Company Assembly Plant, 2700 N. Broad St., operated from 1910 to 1926, putting out about 150 cars each day. After World War I, the company moved to the suburbs. The building is empty today.

Turn around to see the opposite side of the building at North Broad Street and Lehigh Avenue. It reads RISE.

Continue on North Broad Street to ❼ *Tribute to Jackie Robinson.* Originally painted in 1997 and retouched in 2016, this 30-foot-tall mural honors the first player to desegregate Major League Baseball in 1947. The artist said he chose to paint in black and white as a reminder of Robinson's struggles. The image is a compilation of two photos and shows Robinson, a Brooklyn Dodger, stealing home in the 1955 World Series against the New York Yankees. The catcher with his back to you, No. 8, is Yogi Berra. The umpire called Robinson safe at home, although video footage of the play seems to show otherwise. Berra always insisted Robinson was out.

Cross Glenwood Avenue. The large pink building is North Philadelphia Station, opened in the 1870s to serve the city's subway line and Amtrak. To return to downtown, hop on a train here. If not, look one block north at the furniture store with yellow and red signage. This was Joe Frazier's Gym, 2917 N. Broad St. The boxer, an Olympic gold medalist and World Heavyweight Champion, is perhaps best remembered for beating Muhammad Ali in 1971's Fight of the Century. He purchased this gym in 1975 and trained boxers here for 25 years.

(continued on next page)

North Broad Street II

Points of Interest

① **New Freedom Theatre** 1346 N. Broad St., 215-765-2793, freedomtheatre.org

② **Sullivan Progress Plaza** 1501 N. Broad St., 215-232-7070, progressplaza.com

③ **Temple Performing Arts Center** 1837 N. Broad St., 215-204-9860, templeperformingartscenter.org

④ **Berean Presbyterian Church** 2101 N. Broad St., 215-769-5683, bereanpresbyterian.org

⑤ **Uptown Theater (now closed)** 2240–2248 N. Broad St.

⑥ **Philadelphia Doll Museum** 2253 N. Broad St., 215-787-0220

⑦ *Tribute to Jackie Robinson* 2803 N. Broad St. For more information, contact Philadelphia Mural Arts, 215-685-0750, muralarts.org.

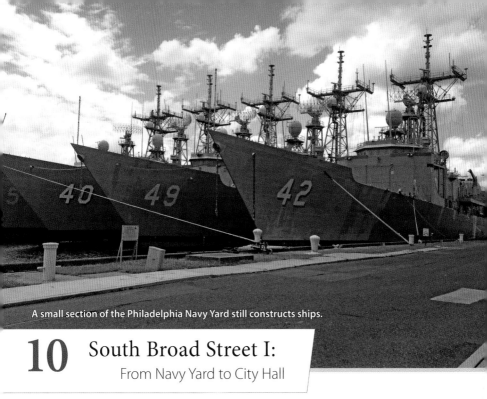

A small section of the Philadelphia Navy Yard still constructs ships.

10 South Broad Street I:
From Navy Yard to City Hall

BOUNDARIES: S. Broad St., Market St., Constitution Ave.
DISTANCE: 3.9 miles; if you loop through the Navy Yard, add another 1.4 miles
DIFFICULTY: Moderate
PARKING: Metered street parking is available once the walk passes the stadium area. The sporting complexes have multiple pay lots.
PUBLIC TRANSIT: SEPTA's Broad Street line stops at AT&T station, near the stadiums, about 0.2 mile away. The Navy Yard also offers a free shuttle between Center City and the Navy Yard. The stop is at N. 10th St. between Market and Filbert Sts. The schedule is available online.

Broad Street is where the city celebrates. This is where mummers have paraded for a century (for more on the Mummers Parade, see Walk 24, page 178), where residents gathered to mark the end of World Wars I and II, and where sports teams have victory parades.

Walk Description

This walk begins at the ❶ **Navy Yard**, which was the first Unites States Navy shipyard. The current facilities were built in the 1870s. During World War II, the yard employed more than 40,000 people who built 53 ships, including the USS *New Jersey*. Workers also repaired almost 600 war-damaged crafts, and scientists developed the liquid thermal diffusion technique that made the Manhattan Project possible.

The Navy closed most programs here in the 1990s. City government, the new landlord, converted the area into a thriving business hub, with more than 150 businesses—including pharmaceutical giant GlaxoSmithKline and retailer Urban Outfitters—employing more than 12,000 people.

To further explore the 1,200-acre property, the Navy Yard's management has designed a self-guided 2-mile walking tour, available online. Enter the main gates and follow Constitution Avenue to the Four Chaplains Memorial Chapel and Foundation, 1201 Constitution Ave., which honors four army chaplains belonging to different religious orders who, when the SS *Dorchester* was sinking after being struck by a U-boat torpedo in February 1945, treated the wounded, calmed the panicked, and gave up their own life jackets and lives.

Legend says the four men linked arms on the ship's deck and sang and said prayers as the boat went down, with one witness saying, "It was the finest thing I have seen or hope to see this side of heaven." Only 230 men of the 904 aboard survived the wreck. In 1988, Congress passed a unanimous resolution establishing February 3 as Four Chaplains Day.

Double back, leaving the Navy Yard, and turn right. Walk north on South Broad Street. On the right past I-95 is the ❷ **South Philadelphia Sports Complex.** This is where the city's professional sporting teams play—Citizens Bank Park for baseball's Phillies; the Wells Fargo Center

The *Theatre of Life* mural is one of the city's most popular.

for hockey's Flyers and basketball's 76ers; and Lincoln Financial Field for football's Eagles. A retail/entertainment center called XFinity Live! is also here.

It was in the Wells Fargo Center, opened in 1996, where Hillary Clinton accepted the Democratic Party's presidential nomination in 2016, becoming the first female presidential nominee from a major political party. The other three facilities opened in the early 2000s.

Continue on South Broad Street. Cars are often parked in the middle of the street, which may seem odd to outsiders but is normal to locals. A 2015 *Philadelphia* magazine article quoted a police captain who said ticketing the vehicles could cause a "minor revolution." Perhaps, the writer mused, the city learned to avoid parking matters after 2,000 residents threw tomatoes at the mayor who suggested changes in 1961.

Continue past I-76 to Marconi Plaza, 2800 S. Broad St. The Guglielmo Marconi statue was dedicated April 25, 1980, the 106th anniversary of the Italian scientist/inventor/Nobel Prize Laureate's birth. The "Father of Modern Communications" is an unimposing figure, wearing a neat suit with his hands by his sides. Marconi's humble nature was one of his beloved traits.

Bambi Cleaners, 2439 S. Broad St., has been in operation since the 1950s and has an old-fashioned sign with a lookalike Disney deer from when copyright laws were, apparently, more lax.

❸ **South Philadelphia High School** was built in 1907 as a trade school for boys, primarily Italian and Jewish immigrants. One alum was Israel Goldstein, who graduated from the University of Pennsylvania at age 17 and went on to become a well-known rabbi and founder of Brandeis University.

"Southern," as locals call it, has a list of notable graduates, including Chubby Checker, Eddie Fisher, Jack Klugman, and Marian Anderson. Less recognizable is Eddie "Mr. Basketball" Gottlieb. In the 1920s, Gottlieb helped found the Philadelphia Sphas, a basketball team named for its sponsor, South Philadelphia Hebrew

Association. Most players were Jewish, and because the team had no home court, they were known as The Wandering Jews.

In 1946, Gottlieb became the first coach of the Philadelphia Warriors, leading them to the NBA's first championship. Gottlieb later helmed NBA's rules committee for 25 years and was in charge of schedules for 30 years. Basketball Hall of Famer Harry Litwack once said that "Gottlieb was about as important to the game of basketball as the basketball."

Six blocks north, at the Tasker Street intersection, Philadelphia Gas Works, 1601 S. Broad St., and Dolphin Billiards Tavern, 1539 S. Broad St., both have interesting signs.

Pennsylvania Burial Company/Baldi Funeral Home, 1327–29 S. Broad St., just past Reed Street, is one of a cluster of funeral homes here bearing Italian surnames. Patriarch Pietro Jacovini, an Italian immigrant, opened his first funeral home in 1921, creating the prepaid funeral. Jacovini was also editor of the city's Italian-language newspaper and a civic leader who annually led the New Year's Day parade on his black stallion.

Philip's Restaurant, 1145 S. Broad St., has been closed since the 1990s, but the sign remains. The restaurant opened in the 1940s, bearing owner Philip Muzi's first name because the nation was at war with Italy. The landscape mural on the building's sides dates to the earliest days of the city's Mural Arts Program, when its primary goal was covering graffiti.

Broad Street Diner, 1135 S. Broad St, on the corner of Ellsworth Street, reopened and renovated in 2011, is open 24/7 and serves classic diner fare.

Cross Ellsworth Street to Boot & Saddle bar, 1131 S. Broad St., long the city's only country-Western bar. Original owner Peter Del Borrello Sr. was a retired US Navy chief petty officer who decorated the walls with dozens of sailor caps. Del Borrello closed the bar in 1995 and the Boot reopened in 2013 as a live-music venue and restaurant. Some signs of the old bar remain, including the folk art cowboy murals.

At the Washington Avenue intersection, note the empty plot at 1001 S. Broad St. This was Citizens Volunteer Hospital, where wounded Union soldiers were

Citizens Bank Park

Statue of Hall of Fame third basemen Mike Schmidt by Zenos Frudakis outside Citizens Bank Park

treated. Opened in 1863, the hospital had 400 beds but routinely treated double that number. The hospital was unique because it was completely financed by citizens.

The Philadelphia High School for Creative and Performing Arts (CAPA) was built in 1907 as a library that contained the tomb of the couple who funded the Greek Revival building. The library closed in the 1960s, and the building suffered, at one point looking so run-down that it was used as a backdrop in the 1995 film *Twelve Monkeys* to show a destroyed city. CAPA moved into this space in 1997. (The entombed couple moved out—or were moved.) Famous alums include members of The Roots.

Arts Bank, 601 S. Broad St., now houses performance spaces, but it was a bank when it was completed in 1886. "South Philadelphia National Bank" is still carved on the facade. Currency collectors know the bank because it printed money—almost $1.5 million between 1886 and 1935—issuing 15 types and denominations. Collectors seek rare $10 "red seal" national bank notes issued in 1902 and $10 "brown back" national bank notes issued in 1882, both printed here. One collecting website notes that the red seals are the rarest bank notes printed by any national bank.

The 1882 Queen Anne–style home at 507 S. Broad St. was built for J. Dundas Lippincott. The Lippincotts founded their eponymous publishing company in 1785, selling it in 1978 to what is now HarperCollins. On the side, *Theatre of Life,* one of the city's most popular murals, shows different figures representing roles people play. The hands holding marionette sticks symbolize external influences that control people. Mosaics accent the painting, which has a 3-D effect. Completing this work required 400 gallons of paint, 10,000 pieces of glass, and 5,000 marbles.

❹ **The Gershman Y** has been a thriving cultural and community center since 1924, when the Young Men's Hebrew Association merged with the Young

Women's Hebrew Society and moved to this building. YM&WHA—Young Men and Women's Hebrew Association—is carved on the building. The Y celebrates Jewish arts and culture. Programs here include art exhibits, film showings, dance and cooking classes, and community events such as Latkepalooza, which invites local chefs to interpret potato pancakes. An Asian-fusion chef added ginger to his version. A Greek chef used spinach and feta.

❺ **Broad Street Ministry** describes itself as a "broad-minded Christian community that practices radical hospitality and works for a more just world through civic engagement." This hub of social activism was founded in 2005. Pastor Bill Golderer calls the weekly community meal "Philadelphia's most dangerous dinner party," bringing together 4,000 diners from the city's wealthiest residents to the poorest.

The building at 309 S. Broad St. formerly housed Philadelphia International Records, a rival to Motown Records where songwriters/producers Kenneth Gamble and Leon Huff created "The Sound of Philadelphia," music that promoted black pride and addressed the nation's political and social climate. Its best-selling acts included Patti LaBelle, Teddy Pendergrass, and Lou Rawls. Songs from the label include "Ain't No Stoppin' Us Now" and "TSOP (The Sound of Philadelphia)," which was used as the theme to *Soul Train*.

The ❻ **Wilma Theater** houses a company that takes its name not from Fred Flintstone's wife but from a character created by Virginia Woolf. This building's unique signage looks especially striking in the evening.

The ❼ **Wells Fargo History Museum** is one of 10 museums highlighting the company's heritage, which dates to the 1850s. Exhibits include a $386 million cashier's check from 1950 and an authentic stagecoach. The lobby is an example of 1928 Beaux Arts grandeur.

The PNB Building, 1 S. Broad St., formerly housed Philadelphia National Bank, and the company's letters once marked the top of the building on all sides. The bell tower of this Art Deco high-rise has a 17-ton bell rung hourly Monday–Saturday to honor department store magnate John Wanamaker.

City Hall is across the street. Consider taking another walk that starts from there.

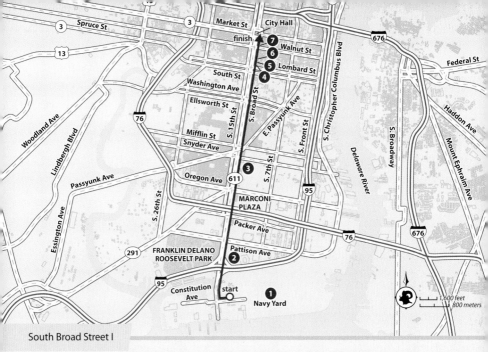

South Broad Street I

Points of Interest

1. **Philadelphia Navy Yard** 4747 S. Broad St., 215-551-0251, navyyard.org
2. **South Philadelphia Sports Complex** 3300 S. Seventh St.
3. **South Philadelphia High School** 2101 S. Broad St.
4. **The Gershman Y** 401 S. Broad St., 215-545-4400, gershmany.org
5. **Broad Street Ministry** 315 S. Broad St., 215-735-4847, broadstreetministry.org
6. **Wilma Theater** 265 S. Broad St., 215-893-9456, wilmatheater.org
7. **Wells Fargo History Museum** 123 S. Broad St., 215-670-6123, wellsfargohistory.com /museums/philadelphia

The Spirit of '61, in front of The Union League, shows a bronze soldier from the First Regiment Infantry National Guard.

11 South Broad Street II: From the Avenue of the Arts to Franklin Delano Roosevelt Park

BOUNDARIES: S. Broad St., S. 15th St., Market St., Pattison Ave.
DISTANCE: 3.9 miles
DIFFICULTY: Moderate
PARKING: Driving around here can be tricky, and parking is difficult. Public transportation is the way to get to City Hall.
PUBLIC TRANSIT: The SEPTA subway system is only footsteps away, and public buses stop at multiple points around City Hall. Bus 38 stops here and at Independence Hall, the Franklin Institute, and the art museum. Bus 21 travels Walnut St. going west and then returns on Chestnut St. going east. Another option is the PHLASH tourist bus, which operates May–October. Tickets are $2 per ride or $5 for a day pass (free for adults ages 65 and over and for children ages 4 and under).

Broad Street is one of the country's earliest planned streets, developed in 1681 and projected as "a unifying government and religious center of the new world metropolis." Still, as late as the mid-1800s, this stretch was rural, with businesses and residents concentrated along the Delaware River to the east. Planners built the Academy of Music here in 1857 because it was quiet and remote.

In the years that followed, this became the city's Wall Street, with financial giants such as Drexel Company, Girard Trust, and Fidelity Bank opening. Residential development followed, and the mansions of what was once called Millionaire's Row still stand, although they've been subdivided into smaller apartments and businesses.

In the 1990s, Mayor Ed Rendell, later governor of Pennsylvania, pushed for the development of the Avenue of the Arts Inc., a nonprofit organization focused on developing the area by pulling in performing arts groups as well as retail and restaurants. Where there was once a single theatre, now there are four, as well as an expanded University of the Arts, high-end hotels, and restaurants. Keep that in mind as you start your tour, as the road has two names—South Broad Street and Avenue of the Arts.

Walk Description

Begin at City Hall, where South Broad and Penn Square meet. When finished in 1901, critics called the building "the white elephant" because the marble facade shone so brightly. Take the crosswalk south to the center median; then turn slightly right and cross again. The Ritz-Carlton, Philadelphia, 10 Avenue of the Arts, is in the former Girard Bank building. The Land Title Building and Annex, 100 S. Broad St., is one of the country's earliest skyscrapers, with the first of its two towers rising 16 stories in 1898. The other, 21 stories tall, was completed a few years later.

Continue on South Broad Street. ❶ **The Union League** was founded in 1862 by supporters of President Abraham Lincoln and the Union during the Civil War. The club occupies an entire city block. Unless a public event is being held, only members are allowed inside. Outside, the sculpture on your right is *Washington Grays Monument,* also known as *Pennsylvania Volunteer,* a tribute to an 1822 volunteer military regiment formed to serve in times of war and peace, similar to today's National Guard. In 1848, the Grays guarded President John Quincy Adams as he lay in state at Independence Hall. Members served in the Civil War.

On the left is a bronze soldier from the First Regiment Infantry National Guard of Philadelphia called *The Spirit of '61.* The First Regiment was the first called to action at the start of the Civil War, following the attack on Fort Sumter in 1861.

Continue to 200 S. Broad St. Formerly the Bellevue-Stratford Hotel, the site currently houses a hotel, a shopping mall, and offices. The Bellevue-Stratford was the most luxurious hotel of its time, the "Grande Dame of Broad Street" when it opened in 1904, with notable guests including members of the Astor, Morgan, and Vanderbilt families; stars such as John Wayne, Bob Hope, and Katharine Hepburn; and almost every sitting American president since Theodore Roosevelt. The 1936 and 1948 Republican National Conventions were held here, as was the 1948 Democratic National Convention.

Cross Walnut Street and look at the sidewalk decor marking the start of the Philadelphia Music Alliance's Walk of Fame. Since 1987, more than 100 plaques have been added to honor local music greats, including Dizzy Gillespie, Dick Clark, John Coltrane, Marian Anderson, Bessie Smith, and Pearl Bailey. The 2015 inductees included Billie Holiday and The Roots.

Continue to the ❷ **Academy of Music,** mentioned in this walk's introduction. The so-called Grand Old Lady of Locust Street is the oldest opera house in the country still used for its original purpose. President Franklin Pierce attended its ground-breaking in 1855. Giuseppe Verdi's *Il Trovatore* was the first production. Pyotr Tchaikovsky and Igor Stravinsky performed here in the 1800s, while stars such as Frank Sinatra, Duke Ellington, and Lynn Fontanne did so in the 1900s. Former presidents, including Ulysses S. Grant, Grover Cleveland, and Richard Nixon, attended productions.

The ghosts of the bygone days apparently still linger, at least in the upper balconies, where women have reported being pinched or having their hair pulled and one man said he saw a black shadow appear and disappear before his eyes.

The Merriam Theater, 250 S. Broad St., was built by the Shubert family in 1918 to honor a brother killed in a train accident. Touring Broadway shows stop here. The University of the Arts, which owns the building, uses it for student activities.

The cornerstone at 260 S. Broad St. reads THE ATLANTIC BUILDING. This 21-story office tower, built in the 1920s for the Atlantic Richfield Oil Refining Company, is now a mixed-use building, with retail, offices, and residences. Check out the lobby's Art Deco designs and detailed murals.

The $180 million ❸ **Kimmel Center for the Performing Arts** is the home of the Philadelphia Orchestra and hosts performances of all types. Built in 2001, it's named for philanthropist Sidney Kimmel, who donated more than $15 million toward its construction.

❹ **Symphony House/Suzanne Roberts Theatre** is a 32-story mixed-use tower named for the wife of the founder of cable giant Comcast. Built in 2007, it replaced a gas station and parking lot. Still, the finished product was not greeted warmly. Pulitzer Prize–winning architecture critic Inga Saffron called it "the ugliest new condo building in Philadelphia," noting its "mixed-use tower flounces onto venerable South Broad Street like a sequined and over-rouged strumpet." While the building may get mixed reviews, the Philadelphia Theatre Company, based here, is well respected.

The new city public health buildings at 500 S. Broad St. stand on the former site of the Dunbar Theater, later renamed the Lincoln Theater. Opened in 1919, it was a showplace for African American acts with its own Harlem Repertory. Owners E. C. Brown and Andrew Stevens Jr. also owned one of the most successful African American banks north of the Mason-Dixon line. Stevens was the only black member of the state's Republican committee, and Brown was president of the largest black realty firm in New York.

The men opened the theater partly because Brown had been denied entry to the Forrest Theatre because of his skin color. The Dunbar, under various owners, thrived until the Great Depression. Some of country's top African American entertainers, including Lena Horne and Duke Ellington, performed here. The building was torn down in 1966.

❺ **The Philadelphia Clef Club of Jazz and Performing Arts** is sometimes called the house that jazz built. It was founded in 1935 by African American musicians barred from joining a whites-only union. The Clef Club moved here in 1995. The union's offices stood at 914 S. Broad St., now a fast-food restaurant.

The stretch of South Broad Street between South Street and Washington Avenue honors the Reverend Charles A. Tindley, who helmed the still-active Tindley Temple United Methodist Church, 750–762 S. Broad St. Born to enslaved parents in 1851, Tindley learned to read and write while working as a teenage janitor at Bainbridge Street Methodist Episcopal Church, where he would eventually lead the congregation. He was an early civil rights leader and is considered the father of gospel music, credited with composing "Stand by Me" and other hymns. The church says he also wrote the lyrics to "We Shall Overcome."

❻ Circle Mission Church is owned by the International Peace Mission Movement, founded by Father Major Jealous Divine, a charismatic, sectarian religious leader whose movement took shape in the 1930s. He preached modesty and moral living, believing his followers should pool resources and live together in racially integrated communes. Some critics called the church a cult. These three buildings were all purchased in 1939. Before that, the twin Victorian homes at the corner had been a hotel.

Approach the intersection of Washington Avenue. The land is currently undeveloped but has a rich history. The city's original passenger train station, built by the Philadelphia, Wilmington and Baltimore Railroad in 1852, stood here. Soldiers reporting for duty during the Civil War left here for points south. President Lincoln's funeral train stopped briefly en route to Illinois.

Cross Washington Avenue. The building at 1100 S. Broad St., now Marine Club Condominiums, was the Marine Quartermaster's Depot, which made soldiers' uniforms during the World Wars.

The stretch of road between Washington and Oregon Avenues is called the Avenue of the States and features two flags from each state. During the 2016 Democratic National Convention, protesters shouting "Take it down! Take it down!" surrounded one of the Mississippi state flags because it includes the stars and bars of the Confederate battle flag. City officials obliged.

The **❼ National Shrine of St. Rita of Cascia and St. Rita's Church** honors the Italian nun known as the Saint of the Impossible and the Peacemaker. Built in 14th-century Renaissance style, the shrine began as a parish church for Italian immigrants.

Look through the graffiti-marred front windows of the long-shuttered Meglio Furs, 1300 S. Broad St., which still has some objects on display. The sign is something of an icon.

The 40-foot-tall painting of opera singer Mario Lanza, 1326 S. Broad St., shows him midtune, wearing a white bow tie and black tails. Artist Diana Keller said she listened to Lanza's music while painting.

The remains of a mural honoring Frank Guarrera can still be glimpsed at 1532 S. Broad St. Guarrera was a baritone who sang at the Metropolitan Opera for nearly 30 years. He died in 2007 at age 83. This mural featured him in his five most famous roles. Blame new construction and building repairs for the loss of this artwork.

The stunning $45.2 million South Philadelphia Health and Literary Center, 1700 S. Broad St., is the result of a collaboration between the city and Children's Hospital of Philadelphia. It opened in 2016, with medical facilities, a library branch, and a recreational center. Note the bright colors and cantilevered upper floors. The statue in front is *See the Moon* by Evelyn Keyser.

The former Bell Telephone Company building, 2000 S. Broad St., will remind some readers of an era when Bell dominated the phone business. This 1962 building is now a Verizon store.

Consider taking a break at ❽ **Melrose Diner:** take a right on Passyunk Avenue. Walk one block to South 15th Street, and turn left. This popular landmark, open around the clock since 1935, formerly promoted itself with a commercial jingle that included the words "Everybody who knows goes to Melrose." The current staff may be persuaded to sing.

Continue on South Broad Street. Renzetti & Magnarelli Clergy, 2216 S. Broad St., on the right past the Jackson Street intersection, "has been serving the vesturing needs of various religious orders and church organizations for over 50 years," its website notes.

Continue on South Broad Street. ❾ **John Lerro Candy,** just before Porter Street, opened in the 1930s and is now run by the fourth generation of the Lerro family. The current owner told Hidden City Philadelphia in 2011 that, "There is no secret to candy. You make it fresh to order. That's the secret." The family's factory is now in the suburbs.

Pass Scannicchio's, 2500 S. Broad St., a relatively new eatery with a largely old-school menu, and the Philadelphia Performing Arts Charter School, 2600 S. Broad St. The green space on the opposite side of Oregon Avenue is Marconi Plaza, a 19-acre park named for Guglielmo Marconi, who created the wireless telegraph and unidirectional radio. Still a gathering place for the city's Italian-American community, the descriptive plaque at the corner describes Marconi as a "deeply religious humanitarian genius, glory of the world in Italy, and glory of Italy in the world . . . His inventions saved millions of lives and will continue to do so as long as this world exists."

Continue to a sculpture surrounded by a low gate decorated with three ships. This is thought to be the first publicly funded Christopher Columbus monument in the country. It's not a good look for Columbus.

Pass the I-76 on-ramps, Packer Avenue, and Pattison Avenue to reach Franklin Delano Roosevelt Park. This 348-acre green space is an oasis in a concrete-heavy area, with a golf course, soccer fields, tennis courts, a boathouse, and a gazebo. Its baseball field is named for Richie Ashburn, an All-Star second baseman who played for the Philadelphia Phillies between 1948 and 1959 and later became a Phillies broadcaster.

Also inside the park is the ❿ **American Swedish Historical Museum.** Designed to look like a 17th-century Swedish castle, the museum opened in the 1920s and is a tribute to the Swedish influence in the area, which dates back to the 1600s. Swedes brought with them a building technique that later took over the American frontier: the log cabin.

To explore the opposite side of South Broad Street, connect with Walk 10 (page 65), which begins at the Navy Yard.

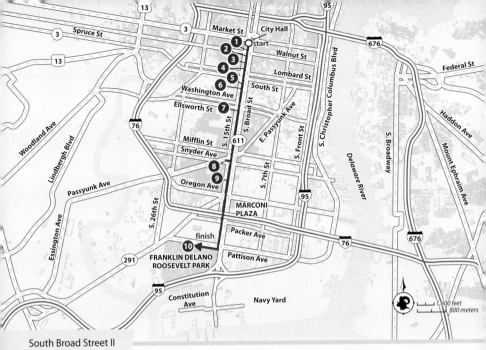

South Broad Street II

Points of Interest

1 The Union League of Philadelphia 140 S. Broad St., 215-563-6500, unionleague.org

2 Academy of Music 240 S. Broad St., 215-893-1999, www.kimmelcenter.org

3 Kimmel Center for the Performing Arts 300 S. Broad St., 215-670-2300, www.kimmelcenter.org

4 Symphony House/Suzanne Roberts Theatre 440 S. Broad St., 215-985-1400, philadelphiatheatrecompany.org

5 Philadelphia Clef Club of Jazz and Performing Arts 738 S. Broad St., 215-893-9912, clefclubofjazz.org

6 Circle Mission Church 764–772 S. Broad St., 215-735-3917

7 National Shrine of St. Rita of Cascia and St. Rita's Church 1166 S. Broad St., 215-546-8333, saintritashrine.org

8 Melrose Diner 1501 Snyder Ave., 215-467-6644, themelrosedinerandbakery.com

9 John Lerro Candy 2434 S. Broad St., 215-336-0411

10 American Swedish Historical Museum 1900 Pattison Ave., 215-389-1776, americanswedish.org

Woody's is a well-known Gayborhood nightspot.

12 Market Street East: The Gayborhood and Reading Terminal Market

BOUNDARIES: Arch St., Pine St., Juniper St., Eighth St.
DISTANCE: 2 miles
DIFFICULTY: Easy
PARKING: While there is some metered street parking, it's hard to get. There are many paid lots. Read signage carefully, as some offer discounts if purchases are made at Reading Terminal Market.
PUBLIC TRANSIT: This tour begins near SEPTA's Jefferson station, and both the Broad Street and Market-Frankford Lines stop here. Buses that stop nearby include the 17, 23, 33, 38, 44, 61, and 78.

Almost every English-speaking town in the 1600s had a main thoroughfare named High Street. Philadelphia was no exception. But Philadelphia founder William Penn may have influenced the eventual name change when he stretched major markets along the road. Locals soon began to call this Market Street, and the name was made official in the mid-1800s.

Market Street remains a commercial stretch dotted with historic sites. Many of Benjamin Franklin's activities were centered around Market Street, President George Washington lived on the road, and Thomas Jefferson wrote the Declaration of Independence while renting lodgings here.

This walk starts at City Hall, wanders through the hub of LGBT culture and nightlife, and includes the can't-miss Reading Terminal Market, a great introduction to the City of Brotherly Love and Sisterly Affection.

Walk Description

Begin on the east side of City Hall in front of the statue of John Wanamaker, inscribed simply with his name and *citizen*. Founder of the department store chain that bore his name, Wanamaker amassed a large fortune during his lifetime and shared that wealth with others. He helped build Presbyterian Hospital, cofounded the Sunday Breakfast Rescue Mission to feed the homeless and hungry, and generously gave to causes such as famine relief in Ireland and help for victims of the 1913 Ohio River flood. When he died in 1922, public schools were closed and flags were lowered to half-mast. About 4,000 residents contributed the $35,000 needed to place this statue of him here.

Directly across from Wanamaker is the 24-story, Art Deco Market Street National Bank, 1319–1325 Market St., built in 1931. The brick and terra-cotta building housed a nickelodeon called Fairyland between 1909 and 1913. The neighboring Courtyard Marriott was built in 1926 and is another Art Deco wonder.

Cross Juniper Street. The historical marker on the island at Market and Juniper Streets remembers Philadelphian Anna Jarvis, founder of Mother's Day, first observed in 1908. Jarvis stressed that the day was Mother's Day, not Mothers' Day, as individuals paid their respects to their own maternal figures. Jarvis was angered as the holiday became commercial. The website explorepahistory.com notes she "objected to greeting cards as 'a poor excuse for the letter you are too lazy to write,' and the sale of flowers and gifts for 'Mother' as turning a day of 'sentiment' into one of 'profit.'" Until her death in 1948, Jarvis fought to reclaim the day, dying penniless.

Cross to the southeast corner of Market Street. Macy's is housed in the **❶ Wanamaker Building,** formerly Wanamaker's department store. The original store had five sales floors, each the equivalent of three football fields. President William Taft attended the store's dedication in December 1911. Inside, the airy marble Grand Court features the Wanamaker Organ, formerly displayed at the St. Louis World's Fair in 1904. It has been played daily since 1910.

The atrium also holds the eagle, a 2,500-pound bronze statue from the same World's Fair. The sculpture was immediately popular with shoppers and remains so, with generations telling friends to "meet me at the eagle." The store's Christmas Light Show has drawn crowds since 1956. Wanamaker's then and now is referenced in pop culture. John Travolta's jeep crashed into a window in 1981's *Blow Out*. A character on HBO's *The Sopranos* says he met his wife at the tie counter.

Turn right onto South 13th Street. St. John the Evangelist Catholic Church, 21 S. 13th St., was chartered in 1839 and has long been one of the city's busiest parishes. The church once offered a Sunday 2:45 a.m. service to accommodate newspaper workers leaving work around that time.

Look at the ghost sign, a remnant of the property's past use, on the second floor of the building, with Old Nelson Food Co. on its ground floor. It reads, LADIES AND CHILDREN'S HAIR DRESSING in beautiful script.

Cross Chestnut Street, entering an area sometimes called Washington Square West or Midtown Village but is best known as the Gayborhood. Long the epicenter of the city's LGBT cultural scene, this once run-down, nine-block pocket is a popular dining and entertainment destination. Philadelphia is considered one of the nation's most gay-friendly cities. In 2003, it was one of the first in the country to actively seek LGBT tourists with the tagline "Get your history straight and your nightlife gay." After the U.S. Supreme Court's 2015 decision allowing same-sex marriage, the city's tourism office released the statement "Brotherly or sisterly, love is love."

Personal Melody, on the second floor of 110 S. 13th St., is the work of twin brothers known for their graffiti.

With so many restaurants and shops, it may be simplest to provide a block-by-block list. For shopping, consider Paper on Pine, 115 S. 13th St., for custom stationery, gifts,

McGillin's offers a large selection of regional microbrews.

and paper goods; Open House, 107 S. 13th St., for home goods and souvenirs; and Marcie Blaine/Verde, 108 S. 13th St., for artisanal chocolates and gifts.

For dining, consider Barbuzzo, 110 S. 13th St., for Mediterranean cuisine or Lolita, 106 S. 13th St., for Mexican fare. Both are owned and operated by Marcie Turney and Valerie Safran, 13th Street pioneers who own nine properties here.

Stop at Drury Street. Above is a mural of urban planner and visionary Edmund Bacon, 102 S. 13th St., sometimes called "The Father of Modern Philadelphia." He's also the father of Kevin. To the right is ❷ McGillin's Olde Ale House, the city's oldest continuously operating tavern, opened in 1860 by Irish immigrants Catherine and William McGillin, who raised their 13 children in an upstairs apartment. Ma McGillin, who ran the bar until dying in 1937, still haunts the premises.

Return to South 13th Street. *Philly Chunk Pack,* on the second floor of 120 S. 13th St., is another work by a well-known graffiti artist. Dining options include Sampan, 124 S. 13th St., offering Pan-Asian cuisine; El Vez, 121 S. 13th St., an early part of the area's revival known for guacamole made table-side; and Charlie Was a Sinner, 131 S. 13th St., a vegan restaurant and bar. Shopping options include Shibe Vintage Sports and Absolute Pop, 137 S. 13th St., for team gear and art.

❸ Woody's is a bustling bar and restaurant that the city's official promotional materials describe this way: "Paris has the Eiffel Tower, and London Big Ben, and the Gayborhood has Woody's, a neighborhood landmark since 1980."

Continue on South 13th Street, noting the rainbow imagery incorporated into the streetscape, including signs, crosswalks, and flags promoting various events.

Philadelphia Muses, 13th and Locust Streets, overlooks an open-air parking lot and celebrates creative expression.

For dining, consider Green Eggs Café, 212 S. 13th St., a busy brunch spot. For children's gifts, there's Nest, 1301 Locust St., a testament to the area's changes: 10 years ago, this property was a strip club. Before that, it was a XXX movie center.

Locust Street between South 12th and 13th Streets is named for Barbara Gittings, the mother of the LGBT civil rights movement. With Frank Kameny, the movement's father, she organized early gay rights marches and challenged the American Psychiatric Association's position that homosexuality was a mental illness. The Association changed the classification in 1973, prompting Kameny to quip it was the day "we were cured en masse by psychiatrists." Gittings edited the nation's first lesbian publication and advocated for more gay and lesbian literature in libraries.

John C. Anderson Apartments, 251 S. 13th St., is an LGBT-friendly apartment building for low-income seniors, the first in Pennsylvania and third in the country. Mark Segal, a longtime gay rights activist and the publisher of *Philadelphia Gay News,* conceived of the project for "the first out generation." It's named for a city council member who died in 1983.

Continue on South 13th Street. At Pine Street, turn left and continue to the corner of South 12th. ❹ **Giovanni's Room** is the oldest gay and lesbian bookstore in the country. It takes its name from a 1956 James Baldwin book.

Turn left on South 12th Street. Toast Philly, 1201 Spruce St., serves more than browned bread. The restaurant is part of the building that once housed the national headquarters of the Grand United Order of Odd Fellows, a loose fraternity of people interested in helping workers. The organization's name is carved over the South 12th Street door.

Turn left on Spruce Street, and make a quick right onto South Camac Street. ❺ **The Plastic Club** was an art club for female artists founded in 1897 by a group of women who challenged the idea that only men could be professional artists. Men were welcomed in the 1990s and today make up about half the membership. The club continues to advance the visual arts, offering exhibitions and lectures.

Next door, the ❻ **Tavern on Camac** may be the oldest continuously operating gay bar in the city. It opened in the 1920s as Maxine's, a gay-friendly speakeasy. One longtime bartender/patron was Mary the Hat. As blogger The Philadelphia Gayborhood Guru (thegayborhoodguru.wordpress.com) writes: Mary, who died in 1984, lived in an apartment across the alley. On rainy nights, when she'd call a cab, the driver would park in front of the bar and open the passenger's side back door. Mary would slide in. The driver would then open the driver's side back door and help Mary to her apartment.

The house at 239 S. Camac St. was formerly the Charlotte Cushman Club, founded in 1907 to provide safe and reasonably priced accommodations for visiting actresses. A local theater patron thought to create such a club after overhearing two young actresses talking about the unwanted male attention they received in city hotels.

❼ **The Philadelphia Sketch Club** was founded in 1860 by six Pennsylvania Academy of Fine Arts students. At one time, the Sketch Club offered classes by esteemed artist Thomas Eakins. It remains a gathering place for member artists and their supporters.

Turn right on Locust Street, passing the Philadelphia Community Women's Center of Philadelphia. The storefront at 1201 Locust St. is part of the Mazzoni Center, which operates multiple programs for the LGBT community. Founded in 1979 as the all-volunteer Philadelphia Community Health Alternatives clinic and named for an early AIDS activist, the nonprofit today has a budget of $11.3 million and offers medical care, addiction/recovery programming, legal services, and safe gathering spaces for LGBT teens and adults.

Turn left on South 12th Street. The ❽ **12th Street Gym** is another neighborhood landmark. As city tour materials note, "Offering day memberships, this sprawling 60,000-square-foot gym is certainly where all the fit boys are (and boys who like looking at fit boys while pretending to work out)." The mural on the building is *A Tribute to Gloria Casarez,* the city's first director of LGBT affairs, who died in 2014.

The building across the street, at 219 S. 12th St., was once part of the SS White Company, makers of dental products. White, a Philadelphia dentist, began making false teeth from feldspar, a common rock-forming mineral, in the 1840s, and the quality of his work soon made him a darling of the dental scene. One advertisement for SS White's toothpaste in *The Saturday Evening Post* in 1918 boasted that "American Teeth Impress Our British Allies" and includes an article from the UK newspaper with the headline "U.S. Teeth." This building is now mostly residential.

Continue on South 12th Street, pausing at Walnut Street. The building at 1125 Walnut St. was an Episcopal Church built in the 1890s that in the 1970s became Philadelphia's version of New York's Studio 54. The disco-loving tenants were evicted in 1986, when the property was sold to a group of personal injury lawyers. Temple University Law School is named for the firm's founding partner, Jim Beasley, whose autobiography is *Courtroom Cowboy.*

The Commonwealth Building, 1201–1205 Chestnut St., was built in 1901 for the Commonwealth Trust Company. Architect John Torrey Windrim designed this building. His father supervised the construction of the US Treasury in 1889. Their firm also built The Franklin Institute and other iconic city structures.

The **9 Loews Philadelphia Hotel** on the corner of Market Street, was commissioned by the Philadelphia Savings Fund Society and completed in 1933. The

Reading Terminal Market offers fresh meat, fish, and produce and prepared delights from around the world.

glowing PSFS letters atop the building were an oddity at the time. The bank kept the letters lit during the Great Depression to reassure customers their bank was secure. Loews, which opened in 2000, maintains the sign.

A blue historical marker in front of the hotel notes this was the site of America's first circus, Ricketts Circus. In 1793, John Bill Ricketts, an equestrian showman, built a horse ring inside a building here. He performed riding tricks for paying customers. As his show's popularity grew, Ricketts added other performers, including tightrope walkers, jugglers, and clowns. President George Washington was a big fan, allowing Ricketts to display his own white steed, Jack, in the building. Ricketts marked Washington's 1797 retirement with a farewell show, and then months later welcomed President John Adams with another show. In 1799, a fire destroyed the theater. A brokenhearted Ricketts left town.

Cross Market Street. The giant spinning guitar is part of the Hard Rock Cafe, which occupies a corner of The Reading Terminal Building, 1115–1141 Market St. In the 1880s, Reading Railroad officials built this Italian Renaissance-style building to rival Pennsylvania Railroad's fortress-like station nearby. The first train departed from here in 1893; the last, in 1984.

Step inside the building. The escalators rise to an entrance of the Pennsylvania Convention Center, which includes the terminal's former soaring train-shed roof. On this main floor, panels tell the story of the building and the railroad. To exit, walk to the rear of the first floor, turn right, and exit onto Filbert Street.

Outside, cross Filbert Street to enter a side door of ❿ **Reading Terminal Market.** When the railroad completed its terminal, it provided space on the ground floor of its train shed for 800 vendors. The market thrived until the early 1970s. By the late 1970s, the building was falling apart and only 23 merchants remained.

The Pennsylvania Convention Center purchased the space in the 1990s and established a nonprofit to manage it. Today it is a must-see attraction for visitors and a favorite of locals, with 80 independently owned businesses. Philbert, the pig statue near the market's seating area, invites visitors to rub his snout for good luck. (Promotional materials call the sculpture "the Market's favorite pork product not topped with broccoli rabe and provolone.") Coins dropped into Philbert's base support a local food charity. Philbert is in a long-term, long-distance relationship with Rachel, a piggy-bank sculpture at Seattle's Pike Place Market.

A few vendors of note include Beiler's Bakery for Amish pies, cookies, and sweet buns; Pennsylvania General Store for local merchandise; Valley Shepherd Creamery & Meltkraft for local cheeses and grilled cheese sandwiches; Keven Parker's Soul Food Cafe for Southern specialties; DiNic's for hot roast beef, pork, and veal sandwiches; and By George! for pizza and Italian delicacies.

Exit via Arch Street. The **⑪ Pennsylvania Convention Center** occupies four city blocks. Originally opened in 1993, the center underwent a $700 million expansion, completed in 2011. It hosts about 250 events each year, including the Philadelphia Flower Show, the world's oldest and largest of its kind.

Turn right, crossing South 11th Street. The Pitcairn Building, 1027 Arch St., was built in 1901 as a distribution center for the Pittsburgh Plate Glass Company. The company, founded by Scottish-born John Pitcairn Jr., was at one point the country's largest manufacturer of plate glass. Pitcairn pursued his future wife for two years until she agreed to be wed. She died young, leaving behind four children. Pitcairn never wed again, saying, "I would no sooner remarry than if Gertrude were standing in the other room."

Turn right onto South 11th Street, walking under a portion of the Pennsylvania Convention Center. Tom's Dim Sum, 59 N. 11th St., is known for good food, including its soup dumplings, even if one local food writer described the decor as "the offspring between a well-off suburban Italian bistro and a Shanghai Chipotle franchise. Plus neon."

Continue to Market Street and turn left. In the 1970s, city leaders developed an urban mall called The Gallery at Market East, which stretched from 11th to Seventh Streets. The Gallery, as locals called it, was anchored by big-name stores such as Strawbridge & Clothier, Kmart, JCPenney, Stern's, and Gimbels. Three of those chains no longer exist. In 2015 many of the interior and exterior stores were closed for remodeling. A full reopening is expected in 2018.

Continue on Market Street. The Robert N. C. Nix Federal Building, 900 Market St., was built in the 1930s, part of a Public Works Administration project as the two bas-reliefs on the building attest. In 1985 it was named for Nix, the first African American to represent Pennsylvania in Congress.

The well-known department store Strawbridge & Clothier, which closed in the 1990s, was located at 801 Market St. It was originally a dry-goods store founded in 1868 by Quakers Justus Strawbridge and Isaac Clothier with the motto, "Small profits, one price, for cash only." This 13-story Beaux Arts structure was built in 1928. Curmudgeon W. C. Fields worked at the store even though it was known for its friendly salespeople.

The Lit Brothers department store formerly occupied 701–739 Market St., an assemblage of 11 buildings. In 1891, Rachel Lit opened a women's clothing store here. Her brothers, Samuel and Jacob Lit, helped her run and advertise the business, marketing it as "A Great Store in a Great City" and a less expensive alternative to Strawbridge & Clothier. The store closed in 1977, but the Lit Brothers name still encircles the property, promising "Hats Trimmed Free of Charge."

⓬ Declaration House, at Market and South Seventh Streets, is a reconstruction of bricklayer Jacob Graff Jr.'s 1775 redbrick home, where Thomas Jefferson wrote the Declaration of Independence in three weeks. Jefferson rented two furnished second-floor rooms, re-created here, including a replica of the small bed into which he squeezed his 6-foot-2 frame. Jefferson allegedly complained about the stables across the street because they attracted horseflies that buzzed around him as he wrote.

This walk ends here. Other tours begin at Washington Square, a few blocks south, and Independence Visitor Center, a few blocks east.

(continued on next page)

Market Street East

Points of Interest

1 **Wanamaker Building (now Macy's)** 1300 Market St., 215-241-9000, macys.com/philadelphia-pa

2 **McGillin's Olde Ale House** 1310 Drury St., 215-735-5562, mcgillins.com

3 **Woody's** 202 S. 13th St., 215-545-1893, woodysbar.com

4 **Giovanni's Room** 345 S. 12th St., 215-923-2960, queerbooks.com

5 **The Plastic Club** 247 S. Camac St., 215-545-9324, plasticclub.org

6 **Tavern on Camac** 243 S. Camac St., 215-545-0900, tavernoncamac.com

7 **The Philadelphia Sketch Club** 235 S. Camac St., 215-545-9298, sketchclub.org

8 **12th Street Gym** 204 S. 12th St., 215-985-4092, 12streetgym.com

9 **Loews Philadelphia Hotel** 1200 Market St., 215-627-1200, loewshotels.com

10 **Reading Terminal Market** 51 N. 12th St., 215-922-2317, readingterminalmarket.org

11 **Pennsylvania Convention Center** 1101 Arch St., 215-418-4700, paconvention.com

12 **Declaration House** 599 S. Seventh St., 215-965-2305, nps.gov/inde

Dilworth Plaza, on the west side of City Hall, features programmed water jets that cool residents in summer.

13 Market Street West:
City Hall and the Skyscrapers

BOUNDARIES: S. 13th St., N. 18th St., John F. Kennedy Blvd., Chestnut St.
DISTANCE: 1 mile
DIFFICULTY: Easy
PARKING: Metered street parking is hard to find. Pay lots are available.
PUBLIC TRANSIT: The best way to reach City Hall is on foot or by using public transportation. There are multiple subway stops here, including City Hall and Suburban Station. There are also numerous buses, including the 16 and the 31.

Construction on City Hall began in 1871 and continued for 30 years. When completed, it was the city's tallest building. It was topped with a bell tower, which was then topped with a 37-foot-tall likeness of William Penn by Alexander Milne Calder.

For years, no building was built higher than the top of Penn's hat. Some thought to do so would violate a gentleman's agreement between the city and local builders. When One and Two Liberty Place broke that agreement in 1987, the curse of Billy Penn began. This downtown tour will tell that story and others.

Walk Description

Start in the courtyard of ❶ **City Hall.** The vibrant compass at the center, featuring zodiac signs and compass points in gold leaf, marks the exact center of the city as established by William Penn in the 1600s. The original painted compass was a gift from legendary city planner Edmund Bacon in 1984 to mark Penn's 350th birthday. (Bacon financed the project by selling a 15th-century illuminated manuscript made by monks.) The art has enlivened this space, and the city hosts concerts and art exhibits here.

City Hall is open for tours, including one to the very top for an amazing city view. Scottish architect John McArthur Jr.'s ornate building has more than 250 architectural reliefs and sculptures, which is odd for a city founded by Quakers, who stressed simplicity. The Penn statue's left hand points to Penn Treaty park, where he signed a peace treaty with the native Lenni Lenape. His right hand holds a rolled-up copy of the Charter of Pennsylvania. From certain angles, that scroll has the unfortunate side effect of making it appear as if Penn is standing at a urinal.

City Hall can be seen in movies such as *Trading Places, Twelve Monkeys,* and *Philadelphia.*

John F. Collins Park is a hidden gem in busy Center City.

Exit the courtyard via the west exit, following the compass. Dilworth Park is named for a former mayor. It was unused open space until a 2014 renovation added programmable fountains that shoot straight out of the ground, a café, a performance and market space, and new glass-encased entrances to the city's subway system. In the winter, the fountains are replaced with an ice rink.

Turn left and walk to the park's southwest corner. Across the street is *Triune* by Robert Engman, installed in 1975. The name means "three in one," and the artist said the bronze curves represent the three rings of people, government, and business.

Across the street, in front of the Centre Square building, is Claes Oldenburg's 45-foot-tall steel structure, ❷ *The Clothespin.* The artist was inspired by Gustav Klimt's *The Kiss.* Some viewers say they see two people with puckered lips, kissing, their little metal arms wrapped around each other. "This is more than a clothes pin," Oldenburg said. "It is my own design with a gothic look and elegance in its sweeping curves." The sculpture is a popular meet-up spot for friends.

Cross the street at the crosswalk at right. After passing 1515 Market St., turn around to look at the unusual sculpture on the second floor of the Centre Square building. *Milord La Chamarre* or *My Lord of the Fancy Vest* is by Jean Dubuffet, a French painter and sculptor credited with founding the art brut movement. Some locals find the sculpture creepy. Even the Association for Public Art describes it as "a giant jigsaw puzzle, an effect both disturbing and humorous."

Continue on Market St. ❸ **One and Two Liberty Place** were the buildings that, in 1987, first topped William Penn's hat. When the project was first proposed, a newspaper poll revealed citizens opposed breaking the height barrier by a vote of 3,809 to 1,822. Edmund Bacon told *The New York Times* the development would decimate "the scale of Center City." Opponents sang a different tune when the buildings were completed. *The Philadelphia Inquirer,* which denounced the project in a 1984 op-ed, published a 1990 piece headlined "Taking It All Back, Liberty Place Turned Out to Be a Swell Idea."

It wasn't all swell. Building higher than Penn's hat apparently triggered the "Curse of Billy Penn." Between 1987 and 2007, none of the city's major sports teams won a championship. The curse broke in June 2007 when, as construction on the city's tallest building (Comcast Center, see page 94) was ending, a small statue of Penn was affixed to a top beam. Penn was back on top and, thus appeased, allowed the Phillies to win the 2008 World Series. The city is waiting for its other teams to follow suit.

Continue on Market Street. The BNY Mellon Center, 1735 Market St., a 54-story office building used as a backdrop in the 1993 film *Philadelphia,* is part of the Penn Center complex, a collection of 11 mid- and high-rise buildings stretching from 15th to 19th Streets and Market Street to John F. Kennedy Boulevard. The mixed-use development was considered radical when Bacon proposed it in the 1950s. Bacon later described introducing the development at a Chamber of Commerce meeting. The mayor, he said, "was so scared he refused to sit at the speaker's table."

Turn right on 18th Street. At John F. Kennedy Boulevard, turn right again. At the corner is the back of the Arch Street Presbyterian Church, 1724 Arch St., built in 1855. The neoclassical Greek Revival style stands in contrast to its neighbor, ❹ **Comcast Center,** the city's tallest building at 975 feet tall and the one bearing the curse-breaking Penn statue. More than 90% of the building houses cable giant Comcast. Architecture critic Inga Saffron praised the structure's clean lines while noting its resemblance to a giant flash drive.

The public outdoor space has seating and a fountain. Inside is The Comcast Experience, a 2,000-square-foot LED screen projecting computer-generated images 18 hours a day. The Market at Comcast Center, located below the main lobby, offers about 20 dining options and smaller stores.

At the corner of North 17th Street, with the Art Deco wonder that is Suburban Street Station in front of you, turn right. Cross Market Street, continuing on South 17th Street. Pop art pioneer Roy Lichtenstein's ❺ *Brushstroke Group* was installed here in 2005. Art critic Edward J. Sozanski of *The Philadelphia Inquirer* said it topped *The Clothespin* in terms of city sculptures, calling it "equally witty, more complex visually, and because of its intense colors, far more animated."

The United Plaza building is the home of Duane Morris LLP. Founded in 1904, the law firm is well respected and among the world's largest.

Continue on South 17th Street, and then make a quick right onto Ranstead Street. Enter the back gate of the oasis that is ❻ **John F. Collins Park,** on the left. Check out the details on the back gate, a tribute to the nearby marshlands of New Jersey and Delaware, featuring iron turtles, fish, and birds. Enter to see the fountain,

a tribute to American Indian totems. Walk through to Chestnut Street, exiting through a gate designed as a tribute to the Wissahickon and Delaware Valleys, with an owl, flowers, insects, and more birds. If the park gates are locked, simply circle the block to examine both gates, and then pick up the walk again.

Across from the park's Chestnut Street gates is an eight-story Art Deco building that once housed Bonwit Teller, an upscale clothing store. The store closed in 1990 but achieved immortality thanks to Philadelphia's favorite fictional boxer, Rocky. In 1979's *Rocky II,* the Rock illegally parks on South 17th Street, next to the store, then runs inside to buy a black satin jacket with a tiger on the back, a fur coat for Adrian, and a watch for Paulie.

Turn left on Chestnut Street, passing One and Two Liberty Place. ❼ **The Art Institute of Philadelphia** opened in 1971 and offers degrees in fashion, media arts, design, and culinary arts. The Art Deco structure, built in 1934, originally housed WCAU, one of the city's first AM radio stations.

Continue on Chestnut Street, noticing the marquee marking . . . a Foot Locker, 1519 Chestnut St. This was the 500-seat Trans-Lux Theater, opened in 1934 with a facade that would bring joy to the heart of Art Deco fans. In 1955, the theater hosted the world premiere of *To Catch a Thief,* an event attended by stars Cary Grant and former local Grace Kelly. Retail moved into the space in the 2000s.

Continue on Chestnut Street. The former First Pennsylvania Bank, 1426 Chestnut St., now has a Del Frisco's Double Eagle Steakhouse on its lower floors, but the 40-foot black iron front gate—along with the words "Pennsylvania Building" and "Insurances on lives and granting annuities" carved above the door—recalls its former life. The bank's safe-deposit boxes are on the wall of the restaurant's private dining room, and the original bank clock remains above the south bar, stopped at 5 o'clock.

The former Jacob Reed's Sons Building, 1424 Chestnut St., was built in 1903 to resemble a Northern Italian palazzo, complete with Byzantine mosaics. This building was meant to convey the clothing company's old-fashioned values and attention to detail.

The top of the American Baptist Publication Society, 1420–22 Chestnut St., built in 1896, resembles a French château.

❽ Prince Theater replaced the Karlton Theatre, which opened on this spot in 1921 with Italian marble floors and fountains. The theater hosted the world premiere of the movie *Adam's Rib* in 1949 and the world premiere of *Rocky II* in 1979.

Continue to Broad Street. The historical marker here recognizes politician Anne Brancato Wood, the first female Democrat elected to the Pennsylvania House of Representatives and the first woman to be named Speaker pro tem. She was an advocate for women and the poor, taking up causes like child labor protection and minimum wage laws. One of her bills was the Hasty Marriage Act of 1936, which required couples to wait three days after applying for a marriage license before marrying. She said that would give women being forced into marriage time to escape.

Continue to The Widener Building, 1327–39 Chestnut St. Philadelphia architect Horace Trumbauer built this for the Widener family in a classical European style with an elaborate arcade and lobby. Trumbauer had a long relationship with the wealthy family, who made their fortune from U.S. Steel and the American Tobacco Company. He also designed Harvard University's Trumbauer Library, built to honor a relative who died on the *Titanic*.

The historical marker on the corner acknowledges that this is where the first American photo was taken, a daguerreotype that took 10 minutes to expose. It showed Central High School, which sat at the corner of Walnut and Juniper Streets in 1839. The camera was made from a cigar box and a lens.

This walk ends here, but return to City Hall to begin another tour.

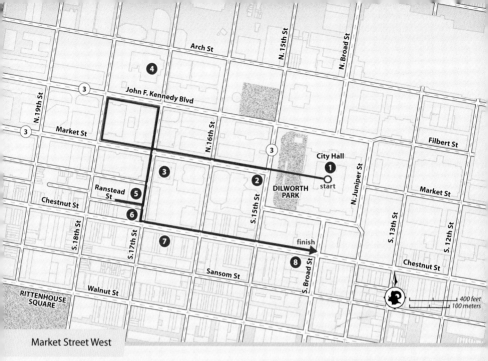

Market Street West

Points of Interest

1. **City Hall** 1401 John F. Kennedy Blvd., 215-686-1776, phila.gov

2. *The Clothespin* 1500 Market St. For more information, contact the Association for Public Art, 215-546-7550, associationforpublicart.org.

3. **One and Two Liberty Place** 1650 Market St., 215-851-9000, phillyfromthetop.com

4. **Comcast Center** 1701 John F. Kennedy Blvd., 215-496-1810, themarketandshopsatcomcastcenter.com

5. *Brushstroke Group* 30 S. 17th St. For more information, contact the Association for Public Art, 215-546-7550, associationforpublicart.org.

6. **John F. Collins Park** 1707 Chestnut St., 215-440-5500, ccdparks.org/john-f-collins-park

7. **The Art Institute of Philadelphia** 1622 Chestnut St., 800-275-2474, artinstitutes.edu/philadelphia

8. **Prince Theater** 1412 Chestnut St., 215-422-4580, princetheater.org

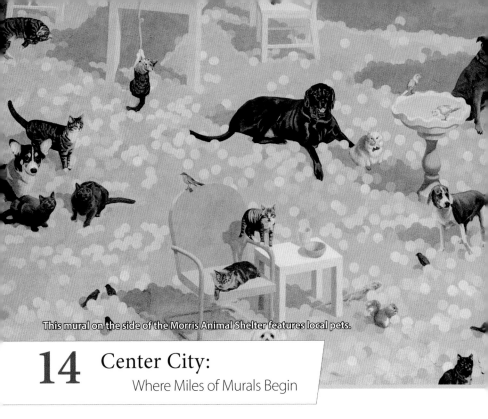

This mural on the side of the Morris Animal Shelter features local pets.

14 Center City:
Where Miles of Murals Begin

BOUNDARIES: Market St., South St., S. Seventh St., Broad St.
DISTANCE: About 2.5 miles
DIFFICULTY: Easy
PARKING: This tour begins in the 700 block of Chestnut St. There is a private parking facility on this block, as well as metered parking on the street.
PUBLIC TRANSIT: Multiple buses stop near the 700 block, including the 9 and the 21. If traveling by subway, take the Market-Frankford Line to the Eighth Street Station.

Philadelphia is called the City of Murals, with more than 3,800 city walls painted with larger-than-life works, creating a massive outdoor art gallery. The city-affiliated agency behind this art, the Philadelphia Mural Arts Program, holds that art can ignite positive change. Mural Arts launched in 1984 as the Anti-Graffiti Network, hiring local graffiti artists and encouraging them to create something positive with their skills. It was an immediate success. Executive director Jane Golden soon realized her group wasn't anti anything; it was pro art. More than 30 years later, Mural Arts is the nation's largest public art program, partnering with diverse groups for projects throughout the city. Mural Arts offers multiple tours, guided and self-guided, on foot, by bike, or via trolley or Segway. This tour, focused in Center City, is a good introduction to both the city and the Mural Arts program. It covers an area called The Mural Mile, although the actual distance is closer to 2.5 miles.

Walk Description

Begin at **❶ *Legacy,*** which overlooks a parking lot. This 4,000-square-foot photo-realistic image honoring Abraham Lincoln is composed of more than 1 million 0.75-inch glass tiles from Italy and France.

On the far left, the mural shows a map of Africa and the deck of a slave ship with iron shackles. Toward the center, a girl wears a necklace with three coins: one featuring Lincoln, another featuring Frederick Douglass, and an 1838 British abolitionist coin showing a freed slave and the words, "Am I not a woman and a sister." In the young girl's palm, an older version of herself rises through flames, signifying the strength she and her ancestors have shown. The text on the lower right comes from the final debate between Lincoln and Stephen Douglas.

With the mural at your back, follow Chestnut Street to South Eighth Street. Turn right. At the corner of Ranstead Street is another mural honoring Lincoln, *A People's Progression towards Equality.* At center, workers construct a statue of Lincoln. The lower level contains images related to slavery and segregation. Near Lincoln's head, people climb ladders to freedom. Across the top is an excerpt from the Gettsyburg Address: "With malice toward none, with charity for all."

Continue on South Eighth Street. Cross Market Street and turn left. At 13th Street **❷ *Tree of Knowledge*** honors its sponsor, the Eisenhower Fellowship, which promotes an international exchange program. Hidden in the tree branches are objects relating to different fields of study, such as musical instruments and carpentry tools. Ladders help people reach these items. The plaque contains a quote from President Dwight D. Eisenhower, "Only justice, fairness, consideration and cooperation can finally lead men to the dawn of eternal peace."

Walk south on South 13th Street, crossing Market Street. **❸ *Finding Home*** aims to shed light on homelessness and to erase its stigma.

The artists asked homeless individuals to write their stories and struggles on strips of fabric, which were woven to create the mural's canvas. Among the images are the words written across the top, which can be read as "Visible Dignity" or "Invisible," depending on your vantage point. Large images of hands painted in different colors come together in prayer to symbolize a community uniting as one. Mixed in are black-and-white depictions of the home life that homeless people say they miss.

Continue on South 13th Street. At Chestnut Street, turn left. Walk to South 12th Street. Turn right. *Building the City,* South 12th and Moravian Streets, was commissioned by the law firm that owns the building. It features several public artworks, including images of the William Penn statue being made.

Continue on South 12th Street. Turn left on Locust Street. At South Sartain Street, turn right. ❹ *Garden of Delight* features swirling Van Gogh–esque images, including trees leaning toward each other as if to embrace. A blue door on the lower left represents a portal to this foreign world. The artist has said this work is meant to be enjoyed, not overanalyzed.

Return to Locust Street. Turn left. ❺ *Philadelphia Muses* reimagines the nine Muses of Greek mythology to represent contemporary concepts such as craft and movement. Each of the human figures is modeled after a local resident. The woman at center worked for the local opera company, while the man at left was part of the city's orchestra. The man in white stretched across the bottom was a Pennsylvania Ballet dancer.

Continue on Locust Street. *Women of Progress,* 1301 Locust St., adorns the New Century Guild, an organization founded in 1882 to highlight women's contributions to society. At the top of the staircase is New Century Guild founder Eliza Turner. Also featured are Anne Preston, one of the country's first female doctors; author Sarah Hale; and First Lady Eleanor Roosevelt.

Continue on Locust Street. At Juniper Street, turn left. ❻ *Pride and Progress* is on the side of the William Way LGBT community center. It celebrates the gay rights movement's strong Philadelphia roots with images of a 1960s-era protest march as well as a modern gay pride event featuring smiling same-sex couples.

The *Famous Franks* mural marks the unmarked bar known as Dirty Frank's.

Barbara Gittings, who is considered the mother of the LGBT civil rights movement, is shown on the left side wearing a rainbow shirt.

Continue on Juniper Street, crossing Spruce Street. ❼ *Taste of Summer* is on Vetri Ristorante, a popular and well-reviewed Italian restaurant. It shows diners gathered at a wooden table in the countryside inspired by Perugia, Italy, with touches of Lancaster, Pennsylvania. The bald man in the chef's coat, on the far right, is restaurant owner Marc Vetri. A young girl in the mural is based on the daughter of one of the parking attendants, a man who came to the United States to work, leaving his family overseas.

Turn left on Spruce Street, then right on South 13th Street. ❽ *Famous Franks* is an inside joke, marking the unmarked bar called Dirty Frank's, a local institution. The mural features famous Franks, including St. Francis of Assisi, Aretha Franklin, and Frankenstein. Former Phillies star Tug McGraw, whose actual first name was Frank, is here too. Pope Francis was added to the mural in 2015 after he visited Philadelphia.

Cross South 13th Street to admire ❾ *Spring.* One of the four *Seasons* murals by David Guinn, it features towering Bradford pears and dogwoods meant to connect to the flowering trees bordering the wall.

With *Famous Franks* and *Spring* behind, follow Pine Street to South Broad Street. Turn left. *Theatre of Life,* Broad and Lombard Streets, is one of the city's best-known murals and one of the first to move beyond two dimensions, incorporating marbles and 3-D masks. Artist Meg Saligman said the mural explores identity and the roles people play. Note the dreamer at left, cutting the strings that control her.

Turn left onto Lombard Street. *Gimme Shelter,* 1236 Lombard St., on the side of Morris Animal Refuge, shows a backyard filled with pets waiting for forever families. Morris sold raffle tickets, with winners having their pets included on the wall. Look for Butch, a gray tabby whose mom worked at the shelter.

Continue on Lombard Street. At South 11th Street, turn right. At South Street, turn left. **10** **Philadelphia's Magic Gardens** is adorned with mosaics, not murals, but it's impossible not to stop here. Isaiah Zagar's distinct works feature broken tiles, painted figures, and trash turned treasure, such as bike tires and broken dishes. Strips of mirrors send messages or outline drawings.

Paying visitors can explore the tunnels and grottoes of the ever-expanding but permanent exhibit. Zagar, a tall, slender man with a white beard rivaling Santa's, may wander by too.

Continue on South Street. At South 10th Street, turn right. **11** *Winter: Crystal Snowscape,* South 10th and Bainbridge Streets, is another in Guinn's Seasons series, this one done in Cubist realism style. Guinn said he is the skier at center moving toward the light and a bright future.

Turn left on Bainbridge Street. At South Ninth Street, turn left. At South Street, turn right. *Mapping Courage: Honoring W. E. B. Du Bois and Engine #11,* South Street and South Sixth Street, pays tribute to Du Bois, the first African American to earn a PhD from Harvard University. He later led the NAACP. He's seen wearing a top hat and tails, which is what he wore while going door to door doing his research in this neighborhood in the late 1800s.

This walk ends here, as does the African American tour (page 14). Consider following that walk in reverse.

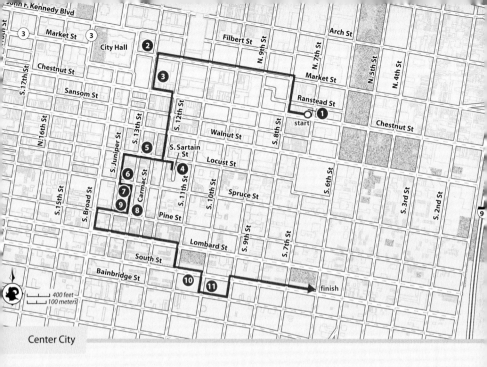

Points of Interest

Unless otherwise noted, call 215-685-0750 or visit muralarts.org for more information.

1 *Legacy* 707 Chestnut St., on the side of an apartment building

2 *Tree of Knowledge* 1301 Market St.

3 *Finding Home* 21 S. 13th St., wrapped around a building managed by Project H.O.M.E. For information about the nonprofit, call 215-232-7272 or visit projecthome.org.

4 *Garden of Delight* 203 S. Sartain St.

5 *Philadelphia Muses* 1235 Locust St., on the side of a private property

6 *Pride and Progress* 1315 Spruce St.

7 *Taste of Summer* 1312 Spruce St., on the side wall of Vetri Ristorante

8 *Famous Franks* 347 S. 13th St., wrapped around Dirty Frank's. For more information about the bar, call 215-732-5010 or visit dirtyfranksbar.com.

9 *Spring* 1315 Pine St.

10 *Philadelphia's Magic Gardens* 1020 South St., 215-733-0390, phillymagicgardens.org

11 *Winter: Crystal Snowscape* S. 10th and Bainbridge Sts.

The Ben Franklin Bridge links Philadelphia to Camden, NJ.

15 Along the Delaware River:
From Industrial Hub to City Playground

BOUNDARIES: Delaware River, N. Seventh St., Monroe St., Callowhill St.
DISTANCE: 2 miles
DIFFICULTY: Easy
PARKING: Public lots and street parking are available.
PUBLIC TRANSIT: Multiple SEPTA buses stop nearby, including the 79 and the 25.

Philadelphia is the city it is today because of the Delaware River. When William Penn arrived on its banks, he saw opportunities for commerce and recreation. The first port was built in 1681. By the 1700s, Philadelphia was the second-busiest port in the world, after London.

The waterfront's fortunes began to wane in the 1800s as commerce moved north to New York and further suffered as the city lost its manufacturing base in the mid-1900s. The construction of I-95 in the 1970s further cut off the river.

The waterfront's upswing began in the 1990s and continues, with more green space and more reasons to visit being added each year. Race Street Pier and Spruce Street Harbor Park have quickly become local and tourist favorites. For more information on the waterfront area, visit the Delaware River Waterfront Corporation's website at delawareriverwaterfront.com.

Walk Description

Start at the Residences at Dockside, 717 Columbus Blvd., where the steel fish swimming in the air, titled *Open-Air Aquarium,* set the mood. The 16-story apartment building is meant to resemble a luxury ocean liner complete with "smokestacks" on top.

Begin walking north along the river. ❶ Battleship *New Jersey,* docked across the river in Camden, New Jersey, was launched in December 1942 and was directly involved in key battles in the Pacific during World War II. The ship was essential to attack plans during the Korean and Vietnam Wars, supported Lebanese forces during the Lebanese Civil War in the 1980s, and supported troops in the Middle East during the First Gulf War. Today the ship is a museum and a memorial to its sailors.

At Lombard Circle, turn right, passing Chart House restaurant, 555 S. Columbus Blvd., and following the path left along the water. ❷ Moshulu is now a floating restaurant and event venue, but it previously traveled the world under different flags. Built in Scotland in 1904, the vessel first carried coal for Germany from Hamburg to Chile, returning to Europe with nitrate. In more than a decade at sea, the ship successfully navigated Cape Horn 54 times.

During World War I, the United States confiscated the ship while it was docked in an American port. President Woodrow Wilson's wife redubbed it *Moshulu,* a native Seneca word meaning "one who fears nothing." Moshulu has occupied its current berth since 2002. Catch the ship in the background in *Rocky,* as the fighter exercises along the waterfront, and in *The Godfather: Part II,* carrying the young Vito Corleone to America.

Across from Moshulu is a plaque honoring citizen-soldiers who patrolled the waterfront in 1747. The group was a predecessor to the Pennsylvania National Guard.

Continue to the ❸ USS *Becuna,* a Connecticut-built submarine that patrolled the Pacific during World War II, sinking four enemy ships. The sub spied on Russian submarines during the Cold War and monitored the Mediterranean and Atlantic Oceans during the Korean and Vietnam Wars. Decommissioned in 1969, the sub is now a museum with guided tours provided by former sailors. One of the guides explained that subs were nicknamed pig boats, sharing this joke: A man wanted to bring live pigs aboard a submarine. A fellow sailor said, "But what about the smell?" The first man replied, "They'll get used to it. We all did."

Next to the sub is the warship USS *Olympia*. Launched in 1892, it is the oldest steel warship afloat in the world. It is also the only survivor from the Spanish-American War fleet. It was from the Olympia's deck that Commodore George Dewey delivered the famous words, "You may fire when you are ready, Gridley," when American forces were fighting in Manila Bay in 1898. The ship's last mission was carrying the body of the unknown soldier from France to the United States in 1921. Next to it is the World War II Submariners Memorial, dedicated to sailors on eternal patrol.

❹ **Spruce Street Harbor Park** is the next stop, a warm-weather pop-up park with free games, a beer garden and food, hammocks, and a water garden. A cantilevered net lounge allows visitors to stretch out 4 feet above the water—with a second net below that one to catch fallen wallets and cell phones.

The Columbus Monument, 201 S. Columbus Blvd., was installed in 1992 to celebrate the 500th anniversary of Columbus's voyage and honor the immigrant groups that have shaped the city.

Pass the Hilton Philadelphia at Penn's Landing, 201 S. Columbus Blvd., and the iron tugboat *Jupiter,* operated by the Standard Oil Company in the early 1900s, which offers educational programming.

Follow the path as it moves along the river and around the ❺ **Independence Seaport Museum,** which has a shipbuilding workshop and other hands-on programming. A historic marker here honors the *Hughes Glomar Explorer,* a ship built in nearby Chester in the 1970s. Workers were told the boat was for billionaire Howard Hughes to explore the deepest oceans. In truth it was a CIA project designed to recover a sunken Soviet submarine. The mission was successful. The bodies of six Soviet sailors were recovered and buried at sea.

Independence Seaport Museum documents the history of the waterways that shaped the city's development.

Continue through the Great Plaza at Penn's Landing, an open-air event space. Across the water is Camden City Hall, built in 1931 and engraved with the Walt Whitman line, "In a dream I saw a city invincible." Camden is one of the most dangerous cities in the United States, known for its political corruption scandals, with three mayors jailed in a 20-year period.

Pass ❻ **Blue Cross RiverRink,** which hosts Winterfest and Summerfest, both free events. Continue to the end of the pier, following it left to exit. Turn right to continue north on Columbus Boulevard.

Pass port buildings converted into residences, restaurants, shops, and offices. ❼ **FringeArts** has a theater, a lauded French restaurant, and a gallery space in a former 1903 pumping station.

Continue to ❽ **Race Street Pier,** in the shadow of the Benjamin Franklin Bridge, This multitiered park is landscaped with 37 swamp white oak trees and more than 10,000 steel planters of sturdy grasses and perennials. The Delaware is a tidal river with fluctuating elevation, and the pier is one of the few places where visitors can get close to the water, guided by the solar lights in the pier's paving.

The ❾ **Benjamin Franklin Bridge,** connecting Philadelphia and Camden, was completed in 1926. The concrete tower piers bear the Seal of Philadelphia on one side and the Seal of Pennsylvania on the other.

While painted blue, the bridge is lit to mark different occasions, becoming red, white, and blue on Pearl Harbor Day and welcoming the new year with a rainbow. In 2013's *World War Z,* military and police officers attempt to block zombies on the bridge.

Pass Dave & Buster's, 325 N. Columbus Blvd. Ahead is *Our Flag Unfurled,* 500 N. Columbus Blvd, originally painted after the 9/11 terrorist attacks. The mural was meant to be temporary but quickly became a landmark. It was refurbished for the 2016 Democratic National Convention.

At Callowhill Street, turn left. The street is named for William Penn's wife, Hannah Callowhill Penn. This was once called Gallows' Hill because it was the site of multiple public hangings. The website hiddencityphila.org notes that this was Philadelphia's first red-light district: "Prostitutes frequented the sector's hostels and boarding houses, and pirates of the Atlantic Coast openly swaggered along Front and Callowhill Streets. Working and retired sea robbers, including Blackbeard and "Captain" William Kidd, liked being in Philadelphia because of the mild temper of Quaker Justice."

Continue on Callowhill Street. *History of Immigration* and *Freedom Wall,* Callowhill and North Second Streets, are murals that look at the city's diversity. The first shows American Indians, ships afloat, and various ethnic groups, including Africans, Chinese, Europeans, and Central and South Americans. The second features images of the Statue of Liberty and Martin Luther King Jr.

Continue on Callowhill Street. At North Seventh Street, turn left. **🔟 Franklin Square** is one of the city's five original green spaces. It was long dangerous and derelict. In 2006, the nonprofit Historic Philadelphia reclaimed the space, adding a carousel, two playgrounds, a minigolf course and dining options.

Before exploring the square, walk across the park to North Sixth Street. *City in Retrospect,* on the wall of the I-676 exit at Callowhill Street, depicts an old-fashioned street scene with certain blocks painted black-and-white and sepia tones.

Walk south along North Sixth Street to the opposite corner of Franklin Square. The 101-foot-tall silver steel sculpture in front of the bridge, near North Sixth Street and the Vine Street Expressway, is *Bolt of Lightning,* a reference to Franklin's famous experiment. A key at the base is topped with a jagged bolt of lightning and hints of a kite. Not everyone is a fan. In 2010, a *Philadelphia* magazine critic called it "the blunder at the bridge," quoting a bridge authority member as saying, "It's so damn ugly, it'll take people's minds off the higher tolls."

This ends this walk. To keep moving, continue three blocks south on Sixth Street to Independence Hall.

Along the Delaware River

Points of Interest

1. Battleship *New Jersey* 62 Battleship Place, 856-966-1652, battleshipnewjersey.org

2. Moshulu 401 S. Columbus Blvd., 215-923-2500, moshulu.com

3. USS *Becuna* Columbus Blvd. and Market St., 215-928-8807, delawareriverwaterfront.com

4. Spruce Street Harbor Park Columbus Blvd. and Spruce St., 215-922-2386, delawareriverwaterfront.com

5. Independence Seaport Museum 211 S. Columbus Blvd., 215-413-8655, phillyseaport.org

6. Blue Cross RiverRink 101 S. Columbus Blvd., 215-925-7465, delawareriverwaterfront.com

7. FringeArts 140 N. Columbus Blvd., 215-413-9006, fringearts.com

8. Race Street Pier Race St. and N. Columbus Blvd., 215-922-2386, delawareriverwaterfront.com

9. Benjamin Franklin Bridge 856-968-3300, drpa.org

10. Franklin Square 200 N. Sixth St., 215-629-4026, historicphiladelphia.org/franklin-square

This statue in Signers Garden is a tribute to the daring men who committed the treasonous act of signing the Declaration of Independence.

16 Old City:
A Place to Play

BOUNDARIES: Vine St., Chestnut St., S. Fifth St., Front St.
DISTANCE: 1.9 miles
DIFFICULTY: Easy
PARKING: Street parking is challenging, but there is a 24-hour secured parking lot underneath the Independence Visitor Center.
PUBLIC TRANSIT: There is a SEPTA subway stop at Market and S. Fifth Sts.

Old City has been called Philadelphia's SoHo because of its boutiques, restaurants, nightclubs, studios, and galleries. On the first Friday of every month, area businesses open their doors, an event that draws thousands.

Proximity to the Delaware River made this the city's earliest commercial area. The tiny alleys were former foot or cart paths as imported goods were moved inland. The cobblestones, gray granite, red bricks, and blue stones paving neighborhood streets hearken back to these early times.

Most of the residential properties in this area are condos or rental apartments, many in former warehouses or readapted industrial spaces. The marked exception is Elfreth's Alley, the nation's oldest residential street.

Walk Description

Begin at South Fifth and Walnut Streets. At left are Independence Mall's gardens, where there's a statue of Robert Morris, a signer of the Declaration of Independence and the Constitution. The so-called financier of the Revolution, Morris was said to be the second-most powerful man in the colonies, after his friend George Washington. Following the war, Morris was jailed for three years for not paying debts. Washington visited his pal in prison.

Walk north on South Fifth Street. Benjamin Franklin founded the ❶ **American Philosophical Society** in 1743 for the purpose of "promoting useful knowledge," he wrote in his memoirs. It is still an active organization.

Continue to Signers Garden, 500 Chestnut St., a park dedicated to the men who risked their lives for what the British viewed as a treasonous act—signing the Declaration of Independence. The statue at center was inspired by Philadelphia-born George Clymer, one of three members of Congress who remained in the city as British soldiers closed in.

Continue on South Fifth Street to the Lafayette Building, 433 Chestnut St. In the 1700s, the US Department of State was at this location. Secretary of State Timothy Pickering, who worked here, was the only Secretary of State to be dismissed from office, according to the State Department. Pickering disagreed with President John Adams's decision to make peace with France. In later years, Pickering led New England's brief and ultimately failed secession plan in 1815.

❷ **The Philadelphia Bourse** originally housed a stock exchange, a maritime exchange, and a grain-trading center. The reddish-orange building, built in the 1890s, was inspired by a similar structure in Germany. The space now houses offices, shops, a food court, and a movie theater.

Continue on South Fifth Street. The ❸ **National Museum of American Jewish History** was established in 1976 at nearby Congregation Mikveh Israel and moved here in 2010. Director Steven Spielberg donated to the building's construction, and his first 8 mm camera is on display inside. The ever-growing Only in America Gallery/Hall of Fame is free to enter; among the first inductees was poet Emma Lazarus, whose most famous work includes the words, "Give me your tired, your poor, your huddled masses yearning to breathe free."

Continue on North Fifth Street. The mirror-polished steel sculpture *Gift of the Winds,* North Fifth and Market Streets, is meant to evoke trees and leaves. ❹ **Congregation Mikveh Israel** stretches between North Fifth and North Fourth Streets, with its main doors at 44 N. Fourth St. It is the oldest continuously operating congregation in the United States and is often called the synagogue of the American Revolution.

Follow the redbrick path at right marked by the statue of Uriah P. Levy, the first Jewish commodore in the US Navy. The Philadelphia-born Levy ran away at age 10 to be a ship's cabin boy, returning home to celebrate his Bar Mitzvah at Mikveh Israel. Years later, he purchased Thomas Jefferson's Monticello, opening the Virginia mansion to tourists.

Continue to four white granite blocks in a square formation, a memorial to Jonathan Netanyahu, brother of Israeli prime minister Benjamin Netanyahu. Jonathan Netanyahu was an Israeli special forces officer killed while leading a mission to rescue 106 hostages taken during a plane hijacking. The Netanyahu family lived in Philadelphia while the patriarch taught here. At the 1986 memorial dedication, Benjamin said the family's time in Philadelphia was a "pivotal passage point" for Jonathan, "when much of his character was formed. Month by month, he grew to appreciate the values of American life—openness, freedom, democracy. Those values stayed with him."

Continue to North Fourth Street. A historical marker remembers congregant Haym Salomon, another Revolutionary War financier who was never repaid and died penniless. In 1975, a commemorative stamp honoring Salomon called him a "financial hero . . . responsible for raising most of the money needed to finance the American Revolution and later to save the new nation from collapse."

Turn right onto North Fourth Street. At Market Street, turn left and then left again on North Third Street. This stretch of road has another name: N3rd, pronounced "nerd." It acknowledges the dozens of tech and design companies that have moved here.

This shopping strip offers: N3rd Collective, 21 N. Third, with vintage goods and new items; Philadelphia Independents, 35 N. Third, selling works by locals, including Philly-centric offerings; Vagabond Boutique, 37 N. Third, specializing in women's clothing and accessories; and BONeJOUR, 53 N. Third, for the beloved canine.

For a bite, try GianFranco Pizza Rustica, 6 N. Third. For a sit-down, consider 26 North BYOB, 26 N. Third, known for seafood; or Bistro 7, 7 N. Third, offering French-inspired farm-to-table dishes.

Continue on North Third for more shopping, including Moderne Gallery, 111 N. Third, for high-end 20th-century furniture and art; Art in the Age and Warby Parker, 116 N. Third, featuring eyewear and unique distilled spirits; Rodger LaPelle Galleries, 122 N. Third, selling fine art; and Sugarcube, 124 N. Third, offering vintage and locally designed clothing.

Dining options include Wedge and Fig, 160 N. Third, a BYOB cheese bistro and La Locanda Del Ghiottone, 130 N. Third, a family-run Italian restaurant.

❺ **The Center for Art in Wood** is a nonprofit supporting wood arts and education to advance the creation and design of wood products. The mural on the side wall highlights 100 objects in the museum's collection.

Cross Race Street. Wireworks, 301 Race St., is a former insulated-wire manufacturing business converted to condos in the 1980s. That business was founded in 1821 by an English immigrant who originally made covered wire for bonnets and hoop skirts then began producing copper wire, supplying all that Samuel Morse needed for the first telegraph from Washington to Baltimore in 1844.

Pass beneath the Benjamin Franklin Bridge. The Chocolate Works, 231 N. Third St., is a residential rental complex in the former H. O. Wilbur & Sons Chocolate

Company. Wilbur and a partner started their company in 1865 making molasses and hard candies for train boys to sell to passengers.

❻ *Growth of a Metropolis* showcases Philadelphia architecture from 1682 to 2015. It wraps around the building; walk through the parking lot to see the second wall. The main wall features well-known buildings such as City Hall and Comcast Center. The side wall features three William Rush sculptures on display at the Philadelphia Museum of Art.

Turn right on New Street to fully appreciate the **❼ Painted Bride Art Center,** housed in a former industrial elevator factory. Artist Isaiah Zagar donated his time to create the mosaic covering the building, *Skin of the Bride*. Take time to examine the mural to find the words and phrases hidden within, and then walk to North Second Street and turn left. Make another left onto Vine Street.

Painted Bride was founded in 1969 to give underrepresented artists a place to showcase their work. The art center's first home was in a former bridal shop on South Street. As the organization's website notes, it is grateful other potential names such as Your Fly is Open didn't stick.

Continue on Vine Street, passing the former K. Strauss & Co., a cigar and cigarette manufacturing building, now condominiums.

Thomas Scientific, Vine and North Third Streets, a company producing lab products, occupies land once owned by Betsy Ross's father. The Essex, 300 N. Third St., is a circa 1830s building that formerly housed various businesses and is now— surprise, surprise—condos.

At North Fourth Street, turn left. **❽ St. Augustine Church** was founded in 1796 as the first permanent establishment of the Augustinian order in the United States. The church school, St. Augustine Academy for Boys, moved to the suburbs and became Villanova University. The exterior can be seen in *The Sixth Sense* and *Shooter*. The congregation today is largely Filipino. The choir sings some songs in Tagalog and honors Santo Nino, the patron saint of the Philippines, each August.

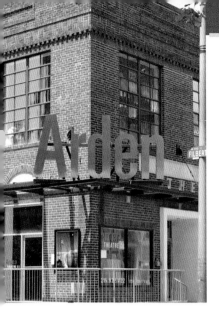
Arden Theatre Company sits in the heart of Old City.

9 **Historic St. George's United Methodist Church** has been called the cradle of American Methodism, in continuous use by Methodists since 1769. In the 1700s, the church welcomed African American worshippers to a special weekly service—held at 5 a.m. This upset two African American parishioners: Richard Allen, who left to found Mother Bethel African Methodist Episcopal Church, and Absalom Jones, who created the African Protestant Episcopal Church. In December 1776, war financier Robert Morris prayed all night here as he sought guidance on securing money for Washington's troops. In 1777, when British soldiers occupied Philadelphia, the church served as a cavalry school because it had a dirt floor and a door that opened onto the street.

Continue on North Fourth Street. Old First Reformed United Church of Christ, 151 N. Fourth St., was founded in the 1700s by German immigrants and was used as a hospital by the British during the Revolution.

Turn left on Race Street, passing DiNardo's Famous Seafood Restaurant, 312 Race St.; Scarlett Alley, 241 Race St., a boutique with clothing, housewares, and crafts; and Sassafras Market, 163 N. Third St.

The Brass Works, 231 Race St., formerly housed Homer Brassworks, manufacturers of beer and ale pumps in the early 1800s. The circa 1885 Pfeiffer House, 222–226 Race St., made coal-transport buckets. Both buildings are now residential.

Continue on Race Street. **10** **Paddy's Pub Old City** is the nominal bar from TV's *It's Always Sunny in Philadelphia*. Race Street Cafe, 208 Race St., is a local favorite, with 15 beers on tap and outdoor seating.

At North Second Street, turn right. Mr. Bar Stool, 167 N. Second St., has been part of the neighborhood for almost 40 years and become a tourist attraction, with people posing for photos with the life-size statues of the Blues Brothers and Elvis.

The Fireman's Hall Museum, 147–49 N. Second St., traces the history of firefighting in Philadelphia.

Retail options here include United by Blue Coffeehouse and Clothier, 144 N. Second St., an environmentally conscious clothing label, and The Clay Studio, 139 N. Second St., which exhibits and sells local works and offers classes.

Continue to ⓫ **Elfreth's Alley,** the oldest continuously inhabited residential block in the country, with homes built between 1720 and 1830. Two adjacent houses, built in 1755, are now a public museum. In the 1800s, eight families—a total of 27 people—shared these two dwellings.

Continue on North Second Street, passing Meadowsweet Mercantile, 47 N. Second St., which specializes in vintage and handcrafted items. ⓬ **Arden Theatre** Company, founded in 1988, offers classes and educational programs in addition to performances of traditional shows.

⓭ **Christ Church,** established in 1695, is sometimes called The Nation's Church. Notable early worshippers included George Washington and John Adams. The church pastor boasts there's been a Sunday service here every weekend for more than 300 years.

Pass The Book Trader, 7 N. Second St., a secondhand bookseller in the city for more than 40 years. The store is crowded, with books falling everywhere, but the owners don't mind people reading among the stacks.

Continue south, crossing Market Street. This block of South Second Street is packed with nightclubs that have given Old City its hard-partying reputation. Among them: The Continental, 138 Market St., one of the first area bars; Cuba Libre, 10 S. Second St., which features a rum bar and salsa nights; and Bleu Martini, 24 S. Second St., a lounge with Asian-inspired fare.

14 *Old City,* 44 S. Second St., is a compilation of local references by street artist Steve "ESPO" Powers. Look for a hoagie; an American flag with a spool of thread; soft pretzels and mustard; John Coltrane; and Philadelphia Phillis, a short-lived mascot of the city's baseball team who appeared with her brother, Phil. Note that Powers wrote "Olde City" with an outlined *E* that seems to have passed out. The joke is there's no *E* on the neighborhood's name. Still, the business housed in this building is called Olde City Tattoo.

The Plough & the Stars is an Irish pub whose name references the design on the banner carried by the Irish citizens who attempted to revolt against the British in the 1916 Easter Rebellion. The pub is housed in the former Corn Exchange National Bank, built in 1903.

At Chestnut Street, turn left. This busy block offers Eulogy Belgian Tavern, 136 Chestnut St., with beers and Belgian *frietjes* (fries), and Buffalo Billiards, 118 Chestnut St., a bar with shuffleboard, darts, and other games.

The latest favorite here is **15 Han Dynasty,** a Chinese restaurant known for its superspicy food and supercranky owner, which may be why one nickname for the place is Handy Nasty. A 2013 *Philadelphia* magazine article described owner Han Chiang this way: "He's famous for cursing at customers. For exploding in the middle of his own dining rooms over perceived breaches in good taste or decorum and refusing to serve people who do something stupid—like asking for Americanized Chinese dishes that exist on his menus but that he thinks no one but children should order. If you don't know him for his restaurants or his food, you likely know him for the legend that has grown up around him. 'Oh, that guy that screams at people who order sweet-and-sour chicken . . . that's Han.'" Still, the food is worth the risk of abuse. Try the Dan Dan Noodles and Three Cup Chicken.

This walk ends here. The South Philadelphia II tour (page 178) begins a few steps away.

(continued on next page)

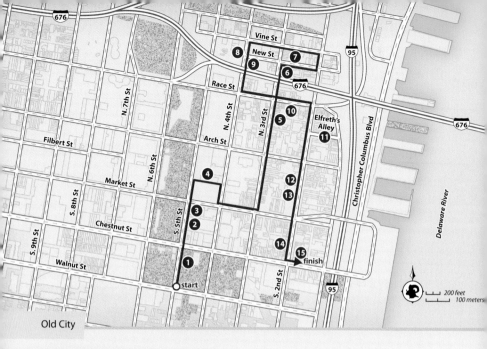

Old City

Points of Interest

1. **American Philosophical Society** 104 S. Fifth St., 215-440-3400, amphilsoc.org

2. **Philadelphia Bourse/The Bourse** 111 S. Independence Mall E., 215-625-0300, tinyurl.com/philadelphiabourse

3. **National Museum of American Jewish History** 101 S. Independence Mall E., 215-923-3811, nmajh.org

4. **Congregation Mikveh Israel** 44 N. Fourth St., 215-922-5446, mikvehisrael.org

5. **The Center for Art in Wood** 141 N. Third St., 215-923-8000, centerforartinwood.org

6. *Growth of a Metropolis* 251 N. Third St. For more information, contact Philadelphia Mural Arts, 215-685-0750, muralarts.org.

7. **Painted Bride Art Center** 230 Vine St., 215-925-9914, paintedbride.org

8. **St. Augustine Church** 243 N. Lawrence St., 215-627-1838, st-augustinechurch.com

9. **Historic St. George's United Methodist Church** 235 N. Fourth St., 215-925-7788, historicstgeorges.org

10. **Paddy's Pub Old City** 228 Race St., 215-627-3532, paddyspuboldcity.com

11. **Elfreth's Alley** Off N. Second St. between Arch and Race Sts., 215-627-8680 (museum house), elfrethsalley.org

12. **Arden Theatre Company** 40 N. Second St., 215-922-8900, ardentheatre.org

13. **Christ Church** 20 N. American St., 215-922-1695, christchurchphila.org

14. *Old City* 44 S. Second St. For more information, contact Philadelphia Mural Arts, 215-685-0750, muralarts.org.

15. **Han Dynasty** 123 Chestnut St., 215-922-1888, handynasty.net/oldcity

A horse-drawn carriage passes Old St. Mary's Church, the city's second Catholic church.

17 Society Hill:
History + Modernity = Charm

BOUNDARIES: Dock St., S. Fourth St., Chestnut St., Lombard St.
DISTANCE: 2.1 miles
DIFFICULTY: Easy
PARKING: There are multiple paid garages but only a few metered street parking spots.
PUBLIC TRANSIT: Via subway, take the Market-Frankford line to Second Street Station.
The buses that stop within a quarter mile are 12, 21, 25, 40, 42, and 57.

Settled in 1682, Society Hill is one of the city's oldest neighborhoods, named for the Free Society of Traders, which had offices here in the 1700s. Immediately before and after the Revolutionary War, the area flourished because of its location between the seat of government and the Delaware River.

Society Hill was neglected as the city expanded west. By 1940, it was completely run-down. City planner Edmund Bacon led the revitalization drive, which included purchasing 31 acres around Dock Street and hiring famed architect I. M. Pei to design three high-rise buildings. Shabby but historic homes were sold to buyers who promised to restore them.

The city added brick sidewalks and replicas of 18th-century street lighting to enhance the atmosphere. Today this is one of the city's safest and wealthiest neighborhoods, with the largest collection of Georgian- and Federal-style brick row houses in the country.

Walk Description

Begin at ❶ **Old Original Bookbinder's.** Founded in 1898 by Dutch Jewish immigrants, it quickly became a popular fine dining spot, famous for its lobster dishes and Bookbinder's Soup, a tomato-based stew made with snapping turtle and vegetables. Regular Frank Sinatra called the place Bookies. The exterior design includes a plaque of Abraham Lincoln and the complete Gettysburg Address. The restaurant is now called Olde Bar and operated by chef Jose Garces.

Walk to South Second Street. ❷ **City Tavern** is a replica of the original building constructed in 1773 and destroyed by fire in 1854. Thomas Jefferson reportedly ate most of his meals at the pub while writing the Declaration of Independence,

City Tavern, rebuilt at this spot, was popular with the Founding Fathers.

while John Jay was renting a tavern room when he signed the document. In 1773, Paul Revere rushed here to share news of the Boston Tea Party. John Adams called this the "most genteel tavern in America." Two ghosts are alleged to haunt the grounds: a young woman killed in a fire as she prepared for her wedding and a young waiter killed in a duel. The female ghost is said to appear in photos. The male likes knocking down silverware.

Turn right to walk north on South Second Street. Welcome Park, between Walnut and Chestnut Streets, is the only city park dedicated to founder William Penn, who lived in a home here with wife Hannah Callowhill Penn. The park is named for the *Welcome,* the 17th-century ship that carried Penn from England. The walls around the park are engraved with Penn's plans for the city. The city's original street grid is imprinted on the ground. The Penn statue here is a miniature of the one atop City Hall.

Continue on South Second Street, passing the Ritz Theater, one of the city's independent movie houses. The Corn Exchange National Bank, 123–25 Chestnut St., was built in 1903 in the Georgian Revival style. Bank robber Willie Sutton attempted to rob this bank in 1933 but failed. He and two partners returned a year later, leaving with more than $21,000.

At Chestnut Street, turn left. The ❸ **U.S. Custom House** occupies an entire block and rises 17 stories. The interior features a three-story rotunda and elaborate murals.

Continue on Chestnut, walking toward South Third Street. The ❹ **Museum of the American Revolution** has a remarkable collection that includes George Washington's war tent, a 1770s mug that still smells of rum, and booties made from a Redcoat's jacket. The Little Lion, 243 Chestnut St., is a pub bearing the nickname of U.S. Treasury Secretary Alexander Hamilton. The ❺ **First Bank of the United States,** which Hamilton founded, is nearby. Turn left onto South Third, and it stands at 116. Chartered in 1791, this was the first national bank, authorized by Congress to hold $10 million in capital.

The ❻ **Merchants' Exchange Building,** built in the 1830s, was the hub of American commercial life for 50 years. The stunning Greek Revival building prompted one newspaper to write that "Philadelphia is truly the Athens of America." It is the oldest existing stock exchange building in the country, now private National Park Service offices.

Walk to the corner of South Third and Walnut Streets. Turn right. The Polish American Cultural Center, 308 Walnut, includes a museum featuring a life-size statue of Pope John Paul II, who visited in 1979.

The ❼ **Bishop White House** is reportedly one of the most haunted structures in historic Philadelphia. Right Reverend William White, rector of Christ Church and the first bishop of the American Episcopalian Church, lived here for almost 50 years. During the yellow fever epidemic of 1793, White tended the sick but stayed healthy, which some attributed to his constant cigar smoking that kept mosquitoes at bay. White died in the third-floor library in 1836, and his ghost is still seen there. A housekeeper haunts the first floor, and a ghost cat has been heard meowing in the garden.

Continue to the circa 1775 Dilworth-Todd-Moylan House, 339–41 Walnut St., the former residence of Dolley Payne Todd, who later married James Madison. Aaron Burr introduced the couple.

At the corner of South Fourth Street, turn left. **❽ The Philadelphia Contributionship** is the oldest property insurance company in America, organized by Ben Franklin in 1752. A museum inside is open by appointment. Homeowners who purchased fire insurance were given fire marks to display on the property exterior. This told firefighters they would be paid by a specific insurer. The Contributionship created the colonies' first fire mark, which showed four hands, each holding the wrist of another, forming a box shape, and the date 1752. Look for fire marks on older homes, including many in Society Hill.

Continue on South Fourth. **❾ Old St. Mary's Church,** built in 1763, was the city's second Roman Catholic church. Although none of the Founding Fathers were Catholic, they gathered here for the first public religious commemoration of the Declaration of Independence. The church cemetery is the final resting place of notables, including Commodore John Barry, Father of the American Navy; George Meade, whose grandson would lead Union forces at Gettysburg; and the great-great-grandfather of Jacqueline Kennedy Onassis.

Continue on South Fourth. **❿ Physick House** is the former home of Dr. Philip Syng Physick, the "Father of American Surgery." Patients treated here included President Andrew Jackson, Chief Justice John Marshall, and Dolley Todd Madison. Inside is a display of Physick's tools, including bloodletting instruments, stomach pumps, and tubes to remove kidney stones. The ghost of Physick's estranged wife is said to haunt the property, crying outside.

Turn right on Cypress Street to reach the cobblestoned cul-de-sac Lawrence Court, a quaint but costly enclave. It's unclear how the three statues of kangaroos by Harold Kimmelman ended up here. A 2015 *Philadelphia* magazine article included *Kangaroos* on a "12 Worst Pieces of Public Art in Philly" list. "Why? Why kangaroos? Why kangaroos here?" the author moaned.

Exit the court by walking past the sculptures to Spruce Street. Turn left. Society Hill Synagogue, 418 Spruce St., was originally a Baptist church, designed by the same architect who conceived the Capitol building. Jews from Romania purchased the building in 1912, and the Yiddish words "Great roumanian Shul" are above the door. The synagogue is still active.

Walk to South Fifth Street, and cross the road; then turn right again, walking back in the direction of the synagogue but on the street's opposite side. Coca-Cola Bottle House, 433 Spruce St., was built in 1972 for the CEO of the Coca-Cola Company. The two lower windows are made from soda bottles.

Continue east on Spruce Street. At South Fourth Street, turn left. At Willings Alley, turn right. ⓫ **Old St. Joseph's Church** is the city's first Roman Catholic parish, founded in 1733. At one point this was the only place in the English-speaking world where Catholics could celebrate Mass publicly. It is thought that the church's odd location—requiring entrance through the small alley archway—was chosen to dissuade protesters. Still, the building suffered damage during the anti-Catholic riots in the 1800s.

Continue to the end of the alley. At South Third Street, look left to catch a glimpse of Thomas Paine Place. Paine's "Common Sense" pamphlet, printed here in January 1776, played a crucial part in galvanizing colonists against England by laying out arguments in simple language. He referred to King George as "a crowned ruffian" with "little more to do than make war and give away places at court."

St. Paul's Episcopal Church, 225 S. Third St., was built in 1761, the city's third Episcopal church. Acclaimed American actor Edwin Forrest is interred in the church graveyard.

Turn right (south) on South Third Street. ⓬ **The Powel House,** built in 1765, was the home of Samuel Powel, the last Colonial mayor of Philadelphia and the first mayor after the Revolutionary War. While Samuel, a pallbearer at Benjamin Franklin's funeral, is remembered as the family's politician, it was his wife, Elizabeth, who was a confidant of George Washington's, advising the first president on personal and state matters. George and wife Martha frequently dined at the Powel home and later hosted the couple at Mount Vernon.

Continue on South Third Street to Pine Street to the ⓭ **Thaddeus Kosciuszko National Memorial.** Polish-born Kosciuszko was a brigadier general during the Revolutionary War, using his engineering background to construct state-of-the-art defenses at various fortifications. Thomas Jefferson called him "the purest son of liberty I have ever known."

After the war, Kosciuszko returned to Poland and continued fighting, organizing an uprising against Russian overlords that led to his capture. He was allowed to emigrate to the United States and briefly lived at this property. The memorial is a single room where Kosciuszko lived for seven months. National Public Radio ran a 2008 piece titled "The Smallest National Park Site," with the host noting, "It's an inspiration to renters everywhere that a cheap studio apartment could become part of the National Park System."

Turn right on Pine Street. ⓮ **Old Pine Street Church** was used as a stable by the British cavalry when they occupied the city during the Revolutionary War. The adjoining cemetery, opened in 1764, holds an estimated 3,000 people. The last person buried here, in 1958, was University of Pennsylvania student In-Ho Oh, a Korean native who was fatally beaten by teenagers seeking cash to buy 65-cent tickets to a dance. During the trial, Oh's family asked city leaders to treat the accused boys leniently. Oh's tombstone contains the words, "To turn sorrow into a Christian purpose." In 2016, his cousin Philadelphia city councilman David Oh successfully led efforts to have the West Philadelphia block where Oh was killed named in his honor.

In 2015, sculptor Roger Wing hand-chiseled the 16-foot-tall stump of a 100-year-old maple tree near the cemetery fence into the likeness of the Reverend George Duffield, co-chaplain of the Continental Army. His prewar sermons inspired John Adams to sign the Declaration of Independence.

At South Fifth Street, turn left. Turn left again on Lombard Street. The ⓯ **Presbyterian Historical Society,** organized in 1852, contains the national archives of the Presbyterian Church. Six 9-foot-tall statues by Alexander Stirling Calder depict Presbyterian leaders such as John Witherspoon, the only clergy member to sign the Declaration of Independence, and James Caldwell, the so-called Fighting

Philadelphia's newest attraction, the Museum of the American Revolution, is the most comprehensive museum on early US history in the country.

Parson, who, when troops ran out of gun wadding during the Revolutionary War, passed out pages of psalm books.

Continue on Lombard Street. The Old Pine Community Center, 401 Pine St., is a nonprofit community hub that hosts programming such as 12-step meetings, wheelchair basketball games, after-school care, and senior activities.

Turn left on South Fourth Street. **16 St. Peter's Church,** founded in 1758 to handle overflow from nearby Christ Church, has an entrance here. The interior is little changed, with a hand-carved pulpit and unusual boxed pews, individual cubes with seating on three sides accessed by a small door on the fourth. The Penn family had a box here, and worshippers reserved boxes as late as 1966. The current rector, Claire Nevin-Field, is the first female leader in the church's history. The church's first leader was Reverend William White. While White may look staid in paintings, Nevin-Field called him "a wild man in his day." One of his bold acts? Ordaining the Episcopal Church's first African American priest.

Continue on South Fourth Street. Turn right on Pine Street, then left on South Second Street. Note the unusual bank building at left with a ground floor designed to look like a Renaissance-era Italian loggia.

At Delancey Street, turn left. The historic touches on the block include horse-head hitching posts and boot scrapers near many front steps.

The home at 205 Delancey has two fire marks, one from The Philadelphia Contributionship. The other, with a tree, was issued by Mutual Assurance of Philadelphia, aka The Green Tree Company, in the 1820s. Its symbol acknowledges the company insured properties near trees, which others did not. The sculpture at 210 Delancey is *Butterfly* by kangaroo-loving sculptor Harold Kimmelman.

At South Third Street, turn right. Turn right again on Locust Street. The 37 contemporary brick and glass houses here are called the I. M. Pei homes. Pei, the celebrated modernist architect whose work includes Louvre Pyramid in Paris, designed them in 1962 to be "sympathetic with the old 18th-century houses, but obviously they had to be designed around contemporary life"—and as cheaply as possible. The boxlike exteriors belie the interiors, which are light and airy, making these hot properties.

Continue on Locust Street. **⓱ Society Hill Towers** are three 31-story high-rises also designed by Pei's firm, completed in 1964. The style is brutalist, which also describes the sculpture here. *Old Man, Young Man, the Future* features figures of a young man standing, an older man sitting, and a bird. Sculptor Leonard Baskin was known for work dealing with "the human-condition in angst-ridden terms. . . . If his figures did not appear to be actively suffering or simply dead, they often appeared to be in numbed, introspective states," noted the 2003 book *I. M. Pei and Society Hill: A 40th Anniversary Celebration*. Baskin said the bird represents the future and the "promising and ominous" nature of external reality.

Walk away from the towers to Spruce Street. Turn left. **⓲ A Man Full of Trouble Tavern,** built in 1759, occupied this shuttered building. It is the only surviving tavern building from pre-Revolutionary Philadelphia. Taverns were central to 16th-century social life; one survey from 1773 tallied 120 in the city, 21 of them on South Second Street alone. Historians say this tavern was originally called The Man Loaded with Mischief. Its sign featured a man carrying a woman on his back.

This tour ends here. Pick up Walk 15 (page 104) by continuing on Spruce Street to the Delaware River.

Points of Interest

❶ Old Original Bookbinder's (now The Olde Bar) 125 Walnut St., 215-253-3777, theoldebar.com

❷ City Tavern 138 S. Second St., 215-413-1443, citytavern.com

❸ U.S. Custom House 211 Chestnut St., tinyurl.com/uscustomhouse

❹ Museum of the American Revolution 101 S. Third St., 215-253-6731, amrevmuseum.org

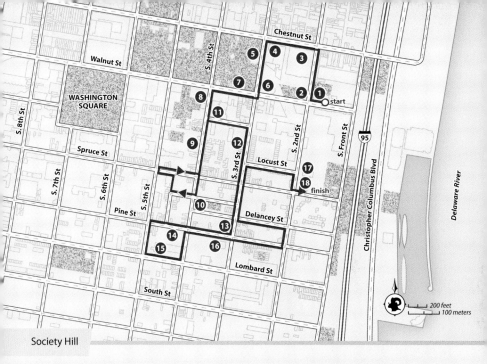

Society Hill

18 Northern Liberties:
A River Ward Gone Upscale

BOUNDARIES: Spring Garden St., Girard Ave., N. Second St., N. Eighth St.
DISTANCE: 3.5 miles
DIFFICULTY: Moderate
PARKING: It's usually fairly easy to find street parking here; there are also paid lots nearby.
PUBLIC TRANSIT: The Spring Garden subway station is located at 600 N. Front St. Area
    buses include the 43.

In 2014, a local museum sponsored a talk titled, "Northern Liberties: From the World's Workshop to Hipster Mecca and the People in Between." That's an easy way to describe how this former industrial neighborhood has changed, but it doesn't tell the whole story.

One of Philadelphia's river wards, the area was outside city limits when William Penn founded Philadelphia. Called the north lands, it was part of the liberties, which were free land parcels granted at government discretion. The area was densely populated in the 1800s, with men, women, and children working mills and factories that produced everything from chocolate to machinery. When industry floundered, so did the neighborhood. Between

1960 and 1980, more than 60% of the population moved away. Blight followed. Its fortune began to change in the 1990s and continues today. Expect construction on this tour.

Walk Description

Start at North Second and Spring Garden Streets. ❶ *Pedal Thru (Bikin' in the O-Zone)* wraps around City Fitness, showing a bicycle moving through a city. The mural is visible to drivers stuck in traffic on nearby I-95.

Cross Spring Garden Street to ❷ **Doughboy Park.** Dedicated in 1920 to local World War I servicemen, this triangle features greenery, benches, cobblestones, and the bronze soldier statue, *Over the Top,* by John Paulding (seen at left).

Walk north on Second Street. This street was laid out in the 1700s and paved in 1761. The area is known for its nightlife, a reputation gained in its earliest days. No police patrolled here until the neighborhood joined the city in the mid-1850s, and the area "has had a history of rioting and disorder—as well as drunkenness and decadence—going back three hundred years," writes Harry Kyriakodis in *Northern Liberties: The Story of a Philadelphia River Ward.*

Shopping and dining options on this stretch include Art Star, 623 N. Second St., featuring works of local artists; Architectural Antiques Exchange, 715 N. Second St.; Bourbon & Branch, 705 N. Second St.; and Green Eggs Cafe, 719 N. Second St.

Continue on North Second. The building at 901 has housed pubs for more than 200 years. The current one, ❸ **Standard Tap,** dates to 1999. Philly is known for its gastropubs, and this considered the first. The bar specializes in local beers. Two ghosts allegedly haunt it: a white-haired woman, who just stands around, and a former male tenant, who has been accused of turning on water and emptying paper towel holders.

Continue on North Second. ❹ **North Bowl** was a mechanic's garage converted in 2006 to a retro-chic bowling alley with a full bar and music. The website thrillist .com included it on its 2013 list of "The Swankiest, Tastiest, Booziest Bowling Alleys in America."

For dining, consider Cantina Dos Segundos, 931 N. Second St. Shoppers have SWAG boutique, 935 N. Second St.

At West Laurel Street, turn right, and then make a quick left onto Hancock Street. Many of the factory buildings, now apartments and condos, operated in the years before child labor laws. A "Guide to Northern Liberties," published in 1982 by the Northern Liberties Neighborhood Association, mentions a weaving mill that in 1832 employed 114 men and women. The men averaged $8.50 per week, and the women, $2.62. The children received $1.37.

Continue on Hancock Street. Turn left on Germantown Avenue. **⑤ The Schmidt's Commons** was the Schmidt's brewery. Established in 1860, it was the last of the breweries in the area to shut down, closing in 1987. It was renovated in 2009 as a mixed-use property. The piazza in the middle hosts events, including major sporting events projected on outdoor screens. Explore the piazza and its businesses, including Creep Records, Gunners Run bar, and Pink Dolphin market and deli.

Continue on Germantown Avenue. Then cross North Second Street. *Bell's Pond,* on the side of Bell Floor Covering Company, 1050 N. Second St., is the work of neighborhood resident Frank Hyder and his art students.

Walk south on North Second Street, with The Schmidt's Commons on the left. **⑥ Liberties Walk** is another mixed-use development. Turn right into the outdoor mall, crossing North American and North Bodine Streets to reach North Third Street. Popular dining spots along the way include Bar Ferdinand, El Camino Real, Baan Thai Thai, and Samwich.

Turn left on North Third Street. **⑦ Liberty Lands Park** occupies the former site of Burks Brothers Tannery and Leather Factory, once the world's second-largest kid glove manufacturer. Near the park entrance, one block farther south on North Second Street, is Dennis Haugh's *Cohocksink: Stand in the Place Where You Live.* It remembers the troublesome Delaware River subsidiary, now filled in, that periodically swallowed neighborhood people and property. After an 1894 storm, phillyhistory.org notes, there was a "familiar 'deep rumbling' heard throughout Northern Liberties. Everyone knew what happened: the Cohocksink claimed yet another chunk of the city."

Continue on North Third Street. Gold Medal Bakery, 901 N. Third St., offers cookies and coffee to further fuel walking. Much of the block across Poplar Street, under construction at press time, was once the site of Ortlieb's Brewery, which closed in 1981. The four-building complex was torn down in 2013. Ortlieb's Lounge, 847 N. Third St., a restaurant/music venue, remains.

Thomas Mifflin School, 808 N. Third St., was built in 1825 and used as a hospital in 1832 during the 1832 cholera outbreak. It is currently being renovated.

Continue on North Third Street, passing North 3rd gastropub, 801 N. Third St., and the park that is part of the Northern Liberties Community Center, 700 N. Third St. At Fairmount Avenue, turn right.

The mural at 306 Fairmount Ave. is *Advocates for Advocacy* by acclaimed street artist Brett Cook-Dizney. **8** **Saint Michael the Archangel Orthodox Church** was built in 1873 and originally housed the Salem German Reform Church. The Saint Michael congregation, residents of Russian, Galician, and Carpatho-Russian heritage, purchased these buildings in 1923. The church has a shop selling Russian goods, including *matryoshka* dolls. In 2016, the congregation hosted its 40th annual Russian Festival.

Continue to North Fifth Street. Turn right. **9** **Saint Andrew's Russian Orthodox Cathedral,** established in 1897, is the oldest Orthodox Christian church in the city. The building exists thanks to representatives of the Russian Imperial Fleet who came to the city in 1898 to help with the construction of two battleships and gave time, money, and icons to the new church. The Cathedral was consecrated in 1902 by Father Alexander Hotovitzky, who later died under Stalin's rule.

Through Cracks in Pavement, 717 N. Fifth St., features medicinal plants, flowers, barks, leaves, and roots. Neighborhood resident Paul Santoleri wrote on philaplace .org that he was inspired by his own brick-paved backyard. He said he used a columbine as the "pinnacle flower" to "reclaim the flower from the news of past years."

Turn right on Olive Street, then left on North Fourth Street. At Brown Street, check out St. Agnes–St. John Nepomucene (Slovak), 319 Brown St., two churches that merged at the St. Agnes property in 1980.

Continue on North Fourth Street. ❿ **Honey's Sit 'n Eat** is a Southern Jewish diner and local favorite featured on Food Network's *Diners, Drive-Ins and Dives.*

Pass City Planter, 814 N. Fourth St. At Poplar Street, turn left. Continue to Lawrence Street, and turn left again to check out the log cabin on the corner of the 800 block. Author Kyriakodis describes it this way: "This house was built by hand in 1986 by artist Jeff Thomas, his inspiration being the 'back to the land' movement of the 1970s. He assembled the house using a truckload of thirty-foot logs from West Virginia. The rustic abode is the only log cabin in a city of brick houses."

Return to Poplar Street and continue west. ⓫ *Philos Adelphos,* by Mexican street artist Saner, bears the city's Greek name.

Cross Poplar Street, passing Bardot Cafe, 447 Poplar St. Then turn right onto St. John Neumann Way, named for the fourth bishop of Philadelphia. This stretch is nicknamed Rosary Row because so many boys who lived here became priests.

At Lawrence Street, turn left and walk to Girard Avenue. The ⓬ **National Shrine of St. John Neumann** offers visitors a view of the lifelike remains of the saint, who is credited with expanding the Catholic school system in the United States.

Turn left on West Girard Avenue, taking in the mural on Haussemann's Pharmacy, 536 W. Girard Ave., that honors the apothecary craft.

Pass the Ramonita de Rodriguez branch of the Free Library of Philadelphia, 600 W. Girard Ave., which is covered in bright mosaics and named for an educator and community leader.

Turn left on North Seventh Street. Mt. Tabor African Methodist Episcopal Church, 961–71 N. Seventh St., was founded in 1931 by a minister who wanted to assist hardworking domestic workers who were being exploited by homeowners.

At Poplar Street, turn right. Then turn left on Franklin Street. The ⓭ **Ukrainian Catholic Cathedral** is a Byzantine structure built in 1966 in the style of Istanbul's Hagia Sophia. A stone from the tomb of Saint Peter the Apostle is part of the

This mural of Edgar Allan Poe is near the home where Poe lived while writing *The Black Cat*.

building, a gift from Pope Paul VI as a symbol of the unity of faith between the two churches.

Continue on Franklin Street to Brown Street. Turn left, and then make a right onto North Seventh Street. ⑭ **Federal Donuts** has a national reputation for its fried chicken and donuts.

Continue on North Seventh Street, passing a mural of Edgar Allan Poe. The ⑮ **Edgar Allan Poe National Historic Site** is where the author wrote "The Black Cat." Poe lived in this house with his wife and mother-in-law in 1843.

At Spring Garden Street, turn right to make a quick detour to see ⑯ **Guild House.** This residence was designed by architect Robert Venturi and is considered one of the most important works of the 20th century. No, not kidding. In *Twentieth-Century American Architecture: The Buildings and Their Makers,* author Carter Wiseman writes that the building combines historic forms with "banal" 20th-century commercialism, hiding a "slyly intellectual agenda" behind its "apparent ordinariness."

Return to North Seventh Street and continue east on Spring Garden Street. The ⑰ **German Society of Pennsylvania** dates back to this street's golden age of grand buildings and a landscaped median. Founded in 1764 and here since 1887, the organization has about 700 members. Nearby is *Building America: German-American Contributions,* 605 Spring Garden St.

Continue past 603 Spring Garden St., where a ghost sign advertises LEATHER BELTING (for engines, not waists). The former Northern Savings Fund Society Building, 600 Spring Garden St., was designed by local architect Frank Furness in 1872.

Just after North Fifth Street, ⓲ **Silk City,** a city institution, began as an old-fashioned stainless steel dining car restaurant and now includes a bar and lounge. The iron-work on the gate and in the beer garden is fun and fabulous.

Northeast Treatment Centers, 499 N. Fifth St., features the block-long mural *The Value of Family,* meant to highlight the work the center does, including adoption and other family support services. Many of the center's clients helped create the work, which features this George Bernard Shaw quote: "Perhaps the greatest social service that can be rendered by anybody to their country and to mankind is to bring up a family."

Turn left onto North Fourth Street. Built in 1902, ⓳ **Integrity Trust Bank** was founded by three leaders in the German immigrant community and was one of the largest banking companies in the city between 1880 and 1940. Much of its success can be tied to the many German brewers who trusted their money to fellow community members.

Turn right on Green Street, then right again on North Third Street. At Spring Garden Street, turn left. The brightly painted block of properties including Finnigan's Wake, 537 N. Third St., was long viewed as an unofficial welcome to Northern Liberties. Finnigan's Wake, which is now closed, was long a popular spot for politicians, with the local Democratic club headquarters next door. Note the Celtic cross and the words "In the Shadow of the Wood" above the door.

This ends this walk. The River Wards tour (page 136) starts a few blocks from here at the Delaware River.

Points of Interest

① *Pedal Thru (Bikin' in the O-Zone)* 200 Spring Garden St.

② **Doughboy Park** N. Second and Spring Garden Sts.

③ **Standard Tap** 901 N. Second St., 215-238-0630, standardtap.com

④ **North Bowl** 909 N. Second St., 215-238-2695, northbowlphilly.com

⑤ **The Schmidt's Commons** 1001 N. Second St., 215-825-7552, theschmidtscommons.com

⑥ **Liberties Walk** 1040 N. American St.

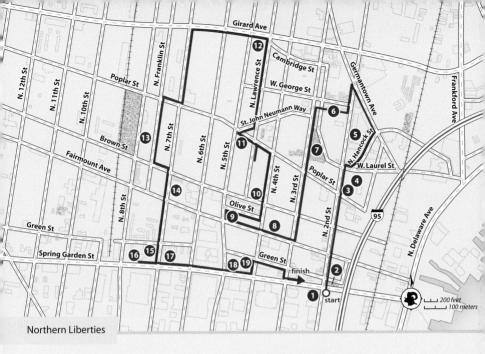

Northern Liberties

7 **Liberty Lands Park** 913 N. Third St., 215-627-6562, nlna.org/liberty-lands

8 **Saint Michael the Archangel Orthodox Church** 335 Fairmount Ave., 215-627-6148, saintmichaelsroc.org

9 **Saint Andrew's Russian Orthodox Cathedral** N. Fifth St. and Fairmount Ave., 215-627-3338, saintandrewscathedral.org

10 **Honey's Sit 'n Eat** 800 N. Fourth St. 215-925-1150, honeyssitneat.com

11 *Philos Adelphos* 440 Poplar St. For more information, contact Philadelphia Mural Arts, 215-685-0750, muralarts.org.

12 **The National Shrine of St. John Neumann** 1019 N. Fifth St., 215-627-3080, stjohnneumann.org

13 **Ukrainian Catholic Cathedral** 830 N. Franklin St., 215-922-2845, ukrcathedral.com

14 **Federal Donuts** 701 N. Seventh St., 267-928-3893, federaldonuts.com

15 **Edgar Allan Poe National Historic Site** 532 N. Seventh St., 215-965-2305, nps.gov/edal

16 **Guild House** 711 Spring Garden St.

17 **German Society of Pennsylvania** 611 Spring Garden St.

18 **Silk City Diner, Bar & Lounge** 435 Spring Garden St., 215-592-8838 silkcityphilly.com

19 **Integrity Trust Bank** 542 N. Fourth St.

This Fishtown mural has become a neighborhood favorite.

19 The River Wards:
Kensington and Fishtown

BOUNDARIES: Delaware River, E. York St., Frankford Ave., Palmer Ave.
DISTANCE: 3.1 miles
DIFFICULTY: Easy
PARKING: Street parking is almost always available on side streets.
PUBLIC TRANSIT: SEPTA bus routes that stop nearby are 5, 25, 43, and MFL.

For years, outsiders considered Kensington dangerous, dirty, and plagued by problems. That would have shocked Anthony Palmer, who founded this once-independent city in the 1700s and named it after Kensington Palace. Indeed, many of the original street names referenced royalty. Girard Avenue, for example, was previously Prince Street.

In the 1800s, Kensington was safe and solid, home to blue-collar dock and factory workers. The decline began when the factories closed and picked up speed as the years passed.

The neighborhood's rebirth began in the late 20th century as artists and young people moved here, attracted by the low prices and the potential. Today transplants live side by side with families who have lived here for generations. Because of the creativity influx, walking these streets is a delight, with random art on walls, sidewalks, and even telephone poles. Fishtown is a small area within Kensington.

Walk Description

Begin at ❶ **Yards Brewing Company,** a brewery founded in a garage in 1994 and relocated here in 2007. It is the first brewery in the state to be completely wind-powered. In 2001, Yards created a limited-edition line of brews called Ales of the Revolution, based on original recipes belonging to George Washington, Thomas Jefferson, and Benjamin Franklin. Franklin's recipe used spruce for flavoring, possibly because hops were difficult to obtain.

Continue on North Delaware Avenue. ❷ **SugarHouse Casino** opened in 2010 after years of protest. Perhaps it was destiny: This waterfront area was once popular with sailors and lined with gambling dens and brothels. Construction uncovered native relics dating back 3,000 years and remnants from a British fort.

At the intersection of North Delaware and Sugarhouse Drive, note the signage at left, a remnant of the Edward Corner Marine Merchandise Company.

Continue to Columbia Avenue. On the right, ❸ **Penn Treaty Park** was where William Penn made a peace agreement with the Lenni Lenape tribe in the 1680s. The deal was made in the shade of the Treaty Elm, which became a symbol of peace and love. The original tree fell during a storm in 1810, which seems fitting as the treaty was broken in 1755, when members of the Delaware tribe killed 24 settlers living nearby. Authorities who followed Penn took revenge on the tribe for the next 300 years. The 7-acre park features picnic areas, a playground, and views of the Benjamin Franklin Bridge. A small museum is open by appointment.

Walk past the park to the former ❹ **Delaware Power Station,** designed in the early 1900s by the architecture firm behind The Franklin Institute. It closed in 2004. It sits on historic land: the US Navy's first submarine—nicknamed Alligator because it was green—was built here in the 1860s. In 1863, as the sub headed south to be unleashed on Fort Sumter's underwater protections, a violent storm struck and it was lost. Efforts to find it are currently under way near Cape Hatteras.

Backtrack to Columbia Avenue, and turn right. At the corner of Columbia and North Delaware Street, *Under the Great Elm Shackamaxon* honors the treaty between Penn and the Lenni Lenape. Shackamaxon was the area's native name.

At Allen Street, turn left. Turn right on Marlborough Street. Old Brick Church, also known as ❺ **Kensington Methodist Church,** has been in continuous use since 1854. The current congregation no longer fills the sanctuary and instead meets in a small church office. Old Brick's future is in doubt.

Continue on Marlborough Street. At Girard Avenue, turn left, crossing Crease Street. Look to the left. The ❻ **Kensington Soup Society** served meals to the hungry in a building nearby from 1844 to 2012. "Kensington Soup House" remains carved on the facade. During the winter of 1876–77, the organization fed about 28,000 people—an average of nearly 400 each day—according to the Preservation Alliance of Philadelphia. Those served included "families widowed or crippled by war, accident or disease; the unemployed; and workers whose wages could not cover the expenses of providing for their families. 'Bummers,' single men without fixed residence, were actively denied aid, as were those suspected of 'double-dipping' from soup kitchens elsewhere in the city."

At the corner of Frankford Avenue, the modern corner bar Garage North, 100 E. Girard Ave., stands across from an 1877 building that now houses a Wells Fargo Bank, 1148 Frankford Ave.

Turn right on Frankford, crossing Girard Avenue to ❼ **Johnny Brenda's.** In the 1960s, a boxer named Johnny Imbrenda ran a rough neighborhood bar here. In the early 2000s, two experienced restaurateurs purchased the place despite the questionable neighborhood and rebranded the spot as a music venue with gastropub leanings. It reopened in 2003 and helped launch the neighborhood's renaissance.

Other dining options on this block include Fette Sau, 1208 Frankfort Ave., a barbecue joint from Brooklyn, and Frankford Hall, 1210 Frankford Ave., a German-style beer garden.

Continue on Frankford Avenue. ❽ *Lotus Diamond* is by Shepard Fairey, an artist perhaps best known for his OBEY design and his 2008 Hope campaign poster of Barack Obama. In the middle of this mural is a star containing Andre the Giant's face. Fairey uses images of the late wrestler/actor in many of his works.

Continue on Frankford Avenue, passing ❾ **Fishtown Tavern** on your right. Fishtown began as a small area within Kensington, so named because of the many commercial fishermen who lived here, working the shad-filled Delaware River, writes Kenneth Milano in *Remembering Kensington and Fishtown: The Story of a Philadelphia River Ward*. Look for fish imagery in sidewalk imprints, in ironwork, on telephone poles, and on trash cans designed to look like a fish's mouth. The original residents here were known for their pride of place, and the newest residents share that.

Pass Jinxed, 1331 Frankford Ave., which offers antiques and curiosities, and Parlour, 1339 Frankford Ave., a salon. ❿ **Lutheran Settlement House,** founded in 1902, continues to serve vulnerable men, women, and children with a variety of services. Two murals of note here: Outside is *Settlement House Roots,* a tribute to the employees who work here and the people they help. It features glass mosaic flowers that pop off the wall. Inside is *You Are Not Alone.* In 2015, Mark Hudson, 26, was shot and killed by his girlfriend. Hudson's mother, Karen, works closely with Settlement House. Representatives from NBC's *Today* show learned of the loss and partnered with Philadelphia Mural Arts to create this tribute to the family. The morning program filmed Karen Hudson first seeing the mural. "Mark is still bigger than life and I'm just overjoyed to see him living forever," she says with emotion.

Dining and drinking options include La Colombe, 1335 Frankford Ave., arguably the best coffee in the city, and Kensington Quarters, 1310 Frankford Ave., a butcher shop that also offers butchering classes. The whole-goat class is popular.

Continue on Frankford. Across from a community garden on the right is ⓫ **The Yachtsman,** a tiki bar with Polynesian cocktails garnished with umbrellas and flowers. Interior decor includes thatched roofs and a stuffed Rastafarian banana. The piña colada is recommended. Note the cool painted waves splashing the exterior.

Ahead on the right, the former gas station on the corner is now 🄬 **Heffe,** a walk-up taco shop with picnic tables outside. Try the fried octopus tacos with tomato jam.

Pass Philadelphia Record Exchange, 1524 Frankford Ave., a go-to vinyl shop, and Steap and Grind, 1619 Frankford Ave., offering a long tea list and interesting ironwork.

Palmer Park, Frankford Avenue and Palmer Street, is named after Kensington's founder. The Fishtown Neighbors Association keeps this tiny park hopping with community events, including movie nights and a farmers market.

About two blocks east, at Palmer and Tulips Streets, early baseball star A. J. Reach, one of the founders of the Philadelphia Phillies franchise, had a manufacturing plant that made baseballs, footballs, boxing gloves, and other sports equipment, historian Milano writes.

🄭 *You Can Be Stronger Than Diabetes* is on the side of Bell Surplus Floor Covering Warehouse. While the title may seem strange, this artwork has become a popular neighborhood symbol. Drug manufacturing company GlaxoSmithKline sponsored the mural as part of a public education project. Fishtown has the city's highest rate of diabetes diagnoses in people ages 18 and younger. The mural promotes healthy eating, with images of fruits and vegetables inside a fish-shaped outline.

Neumann Medical Center, 1601 E. Palmer St., was once the 80-bed St. Mary's Hospital, run by the Order of the Sisters of St. Francis. In the 1840s, the Philadelphia archdiocese sent three nuns to this part of the city to help the poor and infirm. The need for health care was so great that the nuns treated more than 15,000 patients—mostly German and Irish immigrants—in the first five years. The hospital's constitution was written in German.

Just before East Berks Avenue, an enclosed community garden offers interesting ironwork. Across the street is *The Vegetable Garden,* painted on the side of Frankford Auto & Truck, 1833 Frankford Ave.

Invisible Art: An Exploration in Color, 1834 Frankford Ave., is a bright delight on the side of Philadelphia Sculpture Gym, 1834 E. Frankford Ave.

Continue on Frankford Avenue. The signs promoting New City Car Wash & Detail Center, 1868 Frankford, prompt thoughts of the 1970s hit car wash song. Rocket Cat Cafe, 2001 Frankford, offers vegetarian food and bears art by Shepard Fairey.

Other commercial sites here include Furfari's Soft Pretzels, 2015 Frankford, founded in 1954, and Two Percent to Glory, 2031 Frankford, offering vintage clothing and home goods. Circle Thrift, 2233 Frankford, is a great place to shop for used clothing and goods.

⓮ Pizza Brain offers pizza by the pie or the slice, including traditional toppings such as pepperoni and more unusual ones, such as Gruyère cheese and caramelized onions. The restaurant contains a Pizza Museum. In 2011 the Guinness World Records folks certified that company cofounder Brian Dwyer has the world's largest collection of pizza-related memorabilia, including a pizza cutter in the shape of the starship *Enterprise*.

Pizza Brain shares space with Little Baby's Ice Cream, which began selling wares from specially constructed tricycles in 2011. Little Baby's is known for unusual flavors like smoked salmon and Earl Grey Sriracha. It honors other local businesses with flavors such as Yards Brewing Company Brown Butter Brawler, Goldenberg's Peanut Chews Vanilla Molasses, and pizza.

Welcome to the Neighborhood, on AC Auto Repairs, 2300 Frankford Ave., features sketches of residents past and present.

At East York Street, turn right. Horatio B. Hackett Elementary School, 2161 E. York St., named for an American biblical scholar who died in 1875, is currently being revamped inside and out. Note its mural.

Continue to Sepviva Street. Turn right. Konrad Square Park, East Dauphin Street, is named for firefighter Joseph Konrad, who was killed on the job in 1984. A nearby mural of Konrad was covered by new development.

Turn left on East Dauphin Street, passing Summerfield-Siloam United Methodist Church, 2223 E. Dauphin St. Turn right on Memphis Street, and follow the road as it bears right at East Norris Street. **⓯** St. Laurentius Roman Catholic Church was funded by the Polish immigrant workers who contributed every spare nickel and dime to build it in 1885. Now closed, the high Gothic church's brownstone facade remains a neighborhood landmark. Neighbors fought the church's closure and continue to butt heads with the Philadelphia Archdiocese over the building's ultimate fate.

Continue to ⑯ **Palmer Cemetery.** Neighborhood founder Palmer established this 5-acre cemetery, also known as Kensington Burial Ground, as a free final resting place for neighborhood residents. It's still active, offering free space to current residents or property owners. There's a monument inside dedicated to the family of John and Mary Ann Willingmyre, whose five sons fought in the Civil War, according to palmercemeteryfishtown.com. Two were killed, two were wounded, and one was captured. Because of space concerns, cremains are preferred. Palmer himself is not buried here; he lies in Christ Church Cemetery with Ben Franklin.

At East Palmer Street, turn left. At Girard Avenue, turn right. ⑰ **First Presbyterian Church,** another neighborhood landmark, was built in 1859. The structure originally had a 180-foot-tall steeple, but it deteriorated and was replaced with the copper dome in the 1920s.

Milkcrate Cafe, 400 Girard Ave., is a coffeehouse that also sells vinyl records and turntables.

This walk ends here. Consider walking to the start of the Northern Liberties tour (page 128), which is 1 mile away.

Points of Interest

① **Yards Brewing Company** 901 N. Delaware Ave., 215-634-2600, yardsbrewing.com

② **SugarHouse Casino** 1001 N. Delaware Ave., sugarhousecasino.com

③ **Penn Treaty Park** 1199 N. Delaware Ave., penntreatypark.org

④ **Delaware Power Station** 1325 Beach St.

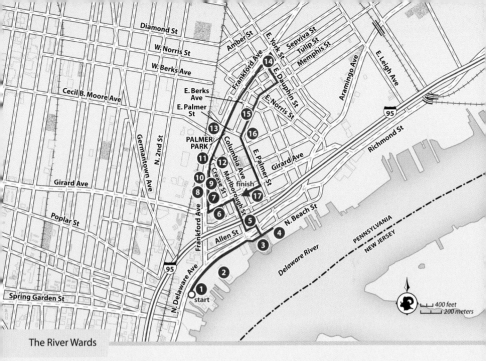

The River Wards

5 **Kensington Methodist Church** 300 Richmond St., 215-634-2495

6 **Kensington Soup Society** 1036 Crease St.

7 **Johnny Brenda's** 1201 Frankford Ave., 215-739-9684, johnnybrendas.com

8 *Lotus Diamond* 1228 Frankford Ave. For more information, contact Philadelphia Mural Arts, 215-685-0750, muralarts.org.

9 **Fishtown Tavern** 1301 Frankford Ave., 267-687-8406, fishtowntavern.com

10 **Lutheran Settlement House** 1340 Frankford Ave., 215-426-8610, lutheransettlement.org

11 **The Yachtsman** 1444 Frankford Ave., 267-909-8740, yachtsmanbar.com

12 **Heffe** 1431 Frankford Ave., 215-423-2309, heffetacos.com

13 *You Can Be Stronger Than Diabetes* 1706 Frankford Ave.

14 **Pizza Brain** 2313 Frankford Ave., 215-291-2965, pizzabrain.org

15 **St. Laurentius Roman Catholic Church** 1600 E. Berks St.

16 **Palmer Cemetery** 1499 E. Palmer St., palmercemeteryfishtown.com

17 **First Presbyterian Church** 410–22 Girard Ave.

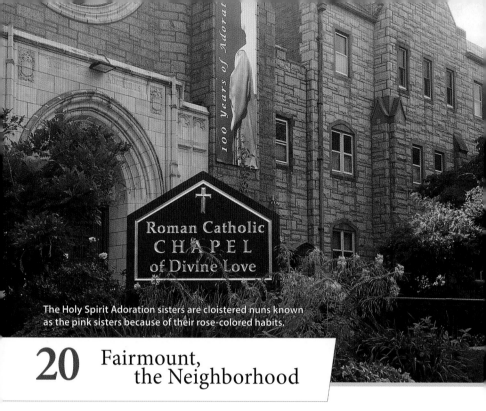

The Holy Spirit Adoration sisters are cloistered nuns known as the pink sisters because of their rose-colored habits.

20 Fairmount, the Neighborhood

BOUNDARIES: W. Girard Ave., Spring Garden St., N. Broad St., N. 25th St.
DISTANCE: 3.7 miles
DIFFICULTY: Easy, with downhill stretches
PARKING: Street parking is usually available unless a special event is taking place; there's a paid lot at N. 22nd St. and Fairmount Ave.
PUBLIC TRANSIT: SEPTA's Broad Street subway line takes you to Fairmount's eastern border. Bus lines include the 7, 32, 33, and 48.

William Penn named this neighborhood just northwest of Center City for the high hill, or "fair mount" on which it sits, giving residents a great view of the Schuylkill River. It's also called the Art Museum area because of its proximity to that landmark. The pocket closer to downtown is also known as Spring Garden.

Walk Description

Begin at Fairmount and Ridge Avenues, looking at the **❶ JBJ Soul Homes.** Local nonprofit Project Home partnered with rocker Jon Bon Jovi to build this four-story, mixed-use building with 55 apartments for formerly homeless and low-income people. Artist Meg Saligman created the stunning two-story mural *Fire Beacon,* which contains a round glass sculpture that is lit at night. There are two murals inside: one in the lobby and one in the second-floor community room. One lobby wall contains a line from a song on Bon Jovi's ninth album, "Who says you can't go home?"

Continue on Fairmount Avenue. Overseas Motor Works, 1501–05 Fairmount Ave., is a 1930s Art Deco building specifically designed to house an auto-related business when nearby North Broad Street was known as automobile row. Note the ram heads, nymphs, and fluted columns.

Another 1930s Art Deco delight and Project Home building, 1515 Fairmount Ave., has offices, apartments, and a café. Note the flower and plant motifs and the carved *B* over the door. Could the builder have foretold Bon Jovi's future involvement with the nonprofit?

Cross North 16th Street. Jobbers Warehouse, 1601 Fairmount Ave., was also designed for an auto business, as evidenced by its garage fronts. It is still used for that purpose. Look at the top floor panel above the door, which lists the construction date and an unusual logo, perhaps a Quaker or Colonial figure holding a tire.

Cross North 17th Street. Condos are now planned for this area, but from the late 1800s through the early 1900s, the smokestack from the A. F. Bornot "French Steam Dyeing and Scouring Establishment" cut into the skyline.

Continue on Fairmount Avenue, passing Tela's Market and Kitchen, 1833 Fairmount Ave., great for light fare. Mugshots Coffeehouse, 1925 Fairmount Ave., was one of the first neighborhood coffee shops. Check out its eclectic interior.

❷ Eastern State Penitentiary opened in 1829 and was conceived as a true penitentiary, one that would reform, not punish. The cells were lit by skylights in the vaulted ceilings, the message being that only God and hard work could provide redemption.

Among the big-name criminals held here were bank robber Willie Sutton and gangster Al Capone. The penitentiary closed in 1970. It has been transformed into a popular tourist attraction. Its best-known events are its Halloween haunted house and its Bastille Day celebration, which features a woman dressed as Marie Antoinette standing on a tower and shouting, "Let them eat TastyKakes!" while the locally made snack cakes rain on the crowds below. A new exhibition looks at how incarceration has negatively affected the nation.

Double back to Corinthian Avenue. Turn left. The white building ahead is ❸ **Girard College's Founder's Hall.** Banker/merchant Stephen Girard was one of the richest men in the country when he died in 1831. His fortune established Girard College, a school for poor, white, male orphans, many of whom were the sons of coal miners, which opened in 1833.

Today the school is open to both genders and all skin hues and offers full scholarships and boarding for academically gifted students from families of limited means. Founder's Hall is considered one of the finest examples of Greek Revival architecture in the country.

Turn right on Girard Avenue. At Ridge Avenue, turn left and then left again on North College Avenue. ❹ *Henry Ossawa Tanner: Letters of Influence* honors a man the artist describes as "the Jackie Robinson of the art world, the Barack Obama of painting." Tanner, who died in 1937, was one of the first African American artists to receive international acclaim. The project was created with adjudicated male youths living in St. Gabriel's Hall.

Continue on North College Avenue, passing *Cancer Support for Life,* which features people who have survived cancer or provide support for those going through treatments.

Moving Forward, 2521 W. Girard Ave., looks at the neighborhood's history and the changing community, featuring images of current residents, local architecture, and the Route 15 Trolley.

Turn left onto West College Avenue. At Poplar Street, turn left again, passing St. Nicholas Ukrainian Catholic Church, 871 N. 24th St. Turn right on North 24th Street; then turn right again on Aspen Street.

Patrick Ward Memorial Park, 24th and Aspen Streets, is named for a 21-year-old neighborhood resident killed in the Vietnam War while serving as a helicopter gunner. A 1997 *Philadelphia Inquirer* article tells of the day Army officials came to the neighborhood to tell Ward's family of his death. Neighbors watched as "the big brown Army car made its way slowly down the narrow Fairmount street." Patrick Ward's father recalled how a few days earlier

Eastern State Penitentiary was conceived as a place that would reform, not punish.

he'd heard there were "rough times for US helicopters in Vietnam. I said to my wife, 'I hope our Patty's not up there.'"

Continue on Aspen Street to the ❺ **former home of director David Lynch.** Lynch filmed his first 4-minute short, titled "The Alphabet," while living here in the late 1960s. The house is a Trinity, an architectural style unique to the city, also called a Father, Son, Holy Ghost house. This style has three floors, with one room on each floor. The kitchen is in the basement. Servants and lower-income workers typically lived in these homes, which had about 100 square feet of space per floor.

At North 25th Street, turn left, passing Philly Fairmount Art Center, 2501 Olive St., a neighborhood hub. At Fairmount Avenue, turn left.

Restaurants here include La Calaca Feliz, 2321 Fairmount, offering Mexican fare; Rybread, 2319 Fairmount, with sandwiches and sweets; London Grill, 2301 Fairmount, featuring New American cuisine; and A Mano, 2244 Fairmount, offering house-made pastas.

Turn right onto North 23rd Street. Walk to Wallace Street and turn right again. At North 24th Street, turn left, walking down Penn's "fair mount." At Green Street, turn left. **❻ St. Francis Xavier Church** was founded in 1839. The church also contains The Philadelphia Congregation of the Oratory, a group of secular priests who have served the community since 1990. In 2014, the church held a Mass mob event, encouraging each parishioner to bring a few guests to a Sunday service. The idea came from flash mobs, in which groups of people converge on a single space.

Continue on Green Street. Prepare yourself for some serious house envy. The home at 2220 Green St. belongs to former Pennsylvania state senator Vincent J. Fumo, who in 2009 was convicted of more than 135 federal corruption charges. The Romanesque brownstone, built in the 1880s, is a 33-room, 19,200-square-foot mansion with wine cellar, shooting range, and servants' quarters, as well as six bedrooms and 10 bathrooms.

Fumo was in a federal prison until August 2013 and then was allowed to serve the rest of his time in his home, prompting one newspaper reporter to call this building "the federal correctional institution at Fairmount, also known as the Fumo mansion."

The **❼ Bergdoll Mansion** has eight bedrooms, nine bathrooms, two kitchens, and hand-painted ceilings. During World War I, Grover Cleveland Bergdoll, grandson of the original owner, lived here with his mother. According to philly.curbed.com, when World War I began, Bergdoll "dodged the draft . . . by hiding in the mansion."

Before he could be arrested, Bergdoll escaped to Germany, using his family's fortune to live well. When found by bounty hunters, he killed one and bit the thumb off the other, earning the nickname the Fighting Slacker. In May 1939 the wildly disliked Bergdoll returned to the United States—but only because he didn't want to be drafted into the Nazi Army.

Continue on Green Street to the Chapel of Divine Love and the convent of the **❽ Holy Spirit Adoration Sisters.** The cloistered nuns who live here are known as the pink sisters because they wear rose-colored habits to signify the joy they feel honoring the Holy Spirit. The chapel never closes, and there is always at least one nun praying. The sisters recently marked more than 100 years of nonstop prayer.

Continue on Green Street, stopping at the yellow buildings at the corner of North 20th Street. In the 1970s, the Reverend Gabriel Real, pastor of mostly Puerto Rican Our Lady of the Miraculous Medal Church, spearheaded the building of these eight structures for low-income congregants. The homes in Spanish Village cost $20,000, but a family could make a down payment as low as $200.

At North 19th Street, turn left. St. Andrew Lithuanian Catholic Church, 1911 Wallace St., offers two Sunday Masses, one in Lithuanian and one in English.

Cross North 19th Street. Sculptor Evelyn Keyser's *People Pyramid* was installed here in 1971. "The figures are meant to represent the members of a family supporting one another, with fathers on the bottom tier, sons on the second tier and their brothers on the top," the website creativephl.org notes.

The fenced-in garden across Wallace Street is Spring Gardens, which provides space to almost 200 local families. The garden also serves as an outdoor class-room, hosting cooking and planting workshops.

Walk to Wallace Street. ❾ **Roberto Clemente Park,** the entrance to which is on North 18th Street, was the heart of the city's original Puerto Rican community, which reached its population peak in the 1970s. Those who grew up here describe falling asleep to the sounds of Puerto Rican music coming from the park per-formed by the 20Gs, a local gang that served as the neighborhood's protectors. As this area changed and the property values increased, many of these residents moved, now returning only for the annual Clemente Fest.

Continue on Wallace Street. *Tribute to Diego Rivera,* North 17th and Wallace Streets, is divided into three sections, each representing a different theme prominent in Rivera's art: the working man, the community, and the family.

Turn right on North 17th Street. At Mt. Vernon Street, turn right again. The church at 1722 Mt. Vernon Street is a condominium building fittingly named The Church. The ❿ **former home of Thomas Eakins** is now the headquarters of the Philadelphia Mural Arts Program, the city-affiliated nonprofit responsible for almost all of the murals featured in this book. Eakins was a realist painter, photographer, and sculptor, and perhaps one of the most important American artists in modern history. The green space in front of the Philadelphia Museum of Art is also named for him.

Walk to North 18th Street. Turn left. The Laura W. Waring School is named for the well-known African American artist. Her 1944 exhibition *Portraits of Outstanding Citizens of Negro Origin* included a painting of Marian Anderson. Many Waring paintings are in the National Portrait Gallery's permanent collection. The school's side doors are flanked by a stained glass floral mosaic, *Doorway to Imagination.*

Continue to Spring Garden Street. ⓫ **Highway Tabernacle** began as a gospel wagon in 1895, with local preachers traveling from town to town. The horse-drawn wagon, decorated with Bible verses, carried the men, an organ, and litera-ture. After four months, they had stopped 35 times and spoken to about 35,000 people. The next year they were even busier. They established the original church soon after. After a fire devastated the building in 1986, congregants gathered outside to sing and pray. When a reporter asked how people could be so happy looking at the burnt building, one woman replied, "We don't cry over things; we cry over people."

Turn left to walk east on Spring Garden Street. The ⓬ **former Stetson Mansion,** now condos, was the home of hat magnate John B. Stetson. His famous hats were manufactured in Philadelphia.

The New Jersey–born son of a hat maker, Stetson traveled through the American West before settling in Philadelphia in 1865. His travels and observations led to his unique hat design. The *Dictionary of the American West* includes this description from a Stetson fan, "It kept the sun out of your eyes and off your neck. It was an umbrella. It gave you a bucket (the crown) to water your horse and a cup (the brim) to water yourself. It made a hell of a fan, which you need sometimes for a fire but more often to shunt cows this direction or that."

This walk ends here. You're three blocks from North Broad Street, if you'd like to continue walking. See Walks 8 and 9 (pages 49 and 57).

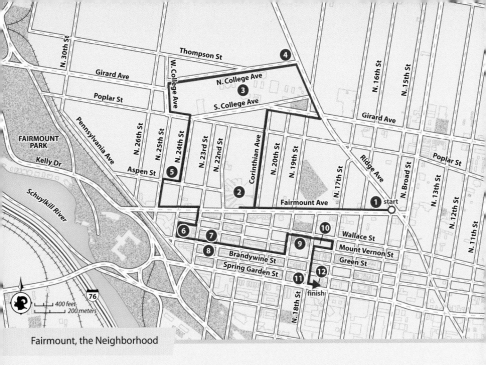

Fairmount, the Neighborhood

Points of Interest

1 **Project Home/JBJ Soul Homes** 1415 Fairmount Ave. and 1515 Fairmount Ave., 215-232-7272, projecthome.org

2 **Eastern State Penitentiary** 2027 Fairmount Ave, 215-236-3300, easternstate.org

3 **Girard College** 2101 S. College Ave., 215-787-2600, girardcollege.edu

4 *Henry Ossawa Tanner: Letters of Influence* 2019 N. College Ave. For more information, contact Philadelphia Mural Arts, 215-685-0750, muralarts.org.

5 **Former home of director David Lynch** 2429 Aspen St.

6 **St. Francis Xavier Church** 2319 Green St., 215-765-4568, sfxoratory.org

7 **Bergdoll Mansion** 2201 Green St.

8 **Holy Spirit Adoration Sisters** 2212 Green St., 215-567-0123, adorationsisters.org

9 **Roberto Clemente Park** N. 19th and Wallace Sts., friendsofclemente.blogspot.com

10 **Former home of Thomas Eakins** 1729 Mt. Vernon St. Now the headquarters of Philadelphia Mural Arts, 215-685-0750, muralarts.org.

11 **Highway Tabernacle** 1801 Spring Garden St., 215-563-9192, highwaytabernacle.org

12 **Former Stetson Mansion** 1717 Spring Garden St.

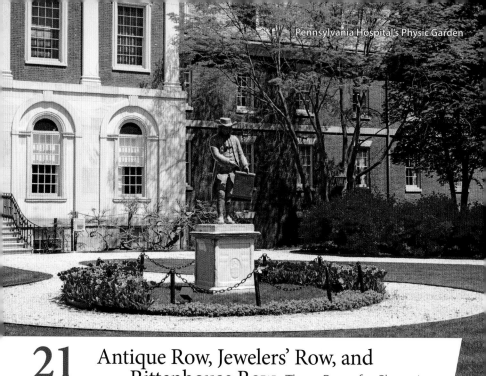

21 Antique Row, Jewelers' Row, and Rittenhouse Row: Three Rows for Shopping

BOUNDARIES: Schuylkill River, S. Sixth St., Pine St., Chestnut St.
DISTANCE: 2.7 miles
DIFFICULTY: Easy
PARKING: There are multiple pay lots throughout this walk, as well as street parking.
PUBLIC TRANSIT: Crosstown buses run back and forth on Pine St., where this tour begins, and Lombard St., one block south of Pine. Consider the 12, 40, and 42.

This Center City walk visits three shopping areas and includes the nation's first hospital, a mural paying tribute to the city's only recent national championship team, and a high-end clothing store occupying a former funeral home.

Walk Description

Start on Antique Row. This stretch of Pine Street between South 12th and South Ninth Streets was so designated in 2001. In August 2016, an article in India's *Hindustan Times* recommended tourists stop here "to pick up a piece of Americana."

While this was a great place to open an antiques shop in the 1980s, many are now closed or have been replaced. There are about half a dozen remaining, including Kohn & Kohn, 1112 Pine St., and Antique Design, 1102 Pine St.

❶ Louis I. Kahn Park is named for the esteemed architect. Kahn was known for his modern buildings. When he died in 1974 at age 73, he was the most celebrated architect in the United States, as a *New Yorker* piece noted two decades after his death. The original park, established in the 1970s was "a low maintenance space with few plantings and an emphasis on concrete; hence its nickname, 'Concrete Park,'" notes the Friends of Louis I. Kahn group, which has worked to transform the area into a more welcome space.

Continue on Pine Street, passing Scarlett's Closet, 1034 Pine; Jeffrey Biber Antiques, 1030 Pine; Happily Ever After, 1010 Pine; and Blendo Past & Present, 1002 Pine.

❷ M. Finkel & Daughter, which specializes in 18th- and 19th-century needlework, is now run by the daughter, Amy Finkel. Her father opened the shop here in the 1940s, and she joined him in 1975. Finkel told hiddencityphila.org how antiquing has changed in the Internet age: She acquired a sampler made in 1832 by an 8-year-old English girl named Thisbe Danson. She found one of Thisbe's direct descendants in England. The man purchased the sampler and now owns something created by his ancestor via a Philadelphia shopkeeper.

Pass Good Karma Cafe, 928 Pine, and Classic Antiques PHL, 922 Pine, en route to the nation's first hospital, **❸ Pennsylvania Hospital,** which was home to other firsts, including the first general vaccine against pneumonia, the first use of intravenous feeding, and the development of magnetic resonance imaging (MRI). Dr. Thomas Bond and Benjamin Franklin founded the hospital in 1751. It's open for guided and self-guided tours.

At South Eighth Street, turn left. At Delancey Street, note the 1938 Richard H. Harte Memorial Building. It honors Harte, who served in World War I, earning the army's Distinguished Service Medal for being "one of the pioneering instructors in the principles of battle surgery."

The Physic Garden, Eighth and Pine Streets, has a statue of city founder William Penn at center. Rumor is his ghost leaves the statue in the evening and walks the grounds.

Continue on South Eighth Street, passing St. George Greek Orthodox Cathedral, 256 S. Eighth St.

At Locust Street, turn right. Ahead is ❹ **Washington Square,** one of the city's original green spaces. The square holds the Tomb of the Unknown Revolutionary War Soldier, and many soldiers are buried under this square.

Continue to the corner of South Washington Square. The Farm Journal Building, 230 W. Washington Square, fittingly has a stone cornucopia above its entrance. In print since 1827, the publication remains the country's largest farming magazine. It's now published elsewhere.

Follow the square to the corner of St. James Street to find The Ayer, a condo building that once housed N. W. Ayer & Son. The advertising firm, founded in 1869, created the memorable tagline, "A diamond is forever."

Bear right, following the park. At Walnut Street, turn right. ❺ **The Curtis Building** housed the Curtis Publishing Company, one of the country's largest publishers in the early 1900s. It printed *Ladies' Home Journal, Jack and Jill,* and *The Saturday Evening Post.* The interior features a waterfall and Maxwell Parrish's glass mosaic *Dream Garden,* which contains more than 100,000 pieces of glass and is seen in *The Sixth Sense.*

At Sixth Street, turn left. ❻ **The Public Ledger Building** housed the daily newspaper of the same name. Founded in 1836, it was known for its bold, tabloid-style headlines and rhyming obituaries. The penny-paper almost folded when its original management opposed the Civil War. New owners rebranded it as a Union supporter and it once again flourished. Its presses—the country's first rotary ones, which quadrupled the speed of newspaper printing—shut down in 1942.

At Chestnut Street, turn left. The sidewalk features plaques commemorating the 56 signers of the Declaration of Independence.

At South Seventh Street, turn left, passing Jones, 700 Chestnut St., a casual spot with a *Brady Bunch*–esque feel, and a sign for the Beck Engraving Company, which in 1908 first made a set of four-color plates, setting an industry standard for creating colored images.

This fountain is Washington Square Park's centerpiece.

At Samson Street, turn right into the heart of Jewelers' Row, which stretches for another block west and includes parts of Walnut and South Eighth Streets. Originally a residential strip, some of the commercial businesses date back to the 1830s, such as J. E. Caldwell & Co., 728 Sansom St. The facades of most of the buildings have changed, including Katz Imports/Penn Diamond Exchange, 723 Sansom St., which now has an Art Deco look.

At South Eighth Street, cross the street and turn right to look at the historical marker in front of the **➐ Craftsman Row Saloon.** It honors Robert Bogle, an African American man whose thriving catering business was here. According to a 1987 *Philadelphia Inquirer* article, Bogle was a favorite of Nicholas Biddle, president of the Second Bank of the United States. "Of the two dozen or so catering dynasties that sprang up in the city in the 1800s . . . a disproportionate number were founded by blacks," the article said. "At a time when most blacks found little or no opportunity to advance, the black caterers achieved money, power—even in some cases, a measure of immortality." When Bogle died, Biddle penned an "Ode to Bogle," suggesting "no human ritual, be it marriage, christening, or even death, was complete if not attended to by the stern, multifarious Bogle."

Head south on South Eighth Street. At Walnut Street, turn right. **➑ The Walnut Street Theatre** is the oldest English-speaking theater in the country, founded in 1809. The first production opened with the Marquis de Lafayette and President Thomas Jefferson in the audience. The Walnut was the first theater to install gas footlights (1837) and the first to feature air conditioning (1855).

➒ Wills Eye Hospital, established in 1834, is the country's oldest continuously operating eye-care center. It's named for James Wills Jr., a Quaker merchant who donated $116,000 to found the hospital, now known for its innovations.

The front sculpture is Brower Hatcher's *Starman in the Ancient Garden,* depicting a space ship that has crash-landed, picking up on its voyage a car, a wagon wheel, snakes, a pineapple, and a falling person. The artist said he hoped the work would prompt viewers to reflect on "what we have been, what we are, and what we may become."

Continue on Walnut Street, passing buildings and offices that are part of Thomas Jefferson University Hospital and Medical School. The university was founded in 1824 by Dr. George McClellan when only four colleges offered medical training. Among its alums: Samuel D. Gross, who graduated in 1828 and was considered the finest surgeon of his time.

⑩ The Forrest Theatre is named for noted thespian Edwin Forrest. Forrest's long feud with actor William Macready was the underlying cause of New York's 1849 Astor Place Riot, which left 22 dead and 100 injured.

Long story short: Forrest was the darling of the working class, while Macready had the support of the largely Anglophile upper classes. In 1849, a group of Forrest's supporters purchased tickets to Macready's performance of *Macbeth* at Astor Place Theater, then shut down the performance by pummeling the stage with rotten eggs, potatoes, lemons, and shoes. Three days later, Macready took the stage and fights broke out among 100,000 people gathered outside.

Forrest Theatre

Two pubs here, Moriarty's, 1116 Walnut St., and The Irish Pub, 1123 Walnut St., are both popular with hospital workers.

The stretch of Walnut Street after South 12th Street is also called Gloria Casarez Way, named for the city's first director of LGBT affairs. A few blocks from here, a mural on the 12th Street Gym also honors her.

⑪ The Witherspoon Building exemplifies the "more is more" school of design. Built in

1897 as the Presbyterian Board of Publications and Sabbath School, the structure is covered with medallions and sculptures of historic figures representing the United States and Europe. The National Register of Historic Places calls each of its entrances "a showcase of sculpture." The architect, James Huston, called it "an attempt to tell the story of the Organization of the Presbyterian Church in this country in Architecture, Painting, and Sculpture." The building is named for John Witherspoon, the only Presbyterian minister to sign the Declaration of Independence.

Continue west on Walnut Street. The **12** **Bellevue-Stratford Hotel** was once one of the country's most glamorous hotels, hosting two Republican National Conventions, a Democratic National Convention, and an American Legion conference that ended with the outbreak of Legionnaire's disease.

Tiffany & Co., 1414 Walnut St., sets the tone for Rittenhouse Row shopping. While there are midrange shops and chains such as McDonald's along this stretch, the high-end retailers have staked their claim here in the last decade.

Butcher & Singer, 1500 Walnut St., is a steakhouse that formerly housed a stock brokerage firm of the same name. The interior salutes old Hollywood.

Continue on Walnut Street, passing The Apple Store, 1607 Walnut; Modell's Sporting Goods, 1608 Walnut; and Paper Source, 1628 Walnut.

The **13** **Icon,** a retail/residential building, is an Art Deco gem. The living spaces were recently remodeled by a company specializing in wellness real estate, meaning baths feature water infused with vitamin C and kitchen surfaces have a coating that prevents the spread of bacteria. The building has a gym, a nutritionist for cooking demos, and an on-site pet groomer.

Continue, passing Aerosoles, 1700 Walnut St., and Zara, 1715 Walnut St. At South 18th Street, turn right. Anthropologie is housed in the 1898 Beaux Arts mansion originally commissioned by Sarah Drexel Fell, widow of a coal magnate, for herself and her new husband. The store retains its beautiful staircase, and one floor has a ceiling featuring gold circular frames with paintings of Italian royalty.

Continue on South 18th Street. Casual dining options include Le Bus Bakery, 129 S. 18th St.; Hip City Veg, 127 S. 18th St.; and Di Bruno Bros., 1730 Chestnut St.

At Chestnut Street, turn left. **⓮ Boyd's** opened in 1938 as a custom shirt shop. It now sells custom suits for men, which can cost more than $5,000, and women's clothing. The founder's grandchildren run the business and employ a team of more than 25 staff tailors.

At South 19th Street, turn left. At Sansom Street, with upscale women's clothing store Sophy Curson, 122 S. 19th St., on the corner, turn right. The mural painted on the second floor of Shake Shack, 2000 Sansom St., is *Summer Rendezvous*. Shake Shack added plantings to this concrete-heavy corner when it opened, and the mural is meant to continue that green idea.

Continue through a mini arts district, home to the Roxy Theater, 2023 Sansom; The Adrienne Theater, 2030 Sansom; and Helium Comedy Club, 2031 Sansom. Porcini restaurant, 2048 Sansom, is a hidden gem.

At South 21st Street, turn left. Walk to Walnut Street. **⓯ The First Presbyterian Church** features Tiffany Studios stained glass windows dating to 1872. One favorite is a 1914 tribute to Emily McFadden, which features two angels with raised arms sitting in a garden.

Turn right on Walnut Street. Note how the buildings on both sides are original structures and retain the feel of the 1800s. Crossing South 22nd Street, the wall overlooking the gas station has trompe l'oeil murals resembling church windows.

Continue on Walnut Street, crossing South 23rd Street and passing an unusual collection of village shops. Continue to the bridge crossing the Schuylkill River and turn around to view the mural at 24th and Walnut Streets, a tribute to the city's Major League Baseball team, the Philadelphia Phillies, which won World Series championships in 1980 and 2008.

This walk ends here. Cross the bridge to begin a West Philadelphia tour (pages 188 and 194), or follow the river south to explore Fitler Square (page 42).

Antique Row, Jewelers' Row, and Rittenhouse Row

Points of Interest

1. **Louis I. Kahn Park** S. 11th and Pine Sts., kahnpark.org

2. **M. Finkel & Daughter** 936 Pine St., 215-627-7797, samplings.com

3. **Pennsylvania Hospital** 800 Spruce St., 215-829-3000, pennmedicine.org

4. **Washington Square** 210 W. Washington Square, 215-965-2305, nps.gov/inde

5. **Curtis Building** 601 Walnut St., 800-627-3999, keystonepropertygroup.com

6. **The Public Ledger Building** 149 S. Sixth St.

7. **Craftsman Row Saloon** 112 S. Eighth St., 215-923-0123, craftsmanrowsaloon.com

8. **Walnut Street Theatre** 825 Walnut St., 215-574-3550, walnuttheatre.org

9. **Wills Eye Hospital** 840 Walnut St., 215-928-3000, willseye.org

10. **The Forrest Theatre** 1114 Walnut St., 215-923-1515, forrest-theatre.com

11. **The Witherspoon Building** 1319–1323 Walnut St.

12. **Former Bellevue-Stratford Hotel (now The Bellevue Hotel)** 200 S. Broad St., 215-893-1234, bellevuephiladelphia.com

13. **Icon** 1616 Walnut St., 844-483-9141, icon1616.com

14. **Boyd's** 1818 Chestnut St., 215-564-9000, boydsphila.com

15. **The First Presbyterian Church** 201 S. 21st St., 215-567-0532, fpcphila.org

Artist Isaiah Zagar has adorned the city with his mosaics.
Philadelphia's Magic Gardens are his most impressive work.

22 Headhouse Square, Fabric Row, and South Street: "Where Do All the Hippies Meet?"

BOUNDARIES: Pine St., Christian St., S. Second St., Schuylkill River
DISTANCE: 2 miles
DIFFICULTY: Easy
PARKING: This tour begins in the 200 block of Pine St. There is a private parking lot at that
    intersection and abundant metered street parking.
PUBLIC TRANSIT: SEPTA's 40 bus stops nearby.

Part of William Penn's original street grid, South Street runs east to west and separates
Center City from South Philadelphia. In 1963, R & B girl group The Orlons earned a gold
record with the song "South Street," which included the line "Where do all the hippies
meet? South Street, South Street." In the 1960s and 70s, the area was best known for its
bars, live-music venues, and the counterculture types—the hippies—who hung out
there. In the late 1970s and early 1980s, South Street attracted punk rock fans.

The bohemian feel faded away in the last part of the 20th century as rents rose and the
funky boutiques gave way to chain stores and tourist traps. Today, however, the street

seems to be undergoing yet another renaissance, with artists reclaiming gallery space and independent vegan and vegetarian food joints opening.

What hasn't changed is the street's popularity on summer evenings. Don't try driving on South Street then, but feel free to walk if you're up for dodging packs of teenagers, hungry diners in line at Jim's Steaks, and the spillover from the many bars and restaurants.

Walk Description

Begin at South Second and Pine Streets at the covered brick ❶ **Headhouse Square.** There were once two headhouses, or fire stations, on the square, but this is the only one still standing. While Philadelphia today is a sea of brick homes, it was originally a collection of tightly packed wooden structures, meaning firefighters were all the more important. The Headhouse, built in 1805, leads to an outdoor market known as the New Market or The Shambles, an Old English term for a butcher stall. Founded in 1745, this is the country's oldest surviving Colonial marketplace, still in use today for farmers markets and craft shows. It was called the New Market to differentiate it from the city's first marketplace on High Street, which is now known as Market Street. The structure is typical of the markets built in rural England at the time, with parallel rows of brick pillars supporting a gabled roof.

Turn south onto South Second Street to walk through the Shambles. The home at 401 S. Second St. belonged to John Ross, flag maker Betsy's uncle by marriage. George Washington reportedly visited for tea.

Continue to South Street. To the left is the Delaware River. Turn right, walking west. Larry Fine of The Three Stooges was born in the house formerly at 300 South St., the current Jon's Bar & Grille.

The comedian, born here in 1902 as Louis Feinberg, is seen in the accompanying mural playing the violin, as he did in many Stooges films, including 1936's *Disorder in the Court.* When Fine was a child, his forearm muscles were damaged by acid that his father, a jeweler, used to test gold. His parents had him take violin and boxing lessons to regain strength.

Continue on South Street. ❷ **Lorenzo and Sons Pizza** is known for the enormous slices it sells to lines of bar patrons in the wee hours of the morning. Experienced patrons know the staff can be a bit gruff; special requests are not encouraged. For years, a sign boasted that this was a place "Where the Customer is Never Right." The restaurant's facade and three-story interior got a postfire face-lift in 2013. The tragedy also prompted owner Giuseppe Pulizzi to update his no-toppings policy: slices with toppings are now available on Tuesday until midnight. South Street Sushi or a Philly Taco is a slice of Lorenzo and Sons' pizza wrapped around a cheesesteak sandwich from nearby Jim's Steaks.

❸ Theatre of Living Arts, better known as the TLA, opened in 1908 as a nickelodeon called the Crystal Palace with room for 500 people. The building has had various uses since, including as a movie theater, a repertory stage, and a nightclub. In 1987, concert company Live Nation Philadelphia purchased and rehabbed TLA, removing 75 pounds of rice that had been thrown at the screen during the weekly midnight viewings of *The Rocky Horror Picture Show*. Today TLA is a popular live-music venue.

Continue on South Street, pausing at the corner of South Fourth Street. Down the block to your right is **❹ Crash Bang Boom.** That's the new home—and new name—of the legendary punk rock shop Zipperhead, which was featured in the song "Punk Rock Girl" from The Dead Milkmen. The former facade at 407 South Street still bears an oversize painted zipper and giant ant sculptures from the second floor to the roof.

❺ Jim's Steaks often has a line snaking from its front door and down the block. Tourists often ask which of the city's two iconic cheesesteak joints is better, Pat's or Geno's. One faction of locals will always reply, "Jim's." Unlike Pat's and Geno's, Jim's has a full sandwich menu and indoor seating.

Turn left on South Fourth Street. **❻ Famous 4th Street Delicatessen,** also called The Famous, is an authentic Jewish deli, in operation since 1923. It's a city landmark, a popular gathering place for politicians and journalists every Election Day. In 2010, President Barack Obama stopped by for a corned beef Reuben and potato pancakes, two of the deli's specialties. The Famous has served as a movie backdrop. In the Oscar-winning 1993 film *Philadelphia*, Denzel Washington leaves the deli with a pastrami sandwich before agreeing to take on Tom Hanks's lawsuit.

If you order a sandwich, be warned: They are called overstuffed for a reason, coming in two sizes, regular and zaftig. The prices may seem a bit high—a zaftig corned beef special, for example, is about $24—but one zaftig can easily be shared by two or three diners. The chocolate chip cookies are another favorite.

Continue on South Fourth Street. This is Fabric Row, the one-time center of the city's Eastern European Jewish community's commercial life, known as Der Ferder ("the fourth" in Yiddish). Textile dealers began selling goods here—either in storefronts or with pushcarts—at the beginning of the 20th century. Pushcarts were outlawed in the 1950s, and many of the textile shops closed in the following decades. The area's revitalization began in the early 2000s.

The sandwiches at Famous 4th Street Deli are enormous.

7 Essene Market has promoted healthy eating since the 1980s. Dining options include The Hungry Pigeon, 743 S. Fourth, and Red Hook Coffee and Tea, 765 S. Fourth. Shopping options include Paper Moon, 520 S. Fourth; Moon + Arrow, 754 S. Fourth; Bus Stop Boutique, 727 S. Fourth; and Digital Underground, 732 S. Fourth.

Continue on South Fourth to Fulton Street. **8 *Harmony and the Window of Curiosities*** 770 S. Fourth St., covers a formerly run-down and oft-vandalized wall. Completed by neighborhood resident Conrad Booker in 2014, this bright, inviting wall now features butterflies made with the handprints of neighborhood children. The map is from 1865 and includes a recently uncovered nearby African American cemetery.

Continue on South Fourth. Turn right at Christian Street. **9 Settlement Music School** was founded in 1908 by two women offering immigrant children piano lessons for a nickel. The school now has six locations. Among the well-known musicians who took lessons here are Chubby Checker, who studied piano, and tenor Mario Lanza. Albert Einstein was a member of the school's advisory board in the 1950s.

Continue on Christian Street. At South Fifth Street, turn right. While walking through this residential stretch, note the many ways residents personalize their properties, including flowers, door decor, outdoor furniture, and front window displays.

Continue on South Fifth Street. Another commercial hub emerges near Bainbridge Street. Philly Aids Thrift, 710 S. Fifth St., is a thrift store with proceeds funding local AIDS organizations.

Continue to South Street and turn left. **⑩ Philadelphia's Magic Gardens** is the next stop. To get an idea of what's coming, look for artist Isaiah Zagar's work—brightly grouted mosaics made of tile and cut mirror—along this stretch. The alley at Schell Street (near Ninth Street) is covered with his works. The door of the building at 824/826 South St. features his self-portrait.

The Headhouse leads to an outdoor market formerly known as The Shambles.

Zagar began work on his half-block-long public art project near his studio in 1994 and continues to expand it. In 2002, the owner of some of the lots called for the art to be removed and the lots sold. After a two-year legal battle and help from the local community, Philadelphia's Magic Gardens was incorporated as a nonprofit that hosts workshops, concerts, and other events. Visitors can enter the indoor art galleries for a small charge.

Continue on South Street. Just past South 12th Street is a historical marker for the Standard Theatre. African American businessman John T. Gibson purchased the property in 1914 to offer "High Class and Meritorious Vaudeville" shows and music, according to explorepahistory.com. It was a tough business for African Americans: in 1927, Duke Ellington and his band were playing the Standard when the white owner of New York's Cotton Club decided he wanted Ellington to play at his club. A tough then went to the Standard and told the theater manager to release the band to travel, saying, "Be big. Or you'll be dead." Still, the Standard did well, appealing to both black and white audiences. The theater and others like it were called black-and-tans.

Continue on South Street to ⑪ *The Atlas of Tomorrow: A Device for Philosophical Reflection.* This is the city's first interactive mural, challenging viewers to ask a question and then spin a 6-foot dial. The spinner stops at a number corresponding with a story detailed on the bottom of the mural, all of the tales modified from *The I Ching,* one of the world's oldest books of wisdom. The person can then interpret the message as desired. The art on the wall itself is a fantastical black-and-white scene, made from thousands of fingerprints.

Continue on South Street, crossing South Broad Street. Govinda's Vegetarian, 1408 South St., offers vegetarian and vegan treats, while Sweet Freedom, 1424 South St., has vegan and gluten-free baked options.

⑫ *Billiards: A Tribute to Edward "Chick" Davis* shows two men playing pool, including one of the sport's greatest, Willie Mosconi (center), a South Philadelphian who picked up a cue at age 6. Between 1941 and 1957, he won 15 straight world championships. During a two-day exhibition in Ohio in the 1950s, he won a record 526 straight games. In the mural, he's seen holding one of his designer cues made by Russian-born craftsman George Balabushka, whose cues are considered the Stradivariuses of the billiards world. Mosconi had several, all inlaid with mother-of-pearl.

The other player is Edward "Chick" Davis, who learned to play billiards at the first YMCA open to African Americans. Since African Americans were barred from playing in pool halls, Davis honed his skills after hours, eventually competing against Mosconi. With his winnings, Davis opened pool halls in the city, including the one where this mural is painted.

⑬ *Legendary,* on the World Communications Charter School, is a tribute to The Roots, the Grammy Award–winning, Philadelphia-born band that gained national renown as the house band for *The Tonight Show Starring Jimmy Fallon.* In the early 1990s, the musicians were buskers hoping to collect change from passersby. The mural is a few blocks from the Philadelphia High School for the Creative and Performing Arts, the alma mater of the band's founders.

Continue on South Street, passing Jamaican Jerk Hut, 1436 South St., and a neighboring seasonal beer garden run by the Philadelphia Horticultural Society.

⑭ The Cambridge offers great food and a fabulous beer selection. It's across from **⑮ Bob & Barbara's Lounge,** a local institution serving its Citywide Special—a can of Pabst Blue Ribbon and a shot of Jim Beam—since 1969.

The now-closed **⑯ Royal Theater,** built in 1919, showcased performers such as Billie Holiday, Cab Calloway, and Pearl Bailey. A mural on the Georgian-style facade shows the building from its days as a hub of African American life. In the 1930s, the theater added movies, with one sign declaring it "America's Finest Colored Photoplayhouse." The theater closed in 1970.

This walk ends here. For more walking, continue to South 18th Street, turn right, and pick up the Rittenhouse Square tour (page 35) by the park.

Points of Interest

① Headhouse Square and The Shambles Pine and South Second Sts., southstreet.com

② Lorenzo and Sons Pizza 305 South St., 215-800-1942, lorenzoandsons.com

③ Theatre of Living Arts 334 South St., 215-922-1011, venue.tlaphilly.com

④ Crash Bang Boom 528 S. Fourth St., 215-928-1123, crashbangboomonline.com

⑤ Jim's Steaks 400 South St., 215-928-1911, jimssouthstreet.com

⑥ Famous 4th Street Delicatessen 700 S. Fourth St., 215-922-3274, famous4thstreetdelicatessen.com

⑦ Essene Market 719 S. Fourth St., 215-922-1146, essenemarket.com

⑧ *Harmony and the Window of Curiosities* 770 S. Fourth St. For more information, contact Philadelphia Mural Arts, 215-685-0750, muralarts.org.

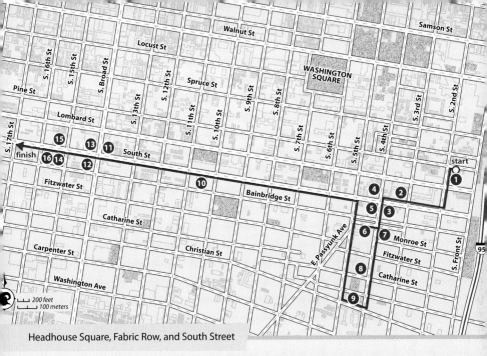

Headhouse Square, Fabric Row, and South Street

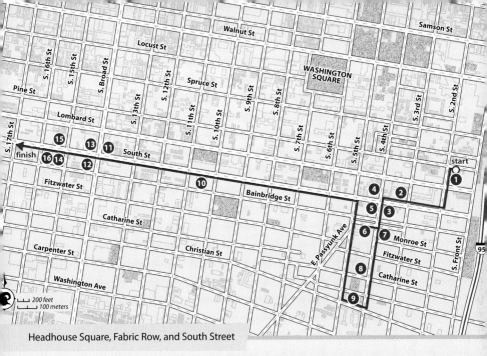

9 Settlement Music School   416 Queen St., 215-320-2601, settlementmusic.org

10 Philadelphia's Magic Gardens   1020 South St., 215-733-0390, phillymagicgardens.org

11 *The Atlas of Tomorrow: A Device for Philosophical Reflection*   South and Juniper Sts. For more information, contact Philadelphia Mural Arts, 215-685-0750, muralarts.org.

12 *Billiards: A Tribute to Edward "Chick" Davis*   1412 South St.

13 *Legendary*   512 S. Broad St. For more information, contact Philadelphia Mural Arts, 215-685-0750, muralarts.org.

14 The Cambridge   1508 South St., 267-455-0647, cambridgeonsouth.com

15 Bob & Barbara's Lounge   1509 South St., 215-545-4511, bobandbarbaras.com

16 Former Royal Theater   1536 South St.

Former Mayor Frank Rizzo watches from a wall in the Italian Market.

23 South Philadelphia I: East Passyunk Avenue and the Italian Market

BOUNDARIES: Broad St., S. Seventh St., Bainbridge St., Passyunk Ave.
DISTANCE: 2 miles
DIFFICULTY: Easy
PARKING: Metered street parking and pay lots are available.
PUBLIC TRANSIT: SEPTA's Broad Street line subway, at Tasker Ave., is about 2 blocks from the start of this walk. Buses that cross E. Passyunk Ave. include the 4, 23, and 29. Buses that stop within a few blocks include the 2, 37, 47, and 47m.

Italian immigrants began settling here as early as the 1700s, but it was the mass migrations at the end of the 1800s and early 1900s that established this area as the city's Little Italy. (No one ever calls it that, though.) The outdoor fruit and vegetable market here—which looks little changed since Rocky Balboa ran through it in the 1970s—is often called the Italian Market although many businesses are now owned by those of Mexican and Southeast Asian descent.

This walk features a section of Italian American—or formerly Italian American—South Philadelphia, including the nation's first Italian American Catholic church, the first Italian mutual aid society and the city's first Italian restaurant. Signs encourage a "Passyunk Passeggiata," an Italian term for a leisurely stroll. That's a good idea.

Walk Description

Begin this walk at South Broad Street and East Passyunk Avenue, following East Passyunk Avenue northeast. This was originally an American Indian trail, the name coming from the word *pachsegink,* which means "in the valley" or "a place of sleep." Locals pronounce it "PASH-yunk" or "PASS-yunk." Manhole covers feature the image of a native man wearing a feathered headdress.

Food and Wine named East Passyunk Avenue one of the 10 best foodie streets in the country in 2013. Many of the restaurants do not have liquor licenses. That means you can BYOB—bring your own bottle—without penalty.

Follow the road as it curves left. Le Virtù, 1927 E. Passyunk, offers food from Italy's Abruzzo region. Tre Scalini, 1915 E. Passyunk, means "three little steps," which made sense before this local favorite moved to this stairless location.

At Mifflin Street, turn right. Cross South 13th Street. The pen-and-ink vinyl panels of *East Passyunk—Crossing through the Ages,* South 13th and Mifflin Streets, were installed on this closed transportation substation in 2015.

Turn around, crossing South 13th Street again, and stop in the median park. The bronze statue honors Joey Giardello, the former middleweight boxing champion of the world, who trained at the nearby Passyunk Avenue Gym.

Continue on East Passyunk. The ❶ **History of Italian Immigration Museum** features the stories of local Italian American families. Inscribed on the sidewalk out front are the names of families who have donated to the museum.

A passeggiata note: Stargazy, 1838 E. Passyunk, serves British meat pies, specializing in one with jellied eels—easy to hold while walking.

Continue on East Passyunk Avenue, passing Saté Kampar, 1837 E. Passyunk, a BYOB offering Malaysian-style meats cooked over coconut bricks; Jinxed, 1835 E. Passyunk, selling antiques and found objects; Occasionette, 1825 E. Passyunk, a popular gift shop; and P'unk Burger, 1823 E. Passyunk, a BYOB with organic and local fare.

② **Marra's Italian Restaurant** was opened by Neapolitan immigrants Salvatore and Chiarina Marra in the 1920s. Three generations later, it's still family owned, using the original oven Salvatore built with bricks from Mount Vesuvius. According to legend, Frank Sinatra got the nickname Ol' Blue Eyes after a Marra's waitress saw him and swooned, "Oh my God, those beautiful blue eyes."

Marra's is what locals consider a red gravy or red sauce restaurant. Some background: Some Northeastern Italian Americans refer to that tomato-based, meat-infused, garlic-enhanced, basil-accented deliciousness on spaghetti as gravy. This confused non-Italians who think of gravy as the brown liquid served on Thanksgiving. In kindness to the confused, those of Italian descent sometimes put the word *red* before gravy. A red-gravy or red-sauce restaurant is one specializing in basics, such as spaghetti and meatballs, lasagna, and manicotti. Marra's also has pizza, but don't expect that at all red-gravy places.

Other shops of interest along this stretch include Nice Things Handmade, 1731 E. Passyunk, featuring local artists; Miss Demeanor, 1729 E. Passyunk, a women's clothing store; and ReUp Philly, 1713 E. Passyunk, a sneaker boutique.

Dining options include Plenty Café, 1710 E. Passyunk, serving American fare; Bing Bing Dim Sum, 1648 E. Passyunk, offering Chinese food with a Jewish twist; and Cantina Los Caballitos, 1651 E. Passyunk, dishing up Mexican fare with potent margaritas.

Di Bruno Bros. cheeses

Two murals overlook the parking lot at 1600 E. Passyunk. On the right, *History of Passyunk* shows the changing street scenes from the area's 125-year history.

On the left is the somewhat puzzling ❸ *Pathology of Devotion,* which, according to a 2008 *Philadelphia Inquirer* article, "appears to depict a World War II–era submariner using a periscope to spy on actor Robin Williams. Curiously, Williams is holding a rosary." The same article quoted a Mural Arts spokeswoman as saying the artist's intent is to represent the intersection of science and religion. (The guy on the right is not Robin Williams in a puffy shirt but a priest hearing confession.)

More passeggiata dining possibilities: Capogiro, 1625 E. Passyunk, sells handmade gelato; Townsend, 1623 E. Passyunk, offers modern French fare; Laurel, 1617 E. Passyunk, is a stylish BYOB bistro with French-American cuisine; and Vanilya, 1611 E. Passyunk, which takes its name from the Turkish word for "vanilla," an ingredient used in every treat baked here.

Shopping options include Beautiful World Syndicate, 1619 E. Passyunk, for used records, and Cloth, 1605 E. Passyunk, to clothe mother and baby.

Continue on East Passyunk Avenue, crossing Tasker Street. ❹ **The Singing Fountain** is a popular pocket park with speakers hidden around the square that allow the fountain to "sing." You'll find locals lounging on the benches and playing chess and visitors killing time before dinner reservations.

Urban Jungle, 1526 E. Passyunk, is a lush garden store. Brigantessa, 1520 E. Passyunk, is a deservedly busy Southern Italian restaurant. On the next block, Essen Bakery, 1437 E. Passyunk, offers Jewish-style breads and baked goods.

The Acme supermarket, with a large parking lot, is built on the former site of Moyamensing Prison, also called Moko or the Philadelphia County Prison. The country's first known serial killer, H. H. Holmes, was put to death by hanging there in 1896, and Edgar Allan Poe and Al Capone each spent a single night there.

Continue on East Passyunk Avenue. At Wharton Street, note the community garden and murals. Until 2011, this empty lot held dumpsters and was a neighborhood eyesore. There was a minor mural controversy because of the panel with "Passyunk's

Finest Pears." Locals griped that pears had nothing to do with South Philadelphia. As one police officer told *The Philadelphia Daily News,* "What do you think might be better? Tomatoes? Basil? Peppers? Garlic?" The beleaguered artist said he'd chosen to paint pears because it started with *P,* like Passyunk. The white-haired man is Harry Olivieri, one of the founders of nearby Pat's King of Steaks.

Cross Wharton Street. Welcome to what some call Cheesesteak Vegas—the neon at night can be blinding—and the city's two best cheesesteak shops, (mostly) friendly rivals. The first is ❺ **Pat's King of Steaks.** The family behind Pat's says theirs was the original cheesesteak, invented in 1930. Across the four-way intersection is ❻ **Geno's Steaks,** which opened in 1966.

So, as cheesesteak-seeking out-of-towners ask, "Pat's or Geno's?" This book takes no stand. But here's some advice: Philadelphians, particularly those who work at these shops, take cheesesteaks seriously. It's best to know how to order before reaching the counter. Here's some help:

1. Decide which type of cheese you would like on your steak. You will generally be offered Cheez Whiz (traditional choice), American (still OK), or provolone (acceptable). To stray is to be mocked: In 2003, Democratic presidential candidate John Kerry asked for Swiss, appalling locals. Once schooled and given a sandwich dripping with processed cheese sauce, Kerry "made matters worse by delicately nibbling at it as if it were tea toast," *The Philadelphia Inquirer* reported.

2. Decide whether you would like onions on your steak. If yes, remember the word *with.* If no, remember the word *without.*

3. Now order. If you'd like one cheesesteak with Cheez Whiz and onions, and a second with American cheese but no onions, say, "I'll have a Whiz with and an American without."

Good luck.

South Philly Musicians, 1231 E. Passyunk Ave., features local musical artists, including Frankie Avalon, Fabian, and Eddie Fisher. Because the wall has deteriorated and is

Locals and guests enjoy the Singing Fountain.

beyond reasonable repair, a new version is scheduled to be installed on Broad Street.

Turn left on South Ninth Street. **❼ Capitolo Playground,** established in 1839, was built on the former site of Lafayette Cemetery. Eventually more than 47,000 people were interred here, including Civil War veterans. In the 1940s, the city decided to reclaim the land, and hired the owner of a suburban cemetery to remove the dead and rebury them respectfully. In 1988, construction workers building a suburban mall stumbled upon 30 unmarked trenches, each filled with hundreds of caskets from Lafayette Cemetery. A memorial plaque was placed on the site. It's unknown if there are still bodies under the playground. *The Melting Pot,* wrapped around the playground's main building, features the faces of neighborhood residents.

Continue on South Ninth Street, entering the so-called Italian Market. Many of the stores and restaurants here are run by Mexican Americans. Immigrants from the state of Puebla began settling here en masse in the 1980s. This strong community hosts El Carnaval de Puebla en Filadelfia, one of the nation's largest Cinco de Mayo celebrations. Most of the unassuming restaurants here serve excellent food, including Moctezuma, 1108–10 S. Ninth St. Anastasi Seafood, 1101 S. Ninth St., is a store/restaurant now run by the fourth generation of the Anastasi family.

Crossing Washington Avenue, the **❽ 9th Street Italian Market** may seem familiar from the *Rocky* movies. In the first, filmed in 1976, the then-unknown Sylvester Stallone ran through the market without drawing much attention. That memorable scene when a vendor throws Rocky an orange? Not scripted. The vendor later said he just wanted to toss something to the dirty guy in the gray sweat suit. It made the movie.

Chef Mario Batali has said the market is "the best Little Italy in America," though locals don't call it that. One of the nicest things about the area is that it has resisted gentrification: It's still crowded and dirty. The vendors still warm themselves via trash-can fires in the winter. Fruits and vegetables are sold in bulk and for cheap.

There are many dining options here, including Paesano's, 1017 S. Ninth St., a sandwich shop that offers unique combinations. Villa Di Roma, 936 S. Ninth St., is a red-gravy joint offering no-frills but solid food and sassy service.

Continue on South Ninth Street to two family-run Italian food shops offering free samples. Both have lines stretching out the door and down the sidewalk during holiday rushes. ❾ **Di Bruno Bros.** was originally a grocery store when brothers Danny and Joe Di Bruno opened it in 1939. In 1965, facing stiff competition from supermarkets, they reinvented themselves as a specialty shop and House of Cheese, which may sound funny but has proven lucrative.

❿ **Claudio's Specialty Foods** was opened by Italian immigrants Salvatrice and Claudio Auriemma Sr. in the 1950s. There's a little more elbow room here, with cheeses taller than the average-sized American woman hanging from the ceiling.

Former mayor Frank Rizzo is featured in the mural on the side of Nina's Trattoria, 910 S. Ninth St. The controversial Rizzo, who also served as the city's police commissioner, was a favorite son of South Philadelphia. He was blunt, often threatening and famously intolerant. This work, completed in 1991, is the most vandalized mural in the city.

Continue to Christian Street and turn left. Monsu, 901 Christian St., is a BYOB featuring Sicilian cuisine. Sabrina's Cafe, 910 Christian St., is another BYOB offering breakfast, lunch, brunch, and long waits on weekends.

Continue on Christian Street, stopping in front of Christopher Columbus Charter School, 916 Christian St. This was Christian Street Hospital, the first Civil War Army hospital. The doctors working at this 220-bed facility developed pioneering treatments for nerve disorders and gunshot wounds. One coined the term *phantom limb* to describe the sensation amputees had.

Pass St. Paul Church, 923 Christian St., and stop at the sweet-smelling ⓫ **Isgro.** This Italian bakery, a neighborhood mainstay since 1904, is known for its cannoli. If there's a line, read the framed letters from satisfied customers on the wall, including tenor Luciano Pavarotti, who had an Isgro's birthday cake.

Double back on Christian Street, turning left on South 10th Street. ⓬ **Dante & Luigi's** opened in 1899 and offers red-gravy dishes and more modern fare. Originally called Corona di Ferro, this was a destination for Italian immigrants, who arrived at the docks with the restaurant's name written on a piece of paper pinned to their lapel. The workers lived in rooms upstairs while working as cooks and waiters. Vice President Joe Biden's family has long had an account at the restaurant.

At Fitzwater Street, turn right. ⓭ **Sam's Morning Glory Diner** is another breakfast/ lunch favorite. (Be prepared: it's cash only.)

Across Fitzwater Street is ⓮ **Palumbo Playground and Recreation Center,** which occupies the full block. Like Capitolo Playground, this was once a cemetery. It was founded by James Ronaldson, first president of the Franklin Institute, in the 1820s as a nonreligious burial space. More than 13,000 people were interred here. In the 1950s, the city reclaimed this space, moving most of the interred to a mass grave in northeast Philadelphia. (A few "celebrity" dead—including several Revolutionary War soldiers—moved less than a mile away to the cemetery at Old Swedes Church.)

Continue on Fitzwater Street. At South Ninth Street, turn right. ⓯ **Sarcone's Deli** opened in 1918 and sells sandwiches on its famous bread, made at nearby Sarcone's Bakery, 758 S. Ninth. Lines snake down the street on weekends and before holidays.

Continue on South Ninth Street. ⓰ **Ralph's** is another popular red-gravy restaurant, a family-run business in operation since 1900. Theodore Roosevelt dined here, according to their website, and Vice President Biden visited frequently when he represented Delaware in the US Senate.

At Catharine Street, turn left. Walk to South Eighth Street, and make a right then a quick left to continue on Catharine Street. *Autumn Revisited* is on the side of ⓱ **Samuel S. Fleisher Art Memorial.** This arts center offers tuition-free lessons and low-cost workshops to children and adults. In the 1890s, Samuel Fleisher became vice president of the yarn company founded by his German Jewish immigrant parents. At the suggestion of his sister, he began offering free art classes to his workers' children. When he died in 1944, his fortune was left in trust to perpetuate these classes. The center welcomes more than 6,000 students annually.

Continue to South Seventh Street. Turn right. Italian American singers Bobby Rydell—born Roberto Ridarelli—and Mario Lanza attended elementary school at the former St. Mary Magdalen de Pazzi Elementary School, 825 S. Seventh St., now condos. Lanza's birthplace, 636 Christian St., is across the street. Born Alfred Arnold Cocozza in January 1921, Lanza was an American opera singer and Hollywood film star in the late 1940s and 1950s.

⓲ John's Water Ice is a neighborhood staple opened by a Sicilian immigrant in 1945. This flavored fruit ice is similar to Italian ice, also popular in the Northeast, but is softer with a less concentrated flavor. The traditional flavors are lemon, chocolate, and cherry. When President Obama visited in 2011, he ordered lemon. Note that the street barriers here are painted in the colors of the Italian flag.

Continue on South Seventh Street, crossing Christian Street. At Montrose Street, turn right. **⓳ St. Mary Magdalen de Pazzi** is the first Italian American Catholic parish in the country. Young Freddy Cocozza allegedly sang in the choir here. The church has a small museum dedicated to the singer and hosts an annual Mass in his honor.

This walk ends here. Continue on Montrose Street for two blocks to return to the Italian Market.

Points of Interest

❶ History of Italian Immigration Museum 1834 E. Passyunk Ave., 215-334-8882, filitaliainternational.com

❷ Marra's Italian Restaurant 1734 E. Passyunk Ave., 215-463-9249, marrasone.com

❸ *Pathology of Devotion* 1644 E. Passyunk Ave.

❹ The Singing Fountain S. 11th St. and E. Passyunk Ave.

❺ Pat's King of Steaks 1237 E. Passyunk Ave., 215-468-1546, patskingofsteaks.com

South Philadelphia I

6 Geno's Steaks 1219 S. Ninth St., 215-389-0659, genosteaks.com

7 Capitolo Playground 900 Federal St., 215-685-1883

8 9th Street Italian Market 215-278-2903, italianmarketphilly.org

9 Di Bruno Bros. 930 S. Ninth St., 215-922-2876, dibruno.com

10 Claudio's Specialty Foods 924 S. Ninth St., 215-627-1873, claudiofood.com

11 Isgro 1009 Christian St., 215-923-3092, bestcannoli.com

12 Dante & Luigi's 762 S. 10th St., 215-922-9501, danteandluigis.com

13 Sam's Morning Glory Diner 735 S. 10th St., 215-413-3999, themorninggglorydiner.com

14 Palumbo Playground and Recreation Center 700 S. Ninth St., 215-592-6007, palumborec.org

15 Sarcone's Deli 734 S. Ninth St., 215-922-1717, sarconesdeli.com

16 Ralph's Italian Restaurant 760 S. Ninth St., 215-627-6011, ralphsrestaurant.com

17 Samuel S. Fleisher Art Memorial 719 Catharine St., 215-922-3456, fleisher.org

18 John's Water Ice 701 Christian St., 215-925-6955, johnswaterice.com

19 St. Mary Magdalen de Pazzi 712 Montrose St., stpaulparish.net

"Oh, Dem Golden Slippers" is the Mummers' unofficial theme.

24 South Philadelphia II:
Migration, Mummers, and Music

BOUNDARIES: Bainbridge St., Washington Ave., Schuylkill River, S. 11th St.
DISTANCE: 3.6 miles
DIFFICULTY: Easy
PARKING: There is 2-hour street parking available here, as well as an outdoor pay lot.
PUBLIC TRANSIT: SEPTA bus stops dot the area where this tour begins, including the 21 to Penn's Landing, the 40 to S. Second and Lombard Sts., or the 64 to Washington Ave. and Columbus Blvd.

South Philadelphia was "the city's first ethnic ghetto," Murray Dubin writes in *South Philadelphia: Mummers, Memories, and the Melrose Diner.* The Irish were its first occupants, arriving in the 1700s.

This area continues to attract immigrants from throughout the world, with those from Mexico and Southeast Asia among the most recent to settle here. This tour looks at some immigrant waves that have passed through by pointing out the institutions they built for themselves.

Walk Description

Begin at Front and Chestnut Streets, where the Old City tour (page 110) ended.

❶ **The Irish Memorial** honors Irish citizens who died during the Irish Potato Famine and those who forged a new path in the United States. In the mid-1800s, after millions died from starvation and accompanying diseases in Ireland, approximately one quarter of the nation's population immigrated to England, Australia, Canada, and the United States. This 30-foot-long sculpture in the round was commissioned to mark the famine's 150th anniversary. It's engraved with a poem by Peter Quinn that begins, "The hunger ended/but it never went away/It was there in silent memories,/From one generation,/to the next. . . ."

Next to The Irish Memorial is the Commemoration of Scottish Immigration to America, the first national memorial acknowledging the contributions of Scottish immigrants, installed here in 2011. It was paid for by the St. Andrew's Society of Philadelphia, an organization named for Scotland's patron saint and founded by Scots in 1747 to help their newly arriving countrymen.

Follow the path on the right to Front Street. A historical marker there marks the former site of Tun Tavern, where the St. Andrew's Society originated.

Turn left onto Front Street. To your left is the Delaware River and the site where, in 1855, an enslaved woman named Jane Johnson and her sons escaped with help from local abolitionists. The two abolitionists were arrested for refusing to reveal Johnson's whereabouts. Johnson returned to the city to testify on their behalf, saying she left on her own, noting, "I don't want to go back . . . I'd sooner die than go back." One of Johnson's sons later served in the U.S. Colored Troops in the Civil War.

At Dock Street, the extensive ❷ **Philadelphia Korean War Memorial** at Penn's Landing, dedicated in 2001, honors the more than 600 men from the Philadelphia area who died in the conflict.

Turn left on Dock Street, then right onto Columbus Boulevard, passing Thomas Foglietta Plaza, named for a former city council member who served in the US House of Representatives and later as the US ambassador to Italy.

Continue to the ❸ **Philadelphia Vietnam Veterans Memorial,** which honors the more than 650 American soldiers killed in Vietnam who identified Philadelphia as their home of record. In 2016, two more names—Master Sergeants George Wilson and Francis Corcoran—were added to the wall. Corcoran's widow attended the dedication.

Walk through the plaza, exiting via the path to the left of the statue of a soldier. Turn left, continuing on Front Street. Crossing South Street, on the left is *Stroll,* a 1995 sculpture featuring three large metal figures crossing the highway overpass. A 2013 *Philadelphia* magazine article described the work this way: "The three figures—strolling hand-in-hand to South Street to buy some novelty t-shirts and bongs, no doubt—have weird, bowling-pin shaped heads and a leg-to-torso ratio not found in any humans I've ever seen." The article also found this hidden meaning in the sculpture: "One day, metal monsters will destroy us all."

Continue on Front Street, passing where US naval officer Stephen Decatur grew up. Decatur became a national hero in 1803 when the USS *Philadelphia* was captured by pirates in Tripoli. He and his crew sailed the harbor disguised as tradesmen and destroyed the ship so America's enemies could not use it. British admiral Horatio Lord Nelson called this "the most bold and daring act of the age."

Turn right on Kenilworth Street. Walk to South Second Street and turn left. Turn right on Monroe Street. Kratchman's Bathhouses once stood at 313–321 Monroe St. Men often played cards after enjoying a *schvitz*. The only remnant of them is a small sign on one house designating BATH HOUSE COURT.

Cross South Fourth Street. This is Fabric Row, a hub of Jewish life in the early 1900s. Many pushcarts here sold fabric, which was known as the rag, or *schmatte,* trade.

While the neighborhood has changed, there are still more than half a dozen fabric businesses here, including the one at the corner, ❹ **Maxie's Daughter.** Russian immigrant Max Wilk moved to the United States as a teenager and began selling fabric, first from a pushcart, then from a storefront a few blocks away. After his death in 1991, his daughter Beverly moved the business here. Her son now manages daily operations. The mural on one side depicts generations of the family.

Continue to South Fifth Street. Turn left. ❺ **Meredith Elementary School** was built in 1931 in the Art Deco style. It's named for William M. Meredith, a Philadelphia attorney who served as secretary of the treasury during the Zachary Taylor administration. The mural on two walls of the Meredith School parking lot is *CornerSmile/ Peace Through Imagination,* named for the oversize lips emerging from the corner.

Walk one block. Turn right on Fitzwater Street, and then turn right again on Passyunk Avenue. At Fitzwater Street, turn left. Continue past Little Fish, 746 S. Sixth St., a BYOB restaurant, and brunch favorite Fitzwater Cafe, 728 S. Seventh St.

❻ **Cianfrani Park** is named for the mother of late politician Henry "Buddy" Cianfrani. Cianfrani, a beloved son of South Philly, saw his star rise, then fall, then rise again. A World War II veteran, he was a state senator when convicted on federal charges of racketeering and mail fraud after it was determined he had two fake employees on his payroll. He left jail and became a highly sought political adviser.

The Southwark Soup Society, 833 Fitzwater St., was one of the first charities dedicated to helping the "deserving poor" with hot meals and free coal during the winter. It was founded in 1805.

Turn right on South Eighth Street. At Bainbridge Street, turn left. ❼ **The Church of the Crucifixion** was founded in 1846 in "the poorest and most violent section of what was to become South Philadelphia," its website says. It was one of the city's first integrated congregations. Young Marian Anderson made her singing debut here. As she told the story, "One day when I was on my way to the grocery store to buy something for my mother, my eyes caught sight of a small handbill lying on the street. I picked it up, and there in a corner was my picture with my name under it. 'Come hear the baby contralto, 10 years old,' it said. I was actually 8. What excitement!"

Continue on Bainbridge Street, passing Chapterhouse Café & Gallery, 620 S. Ninth St., a coffee shop offering organic drinks and a cozy atmosphere.

The Institute for Colored Youth once occupied this residential building at 915 Bainbridge St. It was established by a Quaker philanthropist whose will charged fellow

Quakers to design a school "to instruct the descendants of the African Race in school learning, in the various branches of the mechanic Arts, trades and Agriculture, in order to prepare and fit and qualify them to act as teachers."

Continue on Bainbridge Street, passing *Crystal Snowscape,* by artist David Guinn, at South 10th Street. Frances Ellen Watkins Harper House, 1006 Bainbridge St., was the poet's home from 1870 until her death in 1911. Harper also wrote for antislavery newspapers, leading some to call her the mother of African American journalism.

Continue to South 11th Street. Turn left, passing Hawthorne's, 738 S. 11th St., another dining option.

At the corner of Catharine and South 11th Streets, look at the school building across the street and to the right, built in 1920 in the Art Deco style. Like Meredith School, this one was designed by Irwin T. Catharine, the Philadelphia School District's chief architect at the time. One of his innovations was including a cafeteria so children didn't need to go home for lunch. Hidden City Philadelphia published parts of a 1925 interview Catharine gave with the *Philadelphia Public Ledger* in which he explained why he replaced wooden partitions in school bathrooms with white marble: "There is something in the nature of every boy which makes him want to carve his initial or whole name in a wall. If he isn't clever enough with his pocketknife, he writes his name. White marble partitions and walls make it impossible for him to use his knife." The website notes, "Sadly, Catharine could not foresee the effect that Sharpie markers would have on his marble."

Turn left onto Catharine Street, passing Dante & Luigi's, one of the oldest family-owned Italian restaurants in the country.

Frank Palumbo's Cabaret Restaurant once stood at 824–30 Catharine St., where a Rite Aid drugstore is now. A marker honors the Palumbo family's philanthropy, quoting Frank as saying, "If I stop giving, I stop living." Actor-singer Mario Lanza, who was born and raised a few blocks from here, once said Palumbo was one of the city's unsung heroes. Sinatra was a frequent visitor to the club, where notables such as Jimmy Durante, Louis Prima, and Louis Armstrong performed.

Gloria Dei Church, also known as Old Swedes', was built around 1700.

Continue to Darien Street. Turn right. At Christian Street, turn left to take in a juxtaposition of old and new. ❽ **Fiorella's Sausage** is a butcher shop in operation since 1892. Dan Fiorella, the fourth generation to run the store, told philly.com in 2016 that he still grinds every sausage he sells. The liver sausage is still made with his great-grandmother's recipe using orange peel, garlic, and red pepper. Next door, at 815 Christian St., is Laurentius Salon, a glass-front high-end salon. To date no one has constructed a Venn diagram of the two businesses' customers.

Continue to the corner of South Eighth Street, noting Vietnamese and Mexican businesses along the street. A historical marker near the mural *Moonlit Landscape,* 737 Christian St., notes that the musically gifted Giannini Family lived nearby. (They also operated an Italian opera theater down the block and a boardinghouse for Italian immigrants.) The Gianninis were opera stars: Father Feruccio was a tenor, mother Antoinetta a violinist, daughter Dusolina a soprano, and son Vittorio a composer and teacher at Juilliard.

Continue on Christian Street, passing Mario Lanza's birthplace, 636 Christian St. At South Sixth Street, turn left. At Queen Street, turn right. ❾ **Weccacoe Playground** has been a play space for children for more than a century. During a 2013 renovation, a local historian urged caution after finding evidence of the city's first private African American cemetery beneath the asphalt. Archaeologists found the first tombstone, inscribed AMELIA BROWN, 1819, 26 YEARS OLD, in the playground's southwest corner. Between 3,000 and 5,000 people are believed still buried in roughly one-third of the park.

Continue on Queen Street. Mario Lanza Park, Queen Street between South Second and Third Streets, is named for one of the city's favorite sons. Born Alfred Cocozza,

Lanza did odd jobs to afford voice lessons. His stage name comes from his mother, the Italian-born Maria Lanza.

Across the street is **⑩ St. Philip Neri Church.** Built in the 1840s, the church was targeted during the anti-immigrant, anti-Catholic Nativist Riots of 1844. During four days of violence and destruction over two months, mobs attacked Irish American homes and Roman Catholic churches. At least two churches, a convent, and a handful of homes were destroyed. About 20 people were killed. St. Philip Neri survived because state militia provided protection.

The parish today includes the neighborhood's original Polish church, **⑪ St. Stanislaus Church,** named for Poland's patron saint and founded in the late 1890s. Polish immigrants arriving at the nearby Washington Avenue Immigration Station "only had to walk across Delaware Avenue to find themselves not only in the new land of opportunity, but in a neighborhood where there was a church and school named after the patron saint of their homeland," according to the Polish American Cultural Center's website.

Sparks Shot Tower was the first shot manufacturing facility in the county.

Continue to South Second Street. Turn right. At Carpenter Street, turn left. Signage showcases the city's love of replacing the letter *f* with *ph* to Philafy words. This sign advises drivers to proceed "CarePhilly."

Sparks Shot Tower, 101–31 Carpenter St., was the first shot manufacturing facility in the country, built in 1808. Ammunition was made by dropping dollops of hot lead from near the top of the 142-foot tower through a copper sieve into water below.

Previously projectiles were imported from Britain. The tower became a city recreation center and playground in 1913.

Continue to Front Street. Turn left. At Christian Street, turn right. **⑫ Gloria Dei (Old Swedes') Episcopal Church** was built in 1698, making it the oldest church in the city. It has been in continuous use for more than 300 years, first as a Swedish Lutheran worship site and later as an Episcopal church. Betsy Ross married her second husband, Joseph Ashburn, here in 1777.

Continue to Washington Avenue. Turn left to cross Columbus Boulevard. Follow the trail to Washington Avenue Green, 1301 S. Columbus Blvd., between the Coast Guard building and the union facility. Between 1873 and 1915, more than one million European immigrants passed through Washington Avenue Immigration Station, called Philadelphia's Ellis Island. A neighborhood history group—the Southwark Historical Society—notes that one part of the medical exam room was called the altar, as some single women weren't allowed to disembark until they wed.

The station was torn down in 1915, and this was wasted land for almost a century until the Delaware River Waterfront Corporation reclaimed it. The 1-acre space is inviting and green, with turtles and ducks swimming among the logs in the waterway. The 55-foot-tall spire topped with a blue light at the water's edge, *Land Buoy,* offers a great view.

Leave the water and walk back across Columbus Boulevard. Follow Washington Avenue to *Summary of Mummery,* painted under the I-95 overpass, at 37 Washington Ave. It's hard to explain mummery, but its nearby museum does so this way: "Mummers are people who belong to one of five types of clubs that participate in the annual New Year's Day parade. One group is composed of musicians who compete annually for the title of best string band. The others wear costumes, some fancy and some plain, and perform dance routines. Generations of families often walk together."

The first formal, city-sponsored parade was in 1901 and is believed to be the country's oldest continuous folk parade. In modern times, the parade is associated with first-class musicians—a good thing—and, unfortunately, excessive drinking. Still, that too seems to be part of the tradition, as mummers once went door-to-door chanting, "Here we stand before your door/As we stood the year before/Give us whisky, give us gin/Open the door and let us in."

Continue on Washington Avenue to **⓭ The Mummers Museum.** Opened in 1876 as part of the country's bicentennial celebration, most remaining questions about the mummers can be answered inside. The museum's website has a constant countdown measuring the weeks, days, hours, minutes, and seconds until the next January 1 parade. This stretch of South Second Street—called Two Street by mummers—is the epicenter of mummer life. The walk officially ends here, but continue south on South Second Street to check out the pubs with Irish names and mummer clubs headquartered here.

Washington Avenue Green, a park on the Delaware River, is a peaceful reprieve.

South Philadelphia II

Points of Interest

1. **The Irish Memorial** 100 S. Front St., irishmemorial.org
2. **Philadelphia Korean War Memorial** Penn's Landing
3. **Philadelphia Vietnam Veterans Memorial** Columbus Blvd. and Spruce St.
4. **Maxie's Daughter** 724 S. Fourth St., 215-829-2226
5. **Meredith Elementary School** 725 S. Fifth St.
6. **Cianfrani Park** Fitzwater and S. Eighth Sts.
7. **The Church of the Crucifixion** 620 S. 8th St., 215-922-1128, crucifixionphiladelphia.org
8. **Fiorella's Sausage** 817 Christian St., 215-922-0506
9. **Weccacoe Playground** 400 Catharine St.
10. **St. Philip Neri Church** 220–228 Queen St., 215-468-1922, stphilipneriqueenvillage.org
11. **St. Stanislaus Church** 242 Fitzwater St., 215-468-1922, stphilipneriqueenvillage.org
12. **Gloria Dei (Old Swedes' Episcopal Church)** 916 S. Swanson St., 215-389-1513, old-swedes.org
13. **The Mummers Museum** 1100 S. Second St., 215-336-3050, mummersmuseum.com

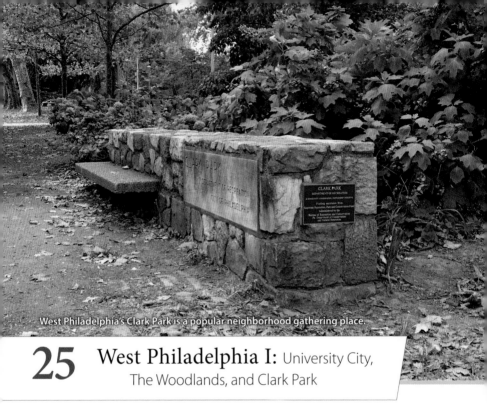

West Philadelphia's Clark Park is a popular neighborhood gathering place.

25 West Philadelphia I: University City, The Woodlands, and Clark Park

BOUNDARIES: Woodland Ave., Baltimore Ave., 30th St., 44th St.
DISTANCE: 1.6 miles
DIFFICULTY: Easy, with very slight changes in elevation
PARKING: Street parking in this area is very hard to find; a few pay lots serve the hospitals nearby.
PUBLIC TRANSIT: SEPTA bus 30 stops nearby, as does LUCY (Loop through University City), a shuttle service.

Philadelphia has two rivers. The Delaware, on the east side, serves as the border with New Jersey, and the Dutch-named Schuylkill, pronounced "skool-kul," serves as the border between Center City and West Philadelphia. The West Philadelphia neighborhood University City is so called because of the cluster of higher-learning institutions here, including the University of Pennsylvania, Drexel University, and the University of the Sciences. This walk introduces the neighborhood, the Woodlands, and Clark Park.

Walk Description

Begin at the University of Pennsylvania's ❶ **Franklin Field,** which has hosted the Penn Relays, the nation's largest track-and-field event, for more than 100 years. The two-tiered stadium, completed in 1925, is the oldest of its kind.

Like many Philadelphia places, this one has been the site of many firsts: the first scoreboard, the first football radio broadcast, the first commercial football game television broadcast, and the first and only place where legendary coach Vince Lombardi's team lost in a playoff game. (It was the 1960 NFL Championship Game. The Eagles beat Lombardi's Green Bay Packers 17–13.)

In 1936, Franklin Delano Roosevelt accepted the Democratic presidential nomination here in front of 100,000 supporters. (But note the field was named for Penn founder Benjamin Franklin.) His speech foreshadowed World War II as he noted the period was "a mysterious cycle in human events. To some generations, much is given. Of other generations, much is expected. This generation of Americans has a rendezvous with destiny." Franklin Field was also a backdrop for the 2000 M. Night Shyamalan movie *Unbreakable;* the main character worked here as a security guard.

Across South Street is ❷ **The University of Pennsylvania Museum of Archaeology and Anthropology,** aka Penn Museum, founded in 1887. It is one of the world's most renowned archaeology and anthropology research museums and the largest university museum in the country. More than 20 galleries feature a collection of about 1 million items, including a 15-ton Egyptian sphinx and clay tablets covered with Sumerian cuneiform, some of the world's oldest writings. Stop in or walk through the museum's public gardens, which feature sculptures by Alexander Stirling Calder and a koi pond.

Head northwest on South Street. Crossing 33rd Street, the road becomes Spruce Street. The buildings on both sides of the street are part of the campus of the ❸ **University of Pennsylvania,** aka Penn. In the 1700s, the colonies had four colleges—Harvard, William and Mary, Yale, and Princeton—but all catered to the clergy. Benjamin Franklin argued that higher education should be open to laypersons, too, stressing practical skills for business and public service as well as the classics. Penn was officially founded in 1740 and moved to this location in 1872.

Penn brought the nation these firsts: medical school, business school, and student union organization. Eight signers of the Declaration of Independence and nine signers of the Constitution attended the school.

Continue on Spruce Street, taking in the Collegiate Gothic architecture inspired by England's Oxford and Cambridge universities. At 38th Street, turn left. This is the city's largest collection of food trucks. Stop for excellent but fairly priced cuisine in a variety of genres—Japanese, Mexican, Indian, Middle Eastern, Chinese, Jamaican, and traditional American. Visit pennfoodtrucks.com for reviews.

Continue to Baltimore Avenue. Turn right, and bear left to continue on Woodland Avenue. Cross Woodland Avenue to reach the entrance of ❹ **The Woodlands.** This national historic landmark includes a Federal-style mansion, a community garden, an apiary, and a cemetery where more than 30,000 people are at rest. William Hamilton developed the property in 1786, combining principles of traditional English garden style with New World plants and practices. Thomas Jefferson called it "the only rival I have known in America to what may be seen in England."

Enter the cemetery and take the 0.7-mile loop through the grounds. The Woodlands Cemetery remains active. Among the notables interred here are artist Thomas Eakins and Campbell Soup Company cofounder Joseph Campbell. Bear right after entering the cemetery, and follow the road as it curves left. Pause at the first intersection. At left is a blackened obelisk topped with an urn, where a young mother who died during childbirth and her son, who lived less than a year, are buried. The difficult to see engraving reads: "Past the struggle, past the pain/Cease to weep for tears are vain/Calm the tumult of the breast/They who suffered are at rest."

Continue following the path left, passing Hamilton's stables and his home. To the right of the mansion is the Drexel Family Mausoleum. Family patriarch Francis M. Drexel was an artist and a financial giant whose bank loaned the US government $49 million to finance the Mexican–American War. Also interred here is his son, Anthony, an adviser to President Ulysses S. Grant and the founder of Drexel University.

Little Nell, of *The Old Curiosity Shop,* looks up at her creator, Charles Dickens.

Continue along the path to the left. The 90-foot-tall obelisk ahead, the tallest funerary monument in America, marks the graves of Philadelphia dentist Thomas Evans and his family. Evans, who died in 1897, was a pioneer in his field: he introduced the use of gold to fill cavities, nitrous oxide as an anesthetic, and vulcanite rubber as a base for dentures. He lived briefly in Paris, where he was dentist to Napoléon III and other members of European royal families. During the American Civil War, Evans apparently advised Napoléon III not to recognize the Confederacy. In his will, Evans designated that a portion of his fortune be used to establish Penn's dental school.

Continue following the path to the Woodlands entrance on your right. Exit here.

Returning to Woodland Avenue, look across the street at the hub for the city's five trolley lines. Known as the Green Lines, the streetcar network is the largest and busiest on the East Coast.

Turn left on Woodland Avenue, passing through the campus of the ❺ **University of the Sciences.** The school, originally called the Philadelphia College of Pharmacy Sciences, was founded in 1821 by a group of local apothecaries who sought to improve standards and professionalize their trade. The university now has four colleges and offers more than 30 degree-granting programs. William Procter Jr., the father of American pharmacy, was a professor here.

Stop in front of the large black-and-white mural flanking a parking lot before 42nd Street. This is ❻ *Communion between a Rock and a Hard Place,* a 2012 tribute to veterans. The designs incorporate photos, words, and phrases contributed by a local branch of Warrior Writers, a nonprofit that helps veterans articulate their experiences. The organization says the works attempt "to give the viewer the sense of being between two worlds, worlds that are separate, but apart. Veterans can never fully leave either of these two worlds."

Continue to 43rd Street. Turn right. A portion of ❼ **Clark Park** is on the left. This 9-acre park, established in 1895 on land donated by banker Clarence Clark, was once an illegal dumping ground. Today it is a major part of community life, with playgrounds, open fields, multiple benches, and dining areas with tables and chairs. The park has a Shakespeare in the Park theater company and the city's largest year-round farmers market.

At the intersection of 43rd Street and Chester Avenue, the fenced garden is the Lower Mill Creek Demonstration Garden and Outdoor Classroom. The University of the Sciences created this open-air classroom on land that formerly housed a brick apartment house in 2001. It features native plants and showcases best practices in storm water management, including grading the landscape and permeable sidewalks.

Cross Chester Avenue, and then cross 43rd Street. Follow the diagonal path on the right to the statue of author Charles Dickens and Little Nell, the tragic heroine of his 1841 novel *The Old Curiosity Shop*. Created for the Chicago World's Fair in 1893, it is one of only three Dickens statues in the world (this despite Dickens's request that no monument be built in his honor so his writings would stand alone). Each year on February 7, Dickens fans gather to celebrate the author's birthday.

Continue along the diagonal path. Stop before what appears to be an oversize tombstone. This rock was taken from Devil's Den, a boulder-strewn hill at Gettysburg Battlefield. It is a monument to the doctors and nurses who served at Satterlee General Hospital, the Union's largest army hospital, as well as the 12,700 patients treated there. Nuns from the Sisters of Charity nursed the soldiers. In 1903's *West Philadelphia Illustrated,* author M. Lafitte Vieira shared soldiers' memories of one sister, Mother Gonzaga, "whose care of the sick and wounded will remain ever memorable. . . . No matter what the creed, her devotion was ever the same, and not a few soldiers recalled in after years the midnight visits of Mother Gonzaga . . . She was one of the purest and loveliest of women."

Continue on the diagonal path to 44th Street and Baltimore Avenue. The walk ends here. Turn left on Baltimore Avenue for food and drink options.

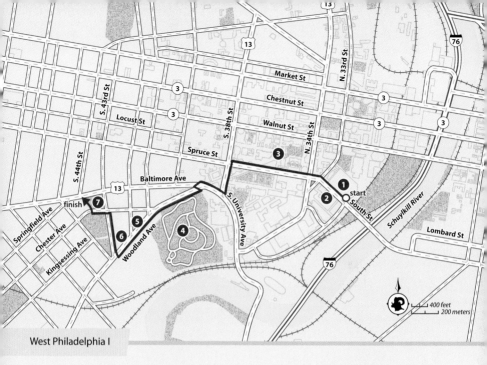

West Philadelphia I

Points of Interest

1 Franklin Field 235 S. 33rd St., 215-898-6151, facilities.upenn.edu/maps/locations/franklin-field

2 The University of Pennsylvania Museum of Archaeology and Anthropology (Penn Museum) 3260 South St., 215-898 4000, penn.museum

3 University of Pennsylvania 215-898-5000, upenn.edu

4 The Woodlands 4000 Woodland Ave., 215-386-2181, woodlandsphila.org

5 University of the Sciences 600 S. 43rd St., 215-596-8800, usciences.edu

6 *Communion between a Rock and a Hard Place* 4129 Woodland Ave., 989-621-1934, warriorwriters.org

7 Clark Park 4300 Baltimore Ave., 215-568-0830, friendsofclarkpark.org

30th Street Station has an amazing Art Deco interior.

26 West Philadelphia II: 30th Street Station, Drexel University, and More

BOUNDARIES: S. 29th St., S. 45th St., Market St., Locust St.
DISTANCE: 3.7 miles
DIFFICULTY: Moderate, with some changes in elevation
PARKING: The tour begins at the train station, which has a pay lot. Street parking can be challenging.
PUBLIC TRANSIT: This tour starts at 30th Street Station, so public transportation is easy. There is a SEPTA subway stop at the station. The following bus lines stop here: 9, 30, 31, 44, 62, 124, 125, and LUCY (Loop through University City).

West Philadelphia is a quick trip from downtown Philadelphia, but early city leaders thought the land on the other side of the Schuylkill River far, far away. In the 1800s, they considered it "a great place to put the city's charitable institutions and to remove the pauper class, the insane, and the sickly from Center City," writes author Robert Morris Skaler in *West Philadelphia: University City to 52nd Street.*

Much has changed. West Philadelphia is home to some of the country's best hospitals and universities. The three-story semi-detached Victorian homes here are in high demand. There's a real community spirit too. Notable locals include actor-rapper Will Smith, who proudly sang he was "West Philadelphia born and raised" in the song for *The Fresh Prince of Bel-Air.*

Walk Description

Begin at ❶ **30th Street Station,** facing the station to take in the grand but simple exterior. Step inside to appreciate the Art Deco–inspired interior with high, coffered ceilings, chandeliers, and cathedral windows. You may recognize the building from movies such as *Witness, World War Z,* and *Unbreakable.*

The Pennsylvania Railroad World War II Memorial honors the more than 1,300 employees killed in the conflict. The sculpture shows the archangel Michael pulling a man's body from flames.

Exit via the doors on the opposite side of the station. Turn left. This is The Porch, a newly developed outdoor space featuring greenery, seating, and food and beverage trucks. The iron fencing features tree branch patterns.

Across the street is the former main United States Post Office, 3000 Chestnut St., built in the 1930s on land that formerly housed stockyards and slaughterhouses. When the building was dedicated in May 1935, the Postmaster General said it was "second to none in the country." The Postal Service moved out in 2008, and the IRS moved in.

Turn right on Market Street. The unique design of the Cira Centre, 2929 Arch St., a 29-story glass-and-steel structure built in 2005, makes the building's shape appear to change when viewed from different angles. The structure is infused with LED lights that change colors and create patterns, including a *P* to honor the city's professional baseball team, the Phillies.

Cross Market Street at 31st Street to Drexel University's ❷ **Paul Peck Alumni Center.** Architect Frank Furness designed this redbrick Gothic building, originally the Centennial National Bank, for the World's Fair of 1876. Drexel purchased it in the 1970s. In 2000, the university restored the building, which is listed on the National

Register of Historic Places, converting it into a gallery that houses a portion of The Drexel Collection.

A large statue of university founder Anthony J. Drexel is nearby. Drexel was a banker and financier who spent more than $1.5 million to found the Drexel Institute of Art, Science and Industry in 1891.

Continue on Market Street to 33rd and Market Streets and Dragon Park. Artist Eric Berg's bronze dragon sculpture, 10 feet high and 14 feet long, is sometimes called Mario the Magnificent to honor late alum Mario Mascioli, who reportedly didn't miss a single basketball game in 25 years.

Continue on Market Street. Drexel's ❸ **Westphal College of Media Arts & Design** is housed in a Robert Venturi–designed building purchased by the university in 2009 with a $25 million donation from the founder of Urban Outfitters. It was transformed into a cutting-edge art center called the URBN Center by 2013.

The Monell Chemical Senses Center, 3500 Market St., is an independent nonprofit that researches taste and smell. *Face Fragment,* the fiberglass sculpture covered in gold leaf near the front doors, has a pronounced nose and mouth, but the rest of the face appears to have broken away.

Cross 37th Street to the ❹ **University City Science Center.** Established in 1963, this nonprofit is the country's first and largest urban research park. The business incubator/networking and community space occupies 17 acres. An independent study found that the center's projects past and present contribute more than $9 billion to the regional economy annually.

Legacy of Richard Allen, 3801 Market St., on the side of First Episcopal District African Methodist Episcopal Church, honors the denomination's founder.

Turn left on 38th Street. The ❺ **Philadelphia Episcopal Cathedral,** built in 1855, is the spiritual home for the 144 congregations of the Episcopal Diocese of Pennsylvania. Its onyx baptismal font was a gift from Anthony Drexel to honor his dead children. The church's stained glass was created by Louis Tiffany.

Continue to Chestnut Street. Turn left. ❻ **St. Agatha–St. James Roman Catholic Church** was the first Catholic Church on the west side of the Schuylkill River, founded in 1850. In a nod to student schedules, the church offers a 9 p.m. service on Sundays. It also has weekly services in Korean and Spanish.

Next door, ❼ **Tabernacle United Church,** which hosts both United Church of Christ and Presbyterian congregations, was built in the 1880s. In the 1980s, the church sheltered El Salvadoran refugees. In the 1990s, they were the first of their denominations in Pennsylvania to welcome LGBT members.

Continue on Chestnut Street. ❽ **University Lutheran Church,** 3637 Chestnut St., is called UniLu and features singing and music-filled services, a nod to St. Augustine's remark, "He who sings prays twice." The church website promises that even the musically challenged are welcome: "Hymns play a major part in how we respond to God's Word. Many members will sing harmony when singing hymns. Others are less musically gifted, but together we always make a joyful noise."

Continue on Chestnut Street. Cross 36th Street through the heart of the Penn campus. This Ivy League university was Ben Franklin's brainchild. The dolphin on the school's coat of arms was adopted from his family crest. Among Penn's distinguished alumni are eight signers of the Declaration of Independence and three US Supreme Court justices. The Electronic Numerical Integrator and Computer, the first all-purpose digital computer, was invented at Penn in 1946, signaling the birth of the Information Age.

Continue on Chestnut Street. *Wave Forms,* 3401 Chestnut St., features six aluminum bell shapes in a courtyard. The 2007 sculpture evokes "history and modernity, freedom and enclosure, silence and speech. The artist brings forth ideas of dwelling place and the organic, unpredictable nature of change," a university website says.

The grand Georgian Revival building on the right corner is Silverman Hall, built in 1900 and part of Penn's law school.

At 34th Street, turn right. Fisher-Bennett Hall, 3340 Walnut St., was originally Bennett College, the first facility built for women on campus, including classrooms, a library, a gymnasium, and a student union. It may have taken its name from Mary Alice Bennett, the first woman to earn a Penn degree. The building now houses the English, Music, and Cinema Studies departments.

Continue on 34th Street. **⑨ Fisher Fine Arts Library** is another Frank Furness work. The exterior of the Gothic red sandstone and terra-cotta building, finished in 1891 and restored in the 1990s, features literary inscriptions chosen by Furness's brother, a Shakespearean scholar and Penn faculty member. Melvil Dewey, creator of the Dewey Decimal System, collaborated with Furness on the interior. Acclaimed architect Frank Lloyd Wright called the building "the work of an artist." It appears in the film *Philadelphia*.

Continue to Spruce Street. Look ahead on 34th Street to see **⑩ Penn Medicine,** the University of Pennsylvania's hospital and the Children's Hospital of Philadelphia, the first US hospital dedicated to children's health. The CHOP site was once Philadelphia Almshouse or Old Blockley, a facility "for the poor, the sick, the elderly and the insane—in other words, those individuals who private hospitals have always turned away," the website philaplace.org notes.

Turn right onto Spruce Street, passing **⑪ Perelman Quadrangle,** a detour-worthy courtyard. The Gothic Irvine Auditorium, 3401 Spruce St., was built in the 1930s by architect Horace Trumbauer. Inside is the 11,000-pipe Curtis Organ, one of the world's largest.

Continue on Spruce Street, walking between buildings that seem suited for Cambridge or Oxford. At 38th Street, lines of food trucks offer cheap but tasty food from around the world. Or stop in the Wawa convenience store, 3744 Spruce St. Wawa is somewhat sacred to locals. Don't mock the name, which comes from the Ojibwa word for a Canada goose. You would also be wise not to question its offerings: one *Philadelphia* magazine writer wrote an opinion piece about not understanding Wawa's appeal. She received more than 300 dissenting emails.

Cross 38th Street, passing Ryan Veterinary Hospital, 3800 Spruce St., part of Penn's School of Veterinary Medicine.

Continue to 40th Street. The **12 Thomas W. Evans Museum and Dental Institute** was appropriately designed with "a frieze of dental tortures," a Penn website notes. Evans, a Philadelphia native, moved to Paris in the 1840s and became the dentist of European royalty. A display case inside contains nearly 200 medals, ribbons, and other gifts from his loyal patients. They included Napoléon III and his wife, whose life Evans allegedly saved when he helped her escape a Parisian mob during the fall of the Second Empire.

Continue on Spruce Street, passing rows of the detached three-story houses described in the introduction. At 42nd Street, turn right. At Walnut Street, turn left. The Restaurant School at Walnut Hill College, 4207 Walnut St., has four full-service restaurants where students receive hands-on training. (The International Bistro is oft praised for its ambience and food.) There's also a pastry shop with student-made products.

13 Masjid Al-Jamia Mosque, the largest mosque in the city, is housed in a 1920s Spanish Revival–Moorish building that was originally the Commodore Movie Theater. The theater closed in the 1950s, and Penn's Muslim Student Association moved into the space in 1973.

At 43rd Street, turn left. The mural on the far side of the CVS pharmacy on the corner is *The Sounds of Philadelphia*. It honors WXPN radio's *Kids Corner,* a weekly live, interactive program for children, on the air since 1988. Local students chose images they thought represented what the sounds coming out of the radio looked like.

Turn right on Locust Street. These largely residential blocks showcase the neighborhood's diversity. You'll see a Jewish deli, a Mediterranean café, an Ethiopian restaurant, and a Chinese takeout spot. **14 The Green Line** is a local coffee chain. (If you have a sweet tooth, the whoopee pies are outstanding.)

Turn right on 45th Street, passing an Egyptian restaurant and a halal deli. Just past Walnut Street, University City Chinese Christian Church, 4501 Walnut St., and The Association of Islamic Charitable Projects Mosque, 4431 Walnut St., are two examples of creative reuse, as Hidden City Philadelphia notes. The church was a strip mall. The mosque was a Methodist church from the early 1900s.

At Chestnut Street, walk left and turn around to see a towering **⓯ mural of Paul Robeson** on the side of The Satterlee Apartments. Robeson, who died in 1976, was an actor, athlete, and academic who was targeted for his civil rights advocacy and Cold War opposition. The New Jersey–born graduate of Columbia University Law School quit practicing law because of racial tensions within his New York firm. He turned to the stage, starring on Broadway in *Showboat* and *Othello*. During World War II, Robeson entertained American troops and sang pro-war songs, but supporters of Senator Joseph McCarthy labeled him subversive, and his career suffered. Testifying before the House Committee on Un-American Activities, Robeson said, "My father was a slave, and my people died to build this country, and I am going to stay here and have a part of it just like you. And no Fascist-minded people will drive me from it. Is that clear? . . . You are the non-Patriots, and you are the un-Americans, and you ought to be ashamed of yourselves."

Double back to 44th Street, continuing on Chestnut Street and passing Igelsia Christina Puente de Vida, 4233 Chestnut St. **⓰ *Building Brotherhood: Engaging Males of Color,*** completed in 2015, came from a series of workshops with men of color, ages 12 and older. The workshops asked, "What obstacles get in the way when you seek education and employment?" Take a moment to find the words and images embedded here, including a Chinese pagoda, bongo drums, and a row of marchers carrying protest signs.

This walk ends here. Continue on Chestnut Street to return to the thick of the university district. Walk another mile to cross the Schuylkill River into Center City.

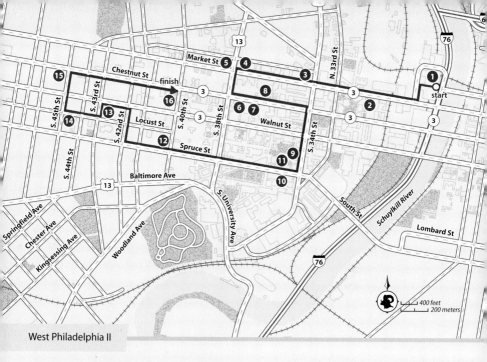

West Philadelphia II

Points of Interest

1 30th Street Station 2955 Market St., 800-USA-RAIL, amtrak.com

2 Paul Peck Alumni Center 3140–3142 Market St., 215-895-2586, drexel.edu/alumni/about/peck

3 Drexel University Westphal College of Media Arts & Design 3501 Market St., 215-895-1834 (visitor center/tours), drexel.edu/westphal

4 The University City Science Center 3711 Market St., 215-966-6000, sciencecenter.org

5 Philadelphia Episcopal Cathedral 23 S. 38th St., 215-386-0234, philadelphiacathedral.org

6 St. Agatha–St. James Roman Catholic Church 3728 Chestnut St., 267-787-5000, saintsaj.org

7 Tabernacle United Church 3700 Chestnut St., 215-386-4100, tabunited.org

8 University Lutheran Church 3637 Chestnut St., 215-387-2885, uniluphila.org

9 University of Pennsylvania Fisher Fine Arts Library 220 S. 34th St., 215-898-8325, library.upenn.edu/finearts

10 Penn Medicine 800-789-7366, pennmedicine.org

11 Perelman Quadrangle 215-898-5552, vpul.upenn.edu/perelmanquad

12 Thomas W. Evans Museum and Dental Institute 4001 Spruce St., dental.upenn.edu

13 Masjid al-Jamia Mosque 4228 Walnut St., 267-275-8087

14 Green Line Cafe 4426 Locust St., 215-822-0799, greenlinecafe.com

15 Mural of Paul Robeson 4500 Chestnut St.

16 *Building Brotherhood: Engaging Males of Color* 4008 Chestnut St.

A mosaic bench provides a resting place for walkers as they travel along the Manayunk canal.

27 Manayunk:
There Will Be Hills

BOUNDARIES: Silverwood St., Manayunk Canal Towpath, Lock St., Fountain St.
DISTANCE: 3.3 miles
DIFFICULTY: Moderate, with some changes in elevation and steps
PARKING: Street parking is usually available unless there's a special event.
PUBLIC TRANSIT: The Manayunk SEPTA rail station is at Cresson and Cotton Sts. Bus routes here include the 35 and 61.

Manayunk takes its name from the Lenni Lenape tribe word *manaiung,* meaning "river" or "place to drink." That's somewhat fitting as this northwest Philadelphia neighborhood's Main Street today is known for its nightlife.

This beautiful area has a rich history and was once called the Manchester of America because of the thriving factories here. During the 1800s, immigrants from Ireland, Poland, Italy, and Germany and freed Africans found work in these mills, many of which were devoted to textiles.

This neighborhood looks unlike any of the others in this book, with unique architecture, street art, and rolling hills. Edgar Allan Poe called it "one of the real Edens of the land."

Walk Description

Begin at Greene Lane and Main Street, in the shadow of the arches of the massive Manayunk Bridge. This concrete span was built in 1928, replacing a steel span.

Walk southeast on Main Street. The ❶ **Philadelphia Fire Department's Engine Company 12** was the first city-owned station, built in 1876 when horses carried firefighters to blazes. "The causes of many fires at this time were machinery and locomotive sparks, gas explosions, and arson," Thom Nickels, a descendant of one of the neighborhood's oldest families, writes in *Images of America: Manayunk*. He also notes there was a fierce rivalry between firefighters from Manayunk and those from neighboring Roxborough.

Next door, the current warehouse for the Loring Construction Company fills the former Empress Theater, 4441 Main St. Built in 1914, this former vaudeville and movie palace closed in the 1960s. The Loring company purchased the building soon after, and one owner told Hidden City Philadelphia that she remembered people attending films there when she was growing up, saying, "For a while it became known as a 'scratch' theater. . . . Movie-goers would come out scratching themselves from flea bites."

Continue on Main Street. The ❷ **U.S. Hotel Bar & Grill** has been in operation since 1903. Cross Conarroe Street, noting the parklike area across the road, an exit for the Towpath later in the walk.

Continue on Main Street. Dining and shopping options here include Beans, 4405 Main St., a beauty supply store; Sweet Elizabeth's, 4409 Main St., a bakery; and Taqueria Feliz, 4410 Main St., offering Mexican fare.

Turn left on Levering Street, which takes its name from the first European family to build a home here. ❸ *Sandy's Dream,* on the back of Propper View Apartments, was created in partnership with the Sandy Rollman Ovarian Cancer Foundation and is the first mural in the country designed to raise cancer awareness. This building formerly housed the Propper Brothers Company, "Manayunk's Busiest Store." In 1911, a woman could buy a summer dress for less than $2.

At Cresson Street, turn right, walking along a cobblestoned street shaded by the elevated train. When the El was constructed in the 1930s as a way to prevent train crossing accidents and deaths, some locals said the tracks ruined their quaint neighborhood, Nickels writes.

Active businesses operate in the El's shadow, including **④ Sorrentino's Deli and Grocery.** The Italian hoagie is a local favorite.

Look left and up—and up and up—to see the continuation of Levering Street. This is the so-called **⑤ Manayunk Wall,** a sacred, if feared, place in the cycling world. The Philadelphia International Championship is a 124-mile annual bike race that's considered the country's most prestigious. The Wall is an 800-meter climb on Levering Street and Lyceum Avenue. The steepest section has a 17% grade.

Continue on Cresson Street. At Cotton Street, turn left to follow the steps to **⑥ Pretzel Park,** originally called Manayunk Park when it opened in 1929. Locals gave it its current name, possibly because the internal sidewalks resemble the twisted treat, or possibly because of a beloved vendor who sold goods here. City leaders officially changed the park's name in 2004. A large silver sculpture of a pretzel was installed in 2005. A scene from *Unbreakable* features Bruce Willis's character in the park, with St. Josaphat Church in the background.

Return to Cresson Street. Walk to Rector Street, and turn left. **⑦ St. John the Baptist Roman Catholic Church** is called Manayunk's Cathedral. This Gothic structure dates to the 1890s, when a visiting Irishman donated the equivalent of $1 million to build it. Inside, the church organ dates to 1906, and the story is that the father of St. Katharine Drexel was the first organist.

At Silverwood Street, turn left (northwest), passing Pretzel Park. **⑧ St. Josaphat Roman Catholic Church** was founded in 1898. For more than 100 years, these two churches flourished within view of each other, each catering to specific populations of immigrants. The Irish went to St. John the Baptist, and the Polish went to St. Josaphat. There were two other Roman Catholic churches nearby: St. Lucy's served Italians, and St. Mary of the Assumption served the Germans.

Continue to Levering Street and turn left. This is the Manayunk Wall—the downhill part. You're welcome.

At Cresson Street, turn right. Turn left on Levering Street and left again on Main Street. The portraits affixed to some businesses honor current or former residents.

Continue east on Main Street. The Nickels Building, 4323 Main St., built in 1906, is now a co-working space, but it originally housed an F. W. Woolworth store on its first floor and a dance hall above. In the early 1900s, Nickels writes, "dancing was almost as controversial as bootlegging." Christian fundamentalists regularly protested outside Saturday evening events.

The 2-mile-long Manayunk Towpath was originally used by mules pulling boats along the canal.

Shopping and dining options on this stretch include Volo Coffeehouse, 4360 Main St.; the Juice Merchant, 4330 Main St.; and Whirled Peace, 4321 Main St., offering frozen yogurt and coffee drinks. The Little Apple, 4361 Main St., and Pineapple on Main, 437 Main St., are popular gift shops.

Canal House, now an upscale apartment building, was originally a mill, built in the 1840s to produce woolen blankets for the Union Army. When the neighborhood was an industrial hub, Nickels writes, "any adult workers or children could quit or be fired from one mill and within the hour get hired in another." Only one mill dating to the 1860s is still in operation. Most of the others have been converted to residences or commercial spaces.

Continue on Main Street, passing Tony Luke's, 4307 Main St., and Winnie's LeBus, 4266 Main St., two places to grab sandwiches. The Bayou Bar and Grill, 4245 Main St., features seafood; Cactus, 4243 Main St., offers Southwestern dishes; and Goat's Beard, 4201 Main St., has New American cuisine. Shopping options include Worn Yesterday, 4228 Main St., a children's consignment shop, and Vamp Boutique, 4231 Main St., a women's clothing store.

The **9 Manayunk Brewing Company** is housed in a former cotton and wool mill from 1822. The first batch of the company's beer was tapped in 1996. It now has more than 600 beers. In 2015, the brewery marked Pope Francis's US visit with Papal Pleasure, an ale infused with oak from Malbec wine barrels. A St. John the Baptist priest blessed the brewing water.

Walk just past the brewery to the **10 G. J. Littlewood and Son Textile Mill,** the only operating mill in the area. The dye factory was founded in 1869. It's currently run by the fourth and fifth generations of the Littlewood family.

Backtrack to Lock Street, and turn left. Opened in 2014, **11 The Venice Island Performing Arts and Recreation Center** has a full theater, sports courts, and a spray garden. The landscaping is designed to handle heavy rains and to provide drainage that helps the entire area.

Begin walking the Towpath along the 2-mile-long Manayunk Canal, which was hand-dug mostly by Irish immigrants in the early 1800s. A towpath is a trail mules walked while towing boats along the canal. This one stretches beyond Valley Forge, about 15 miles away.

Along the path are sets of two to four steps covered in mosaic. This public art project, unveiled in 2006, is called *Manayunk Stoops: Heart and Home.*

Running parallel to Main Street, the Canal Towpath is popular with bikers, runners, bird-watchers, and fishermen.

Artist Diane Pieri made each stoop unique, with images including local plants and animals. Locals often interact with their neighbors on stoops, Pieri said, and the project is "to bring the language of the community to the canal. The stoops are unpretentious yet meaningful reflections of the people and social customs on Manayunk."

Along the walk the ground alternates between gravel, pavement, and wood planks. There are multiple mosaics and paintings. To end the walk early, look for the exit on the right opposite Conarroe Street.

The mural across the canal celebrates Manayunk's industrial past. Exit the Towpath at Fountain Street, which is marked by a pink-and-red, single-lane bridge. A gang called the Schuylkill Rangers once used this bridge to ambush passing boats in the late 1800s.

Leaving the path, turn right to climb the mosaic-covered stairs. While the steps aren't new, the mosaics were added in 2015. The climb may seem steep and intimidating, but there are built-in breaks. Climb the steps. You were spared the Wall. You can do this.

At top, turn right on Umbria Street, passing James Dobson Elementary and Middle School, 4667 Umbria St. ⑫ **Marchiano's Bakery** specializes in tomato pie and other savory breads. Famous fans included Frank Sinatra and The Temptations.

At Leverington Avenue, cross Umbria Street and then Levering Avenue. Turn left on Leverington Avenue, walking to Baker Street. Turn right. Follow the alley until it ends, bearing left onto DuPont Street to see the still active ⑬ **St. David's Episcopal Church** and cemetery. The cornerstone for the original church was laid in 1832. St. David is the patron saint of Wales.

Turn around and continue east on Baker Street. At Green Lane, turn right. Walk under the highway overpass, turning right to see the *Welcome to Manayunk* mural. This walk ends here, near where it began.

(continued on next page)

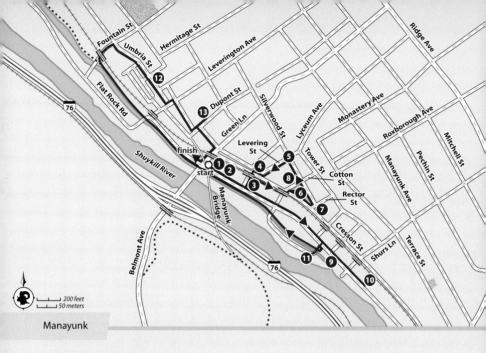

Points of Interest

1 Philadelphia Fire Department's Engine Company 12 4447 Main St.

2 U.S. Hotel Bar & Grill 4439 Main St., 215-483-9222

3 *Sandy's Dream,* 4368 Cresson Ave., tinyurl.com/sandysdream

4 Sorrentino's Deli and Grocery 4361 Cresson St., 215-487-0559

5 Manayunk Wall Starting at Levering St. and Cresson St.

6 Pretzel Park 4300 Silverwood St., manayunkcouncil.org/pretzel

7 St. John the Baptist Roman Catholic Church 146 Rector St., 215-482-4600, stjohnmanayunk.org

8 St. Josaphat Roman Catholic Church 124 Cotton St.

9 Manayunk Brewing Company 4120 Main St., 215-482-8220, manayunkbrewery.com

10 G. J. Littlewood and Son Textile Mill 4045 Main St., 215-483-3970, littlewooddyers.com

11 Venice Island Performing Arts and Recreation Center 7 Lock St., 215-482-9565, manayunk.com/about/dsr/veniceisland.html

12 Marchiano's Bakery 4653 Umbria St., 215-483-8585, marchianosbakery.com

13 St. David's Episcopal Church 150 Dupont St., 215-482-2345, stdavidsmanayunk.org

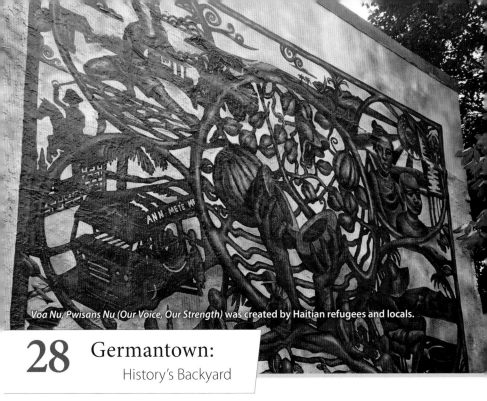

Voa Nu, Pwisans Nu (Our Voice, Our Strength) **was created by Haitian refugees and locals.**

28 Germantown:
History's Backyard

BOUNDARIES: Abbottsford Ave., Upsala St., Germantown Ave., Greene St.
DISTANCE: 2.8 miles
DIFFICULTY: Moderate, with a few gradual hills
PARKING: This neighborhood is about 30 minutes from Center City Philadelphia. Unless a special event is going on, street parking is easy to find.
PUBLIC TRANSIT: SEPTA's regional train, the Chestnut Hill West, will take you from Center City to the Tulpehocken Station. Bus options include the 23 and XH.

It's hard to escape history in Germantown, a neighborhood in the city's northwest pocket. Long before the American Revolution, people with revolutionary ideas—such as ending slavery—settled this rural area known for its rich soil and ample grazing lands.

Germantown, or Germanopolis, was formally founded by 12 families in 1683 as a separate town that was a two-hour walk from Philadelphia. Not surprisingly, many of the original residents were from Germany.

Some stops on this tour reference the Revolutionary War's Battle of Germantown, a British victory. For the rebel army, losing this battle a month after the city of Philadelphia had fallen to the British was a huge defeat. About 1,000 colonials were killed or injured, versus about 500 British fighters. Afterward, Washington took his troops to winter at Valley Forge, from which he launched the sneak attack that would change the course of the war.

Walk Description

Begin at 4650 Germantown Avenue. ❶ **Loudoun Mansion** tops the green hill at left. The original building was built in 1801 on a burial ground, and subsequent generations expanded the structure in different architectural styles. Loudoun is reportedly haunted by at least five ghosts, including a few soldiers; Little Willie, who died at age 8 in 1860; and Maria Dickson Logan, the home's last owner, who died in 1939. In 1994, Loudoun was severely damaged by fire, but many of the antiques were untouched.

Walk north on Germantown Avenue. ❷ *Voa Nu, Pwisans Nu (Our Voice, Our Strength)* was created by members of the city's Haitian community, who were joined by a group of Haitians housed in Germantown after Haiti's 2010 earthquake. The work features images important to Haitian culture, including *Le Negre Marron*, an unknown fighter who used a shell to call Haitians to fight French invaders.

The former Germantown Settlement Charter School, 4811 Germantown Ave., opened to fanfare in 1999 and closed in scandal in 2010. The school's founder reportedly spent millions of taxpayer dollars to fund the institution, only to see its students' test scores drop and its facilities fall apart.

Continue on Germantown Avenue, passing the Fresh Visions Youth Theater, 4801 Germantown Ave. ❸ **Hood Cemetery** was founded in 1692 as the Lower Burying Ground. It was renamed in 1850 to honor William Hood, a Philadelphia native who paid for the wall that separates the cemetery from the road. Hood died in Paris, and his body was returned in a barrel filled with brandy. He rests in a grave near the entrance of the cemetery. It is not known if he is still in the barrel. About 1,000 people are buried here, including soldiers from the Revolutionary War, the War of 1812, and the Civil War.

Continue on Germantown Avenue. The blue historical marker at 5109 marks where the home of Thones Kunders once stood. (Ancestors say the name is incorrectly spelled on the sign.) Kunders was a cloth dyer who moved here with his wife and sons in the 1680s. The first Quaker meeting was held in Kunders's home in 1683, with William Penn in attendance. It was here that four Quakers wrote the first public protest against slavery, 92 years before Pennsylvania was the first state to outlaw the practice.

Continue to Gilbert Stuart Park, 5132 Germantown Ave. Stuart painted portraits of the first six US presidents. His best-known work is the unfinished work of George Washington featured on the dollar bill. Pass Conyngham-Hacker House, 5214 Germantown Ave., which was built in 1775 and is now a multifamily residence.

❹ Grumblethorpe was built in 1744 as a summer home for merchant and wine dealer John Wister. British general James Agnew died on the living room floor during the Battle of Germantown. The bloodstain is still visible, and Agnew's ghost is said to hang around as well. Another ghost who reportedly lives here makes herself known by scent, specifically the smell of baking bread.

❺ Trinity Lutheran Church was founded in 1836, the first neighborhood church to conduct services in English, not German. The steeple houses the area's first town clock, paid for by donations from residents. The church's offices stand in the former home of Christopher Sower, who in 1739 printed the colonies' first German-language newspaper. He also printed the first Bible in Colonial America in 1748, a German translation by Martin Luther that predated an English version by 40 years. Despite providing so much food aid to Revolutionary War soldiers' families that he earned the nickname The Bread Father, Sower was declared a traitor after the conflict for printing a newspaper for British soldiers.

John Fanning Watson House, 5275–77 Germantown Ave., is where author Watson wrote the first history of the city, *Annals of Philadelphia,* published in 1830. The original is online and provides insights into early city life. The "Punishments" section of the book notes that, in 1735, "Frances Hamilton was punished for picking pockets in the market, by being exposed on the court-house steps, with her hands bound to the rails and her face turned toward the whipping post and pillory for two hours. She was then released and publicly whipped."

Continue to West Coulter Street, and turn left to circle the campus of German-town Friends School, 31 W. Coulter St. This well-respected private school opened in 1845 with a class of 33 boys from Quaker families. During the Civil War, students were mocked for their pacifist refusal to fight for either side. In 2002, the school stopped giving out academic awards, concluding that doing so was against Friends' beliefs.

Germantown Friends Meeting House, 47 W. Coulter St., was built in the 1860s, a simple structure in sync with Quaker values. At Greene Street, turn right. The Pennsylvania School for the Deaf, 100 W. School House Lane, opened in 1820. One of the first headmasters was Laurent Clerc, who taught sign language to Thomas Gallaudet, for whom Gallaudet University is named. In 1984, the school moved to this campus, which was used as a hospital during the Battle of Germantown. Six British soldiers are believed to be buried here.

Turn right on West School House Lane. At Germantown Avenue, turn right, walking back toward West Coulter Street. The ➏ **Germantown White House**, also known as the Deshler-Morris House, was built in the 1750s. President George Washington twice used it as a summer retreat. Years before that, British general William Howe claimed the home after his troops defeated Washington's at the Battle of Georgetown. If the building is open—it has limited hours—step inside to see the Washington family's portrait in the hallway. Besides George, Martha, and their grandchildren, slave William Lee is included.

Bringhurst House, 5448 Germantown Ave., was the home of carriage-maker John Bringhurst. In 1780, Washington wrote a letter to one of his officers to "do me a favour by enquiring & letting me know as soon as possible if any good coach-maker in Phila or GermanTown (Bringhurst for instance) will engage to make me a genteel plain chariot with real harness for four horses to go with two postillions."

At West Coulter Street, cross Germantown Avenue, and then turn around to return in the same direction. Pass St. Luke's Episcopal Church, 5421 Germantown Ave., and then stop at 5425 Germantown Ave. The building that formerly stood here, called Pine Place, was the birthplace of Louisa May Alcott. The author of *Little Women* was born on November 29, 1832, her father's 33rd birthday. Alcott's

A statue of John Wister near the entrance of Vernon Park

parents were educators who had moved from New England to Philadelphia to open Alcott's School a few years earlier. When Louisa May was 2 years old, the school closed and the family returned to Boston.

Continue on Germantown Avenue, passing the Cunningham Piano Factory, 5427 Germantown Ave., founded in 1891. When Pope Francis visited Philadelphia in 2016, the company provided the electric organ that accompanied his public Mass. Other customers include Usher and Alicia Keys.

The small half-acre park in the 5500 block of Germantown Avenue includes the **❼ Historic Germantown Visitor Center,** which has a library with genealogy archives, a neighborhood history museum, and tourist information.

The Impacting Your World Christian Center, 5507 Germantown Ave., is a Victorian building built in the 1880s on the site of a British prisoner-of-war lockup used in the Battle of Germantown. The park's centerpiece is a Civil War memorial featuring a Union soldier standing atop granite from Devil's Den in Gettysburg. The cannon on the north side came from a British ship sunk during the American Revolution.

This area was a busy hub of 18th-century life. The prison and stockades were here, as was a busy marketplace and rest area. The website ushistory.org notes that "Indian delegations on their way to Philadelphia broke their journeys here."

Continue on Germantown Avenue to *Healing through Faith and Spirituality,* 5531 Germantown Ave., a 2011 mural weaving bright patterns and a glass mosaic. Pass through a commercial strip with businesses catering to the area's large Muslim population, selling halal meats and women's fashions.

❽ Vernon Park features a sculpture of John Wister near the entrance. Wister—looking oh so dapper with his top hat and cane—was part of the large Wister clan. Other family members include horticulturists, who lent their name to the climbing plant we know as wisteria, and author Owen Wister, whose 1902 novel *The Virginian* first romanticized the American West and the cowboy folk hero. In one memorable scene, the title character responds to a stranger's insult with the gentle threat, "When you call me that, smile."

During the Civil War, John Wister was president of an iron company that supplied ammunition to Union forces. His home, Vernon House, is so named either to honor Washington, whose Virginia plantation was called Mount Vernon, or to refer to Diana Vernon, a character in Sir Walter Scott's *Rob Roy*.

Continue on Germantown Avenue. The interior of the Beaux Arts building that is the Germantown Town Hall, 5928 Germantown Ave., is as ornate as the exterior, containing a memorial plaque with the names of local soldiers who died in World War I and a bell cast in the same shop as the Liberty Bell. Formerly city offices, the building has been empty since 1998.

This Civil War memorial stands in Market Square in Germantown.

Pass First United Methodist Church, 6001 Germantown Ave. ❾ **Wyck House** was a family residence from the 1750s through the 1970s. The members of that family, none of whom were named Wyck, include the founder of the Franklin Institute, a founder of the first horticulture school for women, and a designer of the Mexican railway.

At Walnut Lane, turn left. At Greene Street, turn right. The ❿ **Ebenezer Maxwell Mansion** is a stone Victorian built by Maxwell, a clothing merchant, in 1859 for $10,000. It's now a museum that hosts regular events, including murder mystery games. The mansion's kitchen includes a line of servants' bells. It is whispered that this home inspired Charles Addams, creator of *The Addams Family*. Addams, a University of Pennsylvania student, may have seen the home during his college years.

Turn right on Tulpehocken Street to return to Germantown Avenue, and then turn right. The historical marker in front of Settlement Music School, 6128 Germantown Ave., recognizes Ora Washington, an African American tennis and basketball phenom who is largely unknown because she was not allowed to compete against better-known white players. She played at the YWCA that once stood here.

Between 1932 and 1942, Washington was the coach and leading scorer of the Philadelphia Tribunes. In a 1988 *New York Times* op-ed, tennis legend Arthur Ashe called the Tribunes "black America's first premier female sports team," and noted that white Americans who shunned African American athletics only hurt themselves because "they never got to see Ora Washington of Philadelphia, who may have been the best female athlete ever." During her sporting career, Washington, who died in 1971, earned money doing domestic work.

Continue to Herman Street. Cross Germantown Avenue, and then turn around to see the ⑪ **Mennonite Meeting House and Cemetery.** The first Mennonite church in the colonies was built here in 1708. Before this, Mennonites worshiped with Quakers. This building, made from local stone, replaced the original log structure in 1770.

Continue north on Germantown Avenue. ⑫ **Johnson House Historic Site** was home to four generations of the Johnson family from the 1700s through 1908. During the Revolutionary War, the family's pacifism kept them from defending their property during the Battle of Germantown. Instead, they took refuge in the cellar. The exterior still shows musket ball damage. The Johnsons were abolitionists, and the home was an Underground Railroad stop. Legend has it that Harriet Tubman and William Still both visited. The site's museum hosts an annual Juneteenth celebration to celebrate the end of slavery.

The ⑬ **Upper Burying Ground** is also called Ax's Burying Ground, after caretaker John Frederick Ax, who maintained the space for 22 years in the 1700s. About 1,300 people are believed to be buried here, but there are only about 300 headstones. Adam Chiseler's headstone notes he died in 1777 at "age 969 years." The Concord School House sits in one corner of the cemetery. The original one-room school, built in 1693, is either named for the ship that carried many of the area's first residents or refers to the phrase "in sweet concord" as people with different religions lay side by side.

Continue north on Germantown Avenue. **⑭ Cliveden,** built in the 1760s as a summer home for Dr. Benjamin Chew and seven generations of his family, was the site of the Battle of Germantown's bloodiest skirmishes. It is now a museum with more than 6 acres of grounds to explore.

Multiple generations of the family owned slaves, and one of the museum's permanent exhibits addresses this history. Richard Allen, the founder of the African Methodist Episcopal Church, was born to one of Chew's slaves.

About 70 soldiers died on Cliveden's grounds during the Battle of Germantown. The so-called Blood Portrait is on the floor of a second-floor bedroom. Legend says a wounded British soldier used his own blood to outline a loved one's face. It's difficult to make out the drawing now, but the museum has photos showing the image under a blue light.

Cliveden has its share of ghost stories. A headless woman frequently prowls the grounds; one story says a British soldier lopped off her head during the Battle of Germantown and ran with it into the midst of the American soldiers to intimidate them.

This walk of historic Germantown ends here. The Mount Airy tour (page 218) begins about a mile north of here.

Grumblethorpe was the Wister family home.

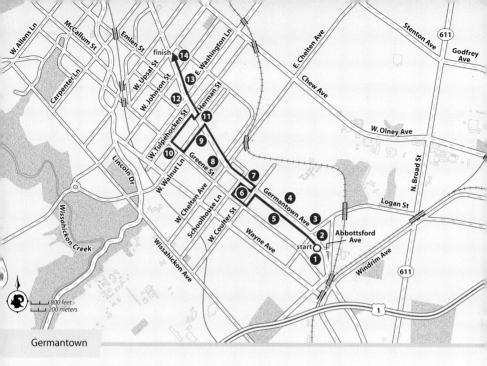

Germantown

Points of Interest

1 **Loudoun Mansion** 4450 Germantown Ave, ushistory.org/germantown

2 *Voa Nu, Pwisans Nu* 4675 Germantown Ave. For more information, contact Philadelphia Mural Arts, 215-685-0750, muralarts.org.

3 **Hood Cemetery** 4901 Germantown Ave., hoodcemetery.org

4 **Grumblethorpe** 5267 Germantown Ave., 215-843-4820, philalandmarks.org/grumblethorpe

5 **Trinity Lutheran Church** 5300 Germantown Ave., 215-848-8150

6 **Germantown White House (Deshler-Morris House)** 5442 Germantown Ave., 215-965-2305, nps.gov/inde

7 **Historic Germantown Visitor Center** 5501 Germantown Ave., 215-844-0514, germantownhistory.org

8 **Vernon Park** 5800 Germantown Ave.

9 **Wyck House** 6026 Germantown Ave., 215-848-1690, wyck.org

10 **Ebenezer Maxwell Mansion** 200 W. Tulpehocken St., 215-438-1861, ebenezermaxwellmansion.org

11 **Mennonite Meeting House and Cemetery** 6119 Germantown Ave., 215-843-0943, meetinghouse.info

12 **Johnson House Historic Site** 6306 Germantown Ave., 215-438-1768, johnsonhouse.org

13 **Upper Burying Ground** 6309 Germantown Ave., ushistory.org/germantown

14 **Cliveden** 6401 Germantown Ave., 215-848-1777, cliveden.org

Walking the Wissahickon is a tribute to Mount Airy's natural beauty.

29 Mount Airy and Wissahickon Valley Park:
City Meets Suburb Meets Wilderness

BOUNDARIES: Germantown Ave., Carpenter Lane, Greene St., McCallum St.
DISTANCE: About 4 miles
DIFFICULTY: Moderate, with some hills
PARKING: There is usually street parking in the area, but note it is zoned for 2 hours only
unless you have a residential permit.
PUBLIC TRANSIT: This tour begins and ends at the Allen Lane SEPTA station, making that a
great option for transportation. Nearby bus stops include 23 and XH.

Like neighboring Germantown, the Mount Airy neighborhood was considered a summer getaway and a haven from city evils such as disease. Europeans began building here in the 1600s. The area's name is the legacy of William Allen, a wealthy merchant who played a role in building Independence Hall and Pennsylvania Hospital. He called his 47-acre estate Mount Airy.

The neighborhood mixes homes that were built for the wealthy with dwellings constructed for laborers, the modern mess of a power station with the nature of Wissahickon

Valley Park. The park is worthy of a return visit, with multiple trail guides available from its supporters. There's a reason CNN's *Money* magazine included Mount Airy in its list of best big-city neighborhoods, along with Park Slope in Brooklyn and Chicago's Lakeview.

Walk Description

Begin at Allen Lane Station, 200 W. Allens Lane at Cresheim Road. Built in 1880, the station maintains its Victorian appearance. The regional rail depot has a comfortable café and a nearby free Little Library, an oversize birdhouse-like structure that encourages readers to take or leave a book.

Note the discrepancy between the station name and the street name. Even locals puzzle over the correct spelling. SEPTA uses Allen. The city stands by Allens. The Fairmount Park Commission has posted signs with Allen's. When asking for directions, try saying Allen with a soft hint of an s to appease whomever you're addressing.

Turn right on Allens Lane. ❶ **Henry H. Houston Elementary School** is a three-story Late Gothic Revival–style building constructed in 1927. Houston, who died in 1895, made his fortune in the transportation industry, working with the Pennsylvania Railroad and investing in the new petroleum field. He oversaw the construction of about 300 homes called Wissahickon Heights and was a trustee for the University of Pennsylvania. Both of his sons attended Penn. Penn's Houston Hall, the first American college student union, is named for his elder son, who died in an accident months after his 1878 graduation.

Continue on Allens Lane. The ❷ **Radha Krishna Temple** moved into the former Cresheim Arms Hotel in 1977. About 500 people worship certain Hindu deities here. Services are open to the public.

Continue to Germantown Avenue. ❸ **Lutheran Theological Seminary** is across the road. The seminary was founded in 1864 and moved to William Allen's former estate in 1889. The oldest building on campus, the refectory, dates to the late 1700s. In January 2016, Lutheran leaders announced this seminary would be closing and joining with another shuttered seminary to launch the United Lutheran Seminary. At press time the campus was still open to visitors.

Turn right on Germantown Avenue. This stretch is part of the National Register of Historic Places' Colonial Germantown Historic District. The road follows a well-used path that natives traveled between the Delaware River and points west. People have lived here for more than 300 years. The 7200 and 7100 blocks are part of the area's earliest commercial district.

The former Mount Airy National Bank, 7208 Germantown Ave., was designed by Norman Hulme, who also assisted with the early planning of Independence Mall. The neighboring Tourison Building, 7200–7206 Germantown Ave., is an Art Deco gem housing a café and other businesses.

Bioluminescence, on the second floor of 7174 Germantown Ave., was inspired by the artist's first snorkeling trip in the Caribbean.

Continue on Germantown Avenue, passing McMenamin's Tavern, 7170 Germantown Ave., a popular hangout for sports fans.

❹ The Sedgwick Theater, now the home of the Quintessence Theatre Group, was built in the 1920s during an era of Art Deco movie palaces that featured silent films. The Sedgwick closed in 1966.

❺ Earth Bread + Brewery is an environmentally friendly restaurant. The mural on the building's side, *Walking the Wissahickon,* is a tribute to the beauty of nearby Wissahickon Valley.

Most of the Mount Airy Presbyterian Church complex, 13 E. Mount Pleasant Ave., will become the city's first cohousing project. Most cohousing developments feature shared kitchens, dining rooms, and laundry and event spaces. Residents also share chores, such as babysitting.

❻ Philadelphia Interfaith Hospitality Network helps homeless families with permanent shelter. It was founded 28 years ago by a marketing executive who noticed the same homeless woman on the streets near her office. One day, she purchased the woman a sandwich, and soon the executive and her young sons were feeding others. Programming grew from there. On the building's side is *Walking Together,* completed in 2009 when another organization occupied this space. The three featured words, *service, justice,* and *faith,* coincidentally reflect the nonprofit's values as well.

Continue on Germantown Avenue, passing the home fields of Mount Airy Baseball and the Mount Airy peewee football team, The Bantams.

The ❼ **Lovett Memorial Library** began in 1885 as the Mount Airy Free Library with 421 books in a rented room in a lumberyard, according to the Free Library of Philadelphia. One of the library's three supporters, Louisa D. Lovett, served as the group's secretary and treasurer, managing the initial $11.20 budget.

Louisa's aunt, Charlotte Lovett Bostwick, then donated land she'd inherited from her brother to build a library there in his honor. The Thomas R. Lovett library opened in 1887. By 1891, it had more than 4,500 books and an annual budget of almost $2,000.

The building was expanded over the years, but some of the original touches remain, including artwork donated by the Lovett family. A multimillion-dollar renovation was expected to be complete by late 2017.

❽ **Germantown Home,** a nonprofit providing affordable housing and skilled nursing care for seniors, originally housed an institution that also helped the very young, according to accessgenealogy.com. In the 1850s, Lutheran reverend William Passavant was visiting the pastor of nearby St. Michael's Church, the Reverend Charles Schaeffer, and his wife, Elizabeth. He wondered if the Lutheran Church could start an orphanage, then gave Elizabeth a dollar, saying, "Now everything must have a beginning: I will give you the first dollar." The Lutheran Orphans Home and Asylum was opened, with Elizabeth as director and other Lutheran women helping her manage the home and children.

The population of the orphanage grew exponentially during the Civil War. A list of orphans from 1894 still exists and details the children's names and ages; many of the last names are of German origin. Sisters Catherine and Rosina Breitweiser, ages 10 and 7, were here, as were siblings Julius and Pauline Goetz, ages 13 and 11. After a century in Germantown, the orphanage moved to the suburbs.

Gorgas House, 6901 Germantown Ave., now office space, takes its name from the wealthy Gorgas family. The family is also associated with the nearby Roxborough neighborhood, where a 5-acre park bearing the family name is a center of neighborhood life. East Gorgas Lane, which begins on the next corner, is considered the north border of the small community of Beggarstown, which extends about 0.5 mile on Germantown Avenue to East Upsal Street. The area's original name is believed to be the German Bettelhausen, which has roughly the same meaning and was given because a poor man was the first to build a shack here.

Continue on Germantown Avenue, crossing Meehan Avenue to reach another small area with an unusual name. Dogtown was so dubbed because, according to William Campbell's book *Old Towns and Districts of Philadelphia*, "when it was the custom in Germantown to tie herrings behind bridal coaches, it is said that most of the dogs that followed came from this section." In the 1970s, a local gang co-opted the name, which is still used. On urbandictionary.com, Dogtown is defined as a "sub-neighborhood in East Mount Airy . . . once a hot-bed of crime . . . that still 'fronts' a hardened appearance." It notes young people wanting to appear tough prefer the name Dogtown to Mt. Airy with this example:

> PERSON #1: *Dogtown Philly, holla!*
>
> PERSON #2: *Whatever, you're from Mount Airy.*

Santander Bank, 6740 Germantown Ave., was built in 1909 for the Pelham Trust Company. In 1911, the bank renovated the basement to create storage vaults for silverware and jewelry "in response to recent robberies in Mount Airy and Germantown," according to *Mount Airy* by Elizabeth Farmer Jarvis.

Continue along Germantown Avenue. Mermaid Bar, 6745 Germantown Ave., is a local hangout that is not to be confused with the nearby Mermaid Inn, which features live folk music. Neighboring Trolley Car Park is a grassy square in front of the former trolley depot. The 23 trolley, once a Germantown mainstay, began rattling down the tracks here in the 1800s. By the 1920s, this was the longest trolley route in the country and perhaps the world, beginning north in the Chestnut Hill neighborhood and ending 25 miles later in South Philadelphia. Buses have taken over most of the transportation runs. One of the trolley's cars is part of the Trolley Car Diner, 7619 Germantown Ave.

Continue to ❾ **St. Michael's Lutheran Church and Cemetery,** which was active from the early 1700s until the mid-1900s. About 80% of the headstones are illegible. The earliest legible stone belongs to Mary Elizabeth Hinkle, who died in 1742. As was tradition at the time, bodies were buried with their heads to the east so they would arise facing the sun on Resurrection day. Two can't-miss graves here: The first, to the left of the entrance, honors four Revolutionary War patriots ambushed—"betrayed," the stone notes—by British soldiers. The second stone, deeper into the cemetery and resembling a table, is the grave of Christopher Ludwig, baker general of the Continental Army. His gingerbread was one of Washington's favorite treats.

Pass Little Jimmie's Bakery Café, 6669 Germantown Ave., located in the former Beggarstown School, a one-room schoolhouse built in 1740.

Cross Germantown Avenue at East Hortter Street, and then turn around. Pass West Phil-Ellena Street. In the 1840s, land speculator and druggist George Carpenter built a mansion here and named it Phil-Ellena, meaning "for the love of Ellen," to honor his wife.

Turn left on Westview Street, then right onto Cresheim Road. Stop at Pelham Road. This part of the walk takes you into a more residential stretch where amazing architecture is almost de rigueur. Styles include Italianate, Georgian, Queen Anne, Norman, Classical, Tudor, Jacobean, and Flemish. "Young architects, who later achieved great distinction, designed these stately homes for newly wealthy Philadelphia businessmen and their families," notes the West Mt. Airy Neighbors group.

Turn left on Pelham Road. Pelham was a streetcar suburb, within city limits, a short trip to downtown by streetcar that still seemed far from the hustle and bustle. The Robert M. Hogue home, 100 Pelham Road, was designed for Hogue in the 1890s by the Boyd brothers, respected architects at the time, for $20,000.

Continue on Pelham Road. The castlelike building at 232 Pelham Road is a 7,600-square-foot home with six bedrooms and five baths, built in 1897 for William M. P. Braun. Note the expansive lawn. Perhaps Braun wasn't worried about tending to it because his father developed lawn-mowing technologies that are still used today.

At Emlen Street, turn right. The Emlen Arms, 6723 Emlen St., is now a public housing complex. Neighboring Pelham Court Apartments, 6803–09 Emlen St., has an

open-air entrance that demands a second look. Follow the road as it bears right.
❿ Commodore Barry Club, also known as the Philadelphia Irish Center, is housed in what was originally the Pelham Auto Club, built in 1905. The Commodore John Barry USN Society purchased the building in 1958. The center promotes Irish culture through music and dance lessons, lectures, and parties. Membership is $25 per year, no Irish heritage required.

The Carpenter Lane regional rail station on the left allows some to end this walk here. To continue, turn left on Carpenter Lane. Pass the Episcopal Church of the Annunciation of the Blessed Virgin Mary, 324 Carpenter Lane, and a home that will remind *Lord of the Rings* fans of Bilbo and Frodo's place in the Shire. Continue on Carpenter Lane, crossing Lincoln Drive. Big Blue Marble Bookstore, 551 Carpenter Lane, is an independently owned shop and hub of community life with a café inside. Nearby is **⓫ Weavers Way Co-Op.** Established in 1973, the co-op moved to this corner in 1974 and has since expanded, now counting more than 5,000 households as members. Local favorite High Point Cafe sits at 602 Carpenter Lane.

Look across Carpenter Lane at **⓬ Charles Wolcott Henry School.** Henry was a descendant of a signer of the Declaration of Independence and served on the Fairmount Park Commission, the Philadelphia City Council, and the leadership team of the Young Men's Christian Association of Germantown. When he died in 1903 at age 51, *The Public Ledger* wrote that "the death of a man like Charles W. Henry in the fullness of his activities is a public calamity. He was one of those broadminded and forceful citizens who do not weary nor despair, but keep on doing." Henry's wife, Sallie B. Houston, was the daughter of Henry H. Houston, for whom the first school on this walk was named.

Turn right on Greene Street, walking slightly uphill then moving downhill after Mount Pleasant Road to reach Carpenter's Woods. "This is a corner of heaven here," poet Gerald Stern wrote, adding he enjoyed lying "for hours with my eyes closed listening to the great sounds." While this walk does not include traversing these woods, it's worth getting lost in its dense, fairy-tale greenery. Bird-watchers will be particularly pleased.

Continue on Greene Street. At West Mount Airy Avenue, turn right. Walk to McCallum Street and turn left. (At some points, neighboring bushes almost completely cover the sidewalk.) Make a quick right onto Allens Lane and then a left onto Elbow Lane to enter French Village, a collection of Gothic-style homes built by George Woodward and his father-in-law, Henry H. Houston. These houses are privately owned today but were rentals in Woodward's time. In *Intimate Bicycle Tours of Philadelphia,* author Patricia Vance describes Woodward as a bit of an eccentric: "He always wore golf knickers and knee socks . . . He used kerosene lamps to read and refused to drive cars with gas engines." The development has some of Woodward's trademarks, including slate sidewalks.

Turn right on McCallum Street. A sign at the driveway across the street says 615/ PRIVATE/CLOSED. Cross the street and walk a few steps down the driveway to reach the public entry to **⓭ Wissahickon Valley Park.** Turn right at the trailhead.

Wissahickon Valley has 50 miles of trails. (The Friends of the Wissahickon offers printable trail maps online.) Follow the path to the right, walking under the McCallum Street Bridge. Continue to a slight clearing. At left is a bridge over Cresheim Creek. On your right is a trail guide. Next to the sign on the left is a singletrack path. Take this trail to exit the park. It's a rocky walk, passing under arched tree branches and through fallen but split trees.

At the end of the trail are the remains of Buttercup Cottage, built in the early 1800s and named after the flowers that filled the grounds. In the late 1800s, two Protestant nuns ran a summer rental property for working girls—young women who took seasonal jobs cleaning cottages here. Rent in 1896 was $1/week.

Exit the park on Emlen Street. Turn right and walk up the hill. At Allens Lane, turn left to return to the starting point.

(continued on next page)

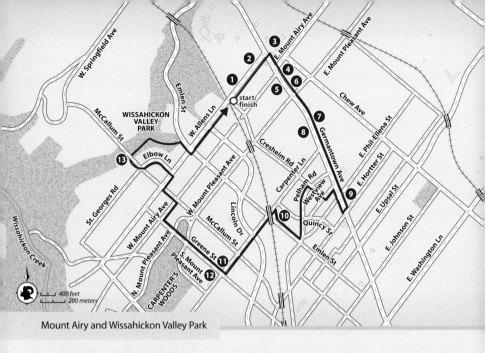

Mount Airy and Wissahickon Valley Park

Points of Interest

1 Henry H. Houston Elementary School 135 W. Allens Lane

2 Radha Krishna Temple 41 W. Allens Lane, 215-247-4825, iskconphiladelphia.com

3 Lutheran Theological Seminary of Philadelphia 7301 Germantown Ave., 215-248-4616, ltsp.edu

4 Quintessence Theatre Group (formerly The Sedgwick Theater) 7137 Germantown Ave., 215-987-4450, quintessencetheatre.org

5 Earth Bread + Brewery 7136 Germantown Ave., 215-242-6666, earthbreadbrewery.com

6 Philadelphia Interfaith Hospitality Network 7047 Germantown Ave., 215-247-4663, philashelter.org

7 Lovett Memorial Library 6945 Germantown Ave. For more information, contact the Free Library of Philadelphia: 215-686-5322, freelibrary.org.

8 Germantown Home 6950 Germantown Ave., 215-848-3306, germantownhome.org

9 St. Michael's Lutheran Church 6671 Germantown Ave., 215-848-0199, stmichaelsgermantown.org

10 Commodore Barry Club (Philadelphia Irish Center) 6815 Emlen St., 215-843-8051, theirishcenter.com

11 Weavers Way Co-op 559 Carpenter Lane, 215-843-2350, weaversway.coop

12 Charles Wolcott Henry School 601–645 Carpenter Lane

13 Wissahickon Valley Park McCallum Street between West Mermaid Lane and West Allens Lane, 215-247-0417, fow.org

Boathouse Row is a collection of buildings housing the Schuylkill Navy clubs.

30 Fairmount Park: Two Tours of One of the World's Largest Park Systems

East Fairmount Park

BOUNDARIES: Waterworks Dr., Mount Pleasant Dr., Schuylkill River, N. 33rd St.
DISTANCE: 3.8 miles
DIFFICULTY: Moderate, with some changes in altitude
PARKING: Street parking is available on side roads.
PUBLIC TRANSIT: SEPTA bus routes include the 25, 43, 89, and MFL.

Fairmount Park is the overarching name for the city's park system, composed of 63 parks and more than 9,000 acres of greenery. This walk focuses on the continuous portion of the park that most Philadelphians consider the "real" Fairmount Park.

In 2016, the website SquareFoot decided to compare the size of this one section of Philadelphia's premier municipal park with Manhattan's often-vaunted Central Park. The results were embarrassing—for New York, that is. This single segment of Philadelphia's park system tops 4,000 acres, making it almost five times as large as Central Park, which covers 843 acres.

There are many guides exploring the park system. The first tour below explores the eastern segment of the park; the second, the western part. While the distance traveled in each may seem significant, the written tours are actually shorter, as there are stretches that simply feature nature.

At the end of the East Fairmount Park walk, it's easy to reach the start of the West Fairmount Park tour.

Walk Description

Begin at ❶ **Fairmount Water Works,** the nation's first municipal water-treatment center, tucked behind the Philadelphia Museum of Art. Access the entrance via Kelly Drive, that long road on the east side of the Schuylkill River. The water part of this complex, made up of a dam, pump house, and reservoir, was built between 1819 and 1822 as a way to ensure clean drinking water. The accompanying buildings—including the superintendent's house and the pavilions—are considered some of the city's loveliest architecture. The whole project was such a marvel that it was a popular tourist draw in the 1800s. Only Niagara Falls drew more visitors.

The Fairmount Water Works Interpretive Center is an interactive museum that allows visitors to create a rainstorm and then follow the water as it drains. The restaurant here is a special event space. Even without an invite, you can wander among the buildings to enjoy the fabulous view. At night, look for Edgar Allan Poe's ghost, reportedly seen walking near the water. Poe's ghost has a busy haunting schedule, as he's also been spotted at the Spring Garden home where he wrote part of "The Raven" and in multiple locations in Maryland and Virginia.

Exit the property by walking toward Kelly Drive. Near the road is the Garden of Heroes, funded by a Philadelphia National Guard general who wished to honor Europeans, including Marquis de Lafayette of France, Poland's General Casimir Pulaski, General Friedrich von Steuben of Prussia, and General Richard Montgomery of Britain, who "threw themselves into the cause of emancipating the colonies from the yoke of British tyranny."

Turn left on Kelly Drive. ❷ **Boathouse Row** is the collective name for the boating clubs here, each a member of the Schuylkill Navy, the oldest amateur athletic governing body in the country. The Schuylkill Navy is nationally known for its major rowing competitions, including the Aberdeen Dad Vail Regatta, the Head of the Schuylkill, and the Stotesbury Cup Regatta. Many Olympic athletes have trained on the river, including the man for whom Kelly Drive is named, John B. Kelly Jr., a four-time Olympian in the single scull who brought home a bronze medal after the 1956 games in Australia. Kelly was the brother of actress Grace Kelly. Their father, John B. Kelly Sr., was also an accomplished rower, winning three gold medals in two Olympic Games. While the road is named for his son, there's a statue of Kelly Sr. along the river near the viewing stands.

Continue to follow the path along the river. The sculpture *Thorfinn Karlsefni* remembers a Viking believed to have come to America in 1004. *Stone Age in America* depicts an American Indian woman trying to protect her child from attack. The trail ahead splits in two. Following either path is fine as they reconnect later.

The plaza-type area with statues is the central terrace of the Ellen Phillips Samuel Memorial sculpture garden. The bronze work at center is *The Spirit of Enterprise.*

Continue along the river, passing Brewery Hill Drive. *Playing Angels* features three winged figures dancing to unheard music.

This walk leaves the river on Fountain Green Drive. But to see the statue of John B. Kelly Sr. and the race-viewing stands, continue on the path about 0.5 mile, and then double back to this point.

On Fountain Green Drive, a sign says THE BOXERS' TRAIL. Forget Rocky; this path has been used by real boxers past and present for training. Muhammad Ali came here looking for Joe Frazier before their famous bout.

Continue to Mount Pleasant Drive. Turn left and follow the road to ❸ **Mount Pleasant Mansion,** an 18th-century Georgian home built by Captain John Macpherson, who made his living as a privateer, which is a nice way of saying pirate. He called this property Clunie, the name of his family's seat in Scotland. John Adams once said that Macpherson had "an arm twice shot off." Benedict Arnold also owned this house, but he never lived here, as he fled the country after being charged with treason.

Leaving the property, continue on Mount Pleasant Drive until it ends, and then turn right onto Reservoir Drive. Bear left as the road winds, and then make a definitive right on an extension of Reservoir Drive to visit ❹ **Smith Memorial Playground and Playhouse.** The 16,000-square-foot play mansion, open to all, features a 44-foot wooden slide, a giant seesaw, and other delights for the 10-and-under crowd.

The Richard and Sarah Smith Trust created this 6.5-acre play area, including the house that was never lived in, in the late 1880s to honor their son, Stansfield, who died at age 40. The Smiths lived in North Philadelphia, and the family fortune came from the typesetting business.

Leave Smith Playground and follow the driveway back to Reservoir Drive. Turn right. ❺ **Sedgley Woods Historic Disc Golf Course** is free to the public; BYOF (bring your own Frisbee).

Walk to North 33rd Street. Turn right. The 33rd Street Bridge is covered with black-and-white scenes paying homage to the surrounding neighborhoods, including Brewerytown and Strawberry Mansion. Look for John Coltrane, the late jazz great who lived nearby.

Continue to Girard Avenue. Turn left to return downtown. Turn right to pick up the West Fairmount Park walk, which begins a few blocks away at Lansdowne Drive.

The Please Touch Museum is one of the country's finest children's museums. It's housed in a building that was constructed for the 1876 centennial celebration.

West Fairmount Park

BOUNDARIES: Girard Ave., Montgomery Dr., Lansdowne Dr., States Dr.
DISTANCE: 3.9 miles
DIFFICULTY: Moderate, with some changes in elevation
PARKING: There are multiple pay lots near the zoo.
PUBLIC TRANSIT: SEPTA bus routes include the 5, 15, 15B, and MFL.

In 1876, Philadelphia hosted the first World's Fair in the United States, also called the Centennial International Exposition in honor of the nation's 100th birthday. More than 10 million people visited during the six-month event. Several of the buildings from that event still stand, the most notable of which is now the home of the Please Touch Museum, perhaps the nation's best children's museum.

Walk Description

Start at ❶ **The Philadelphia Zoo.** The nation's first zoo was established by charter in 1859, but the Civil War postponed its opening for 15 years. Admission was 25 cents for adults and 10 cents for children, which held for the next 50 years. When it opened, the zoo had its own wharf so visitors could arrive by steamboat.

Today, the 42-acre property is home to more than 1,300 animals, including two red pandas born in 2015 named Betsy and Benjamin. The zoo had more than 1.35 million visitors that year. Just inside the main gates is The Solitude, a home designed and built by William Penn's grandson. George Washington once dined here.

From the zoo entrance, cross North 34th Street, and turn left (north) on North 34th Street (which turns into Lansdowne Drive), taking the sidewalk under the bridge decorated with mosaics of giraffe necks. Just past School of the Future (the large white building on the left), Lansdowne Drive splits; turn right.

At the traffic circle, take the second right to walk under the Smith Civil War Memorial Arch. Built between 1897 and 1912, the arch honors many of the military leaders involved in the Civil War, including McClellan, Meade, Reynolds, and Porter. It was financed by Richard Smith, who, with wife Sarah, also endowed Smith Playground. There's a tiny statue of Smith, in his typesetter's apron, high on the memorial.

Passing through the arch, look left, toward the street outside the park gate, to see some of the incredible homes that flank the property. Many of these are now run-down, but the architecture hints at what was.

Now look right. The ❷ **Please Touch Museum** is housed in Memorial Hall, once part of the Centennial Exposition. The building cost $1.5 million to complete, an incredible amount for 1876. It was built without wood to be fireproof. The museum has 25,000 toys. Popular exhibits include the Alice in Wonderland area and the grocery store. The piano from the movie *Big* is here, and young guests are invited to jump on the keys. The Woodside Park Dentzel Carousel was built in the early 1900s and includes more than 50 hand-carved animals, with a few cats, pigs, goats, and rabbits mixed in with the horses.

Continue on what is now Avenue of the Republic. Cross Belmont Avenue. At the center of the circle at the end of Avenue of the Republic is the ❸ **Catholic Total Abstinence Union Fountain.** Also commissioned for the Centennial Exposition, the fountain was designed by a German sculptor, which is only relevant as one part of the fountain was meant to symbolize "the Irish Catholic love of patriotism and liberty." Moses is in the center, holding the Ten Commandments. Medallions around the base represent high-profile Catholics from the Revolutionary War, including the Marquis de Lafayette. All four larger-than-life statues outside the basin had working water fountains when the monument was unveiled.

Beyond the fountain is ❹ **Mann Center for the Performing Arts,** which originally opened in 1935 as Robin Hood Dell Concerts, as some locals still refer to it. It was renamed to honor businessman and supporter Frederic R. Mann. Originally built to be the summer performing space of the Philadelphia Orchestra, it now features performers in all musical genres.

Exit the circle via States Drive, the unmarked road to the right. Follow it to Belmont Avenue. The Ohio House, 4700 States Drive, will be to your left. It is the only other building remaining from the Centennial Exhibition.

Turn left onto Belmont Avenue, then right onto Montgomery Drive. At Belmont Mansion Drive, turn right. This becomes Horticultural Drive and leads to the

The Philadelphia Zoo, the nation's first, averages more than one million visitors each year.

⑤ Fairmount Park Horticulture Center, which includes an arboretum, a demonstration garden, a flower bed, a vegetable garden, a reflecting pool, a pavilion, and a butterfly garden. Picnics are popular here, but note that permits are required for large groups.

Follow the road off to the left, and check out *The Journeyer,* a statue commissioned for the bicentennial celebration. There's something lovable about the tall wanderer carrying a walking stick. Across from him are a few of the Horticulture Center's greenhouses.

Continue following the road to **⑥ Shofuso Japanese House and Garden.** Originally on display on the grounds of New York's Museum of Modern Art, this small building is a reconstruction of a 17th-century scholar's home and teahouse. The garden has a pool and cherry blossoms. Shofuso hosts an annual Cherry Blossom Festival, as its collection of the trees rivals Washington, DC's.

Shofuso also features tea ceremonies performed by members of the Urasenke tea school, which is based in Kyoto, Japan. The tea ceremony is a 450-year-old ceremony considered an art form. Shofuso's ceremonies require advance registration. Other programming includes lessons in Japanese flower-arranging and mask-making workshops.

Turn left (east) on Lansdowne Drive, passing the rear of the Please Touch Museum. At the T intersection, turn right, continuing on this extension of Lansdowne Drive to return to the Philadelphia Zoo, ending your walk.

(continued on next page)

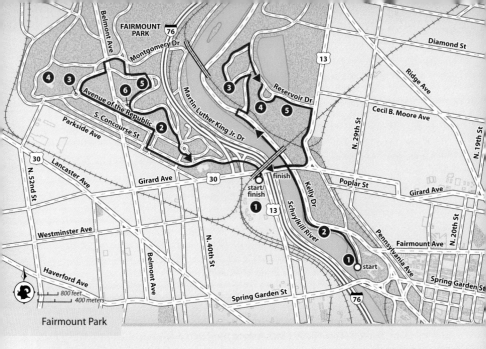

Points of Interest

East Fairmount Park

1 **Fairmount Water Works** 640 Waterworks Dr., 215-685-0723, fairmountwaterworks.org

2 **Boathouse Row** 1 Boathouse Row, 215-685-3936, boathouserow.org

3 **Mount Pleasant Mansion** Mount Pleasant Drive, 215-685-0274, parkcharms.org

4 **Smith Memorial Playground and Playhouse** 3500 Reservoir Drive, 215-765-4325, smithplayground.org

5 **Sedgley Woods Historic Disc Golf Course** N. 33rd and Oxford Sts., sedgleywoods.com

West Fairmount Park

1 **The Philadelphia Zoo** 3400 W. Girard Ave., 215-243-1100, philadelphiazoo.org

2 **Please Touch Museum** 4231 Avenue of the Republic, 215-581-3181, pleasetouchmuseum.org

3 **Catholic Total Abstinence Union Fountain** Avenue of the Republic and States Street

4 **Mann Center for the Performing Arts** 5201 Parkside Ave., 215-546-7900, manncenter.org

5 **Fairmount Park Horticulture Center** 100 North Horticultural Drive, 215-685-0096, phila.gov

6 **Shofuso Japanese House and Garden** Lansdowne Drive and Horticultural Drive, japanesehouse.org

Appendix 1: Walks by Theme

Architectural Tours

Arts and Culture

Family Fun

South Broad Street II: From the Avenue of the Arts to Franklin Delano Roosevelt Park (Walk 11)
Market Street East: The Gayborhood and Reading Terminal Market (Walk 12)
Along the Delaware River (Walk 15)
Old City (Walk 16)
Northern Liberties (Walk 18)
The River Wards: Kensington and Fishtown (Walk 19)
Fairmount, the Neighborhood (Walk 20)
South Philadelphia I (Walk 23)
West Philadelphia I: University City, The Woodlands, and Clark Park (Walk 25)
Manayunk (Walk 27)
Mount Airy and Wissahickon Valley Park (Walk 29)
Fairmount Park (Walk 30)

Green Spaces

The Museum District: From Love Park to the *Rocky* Steps (Walk 4)
The Museum District: From the Art Museum to the Cathedral (Walk 5)
Rittenhouse Square (Walk 6)
Fitler Square and the Schuylkill River (Walk 7)
South Broad Street II: From the Avenue of the Arts to Franklin Delano Roosevelt Park (Walk 11)
Along the Delaware River (Walk 15)
Old City (Walk 16)
South Philadelphia II (Walk 24)
West Philadelphia I: University City, The Woodlands, and Clark Park (Walk 25)
Manayunk (Walk 27)
Germantown (Walk 28)
Mount Airy and Wissahickon Valley Park (Walk 29)
Fairmount Park (Walk 30)

History

Independence National Park (Walk 1)
African American Philadelphia (Walk 3)
South Broad Street II: From the Avenue of the Arts to Franklin Delano Roosevelt Park (Walk 11)
Market Street East: The Gayborhood and Reading Terminal Market (Walk 12)
Old City (Walk 16)
Society Hill (Walk 17)
Antique Row, Jewelers Row, and Rittenhouse Row (Walk 21)
Headhouse Square, Fabric Row, and South Street (Walk 22)
Germantown (Walk 28)

Appendix 2: Points of Interest

Cemeteries

Christ Church Burial Ground Arch and N. Fifth Sts. (Walk 1)

Hood Cemetery 4901 Germantown Ave., hoodcemetery.org (Walk 28)

Palmer Cemetery 1499 E. Palmer St., palmercemeteryfishtown.com (Walk 19)

Upper Burying Ground 6309 Germantown Ave., ushistory.org/Germantown (Walk 28)

Educational Institutions and Libraries

The Art Institute of Philadelphia 1622 Chestnut St., 800-275-2474, artinstitutes.edu/Philadelphia (Walk 13)

Charles Wolcott Henry School 601–645 Carpenter Lane (Walk 29)

Drexel University Westphal College of Media Arts & Design 3501 Market St., 215-895-1834 (visitor center/tours), drexel.edu/westphal (Walk 26)

Free Library of Philadelphia 1901 Vine St., 215-686-5322, freelibrary.org (Walk 5)

Girard College 2101 S. College Ave., 215-787-2600, girardcollege.edu (Walk 20)

Henry H. Houston Elementary School 135 W. Allens Lane (Walk 29)

Lovett Memorial Library 6945 Germantown Ave. For more information, contact the Free Library of Philadelphia: 215-686-5322, freelibrary.org. (Walk 29)

Lutheran Theological Seminary of Philadelphia 7301 Germantown Ave., 215-248-4616, ltsp.edu (Walk 29)

Meredith Elementary School 725 S. Fifth St. (Walk 24)

Moore College of Art & Design 1916 Race St., 215-965-4000, moore.edu (Walk 4)

Pennsylvania Academy of the Fine Arts 118–128 N. Broad St., 215-972-7600, pafa.org (Walk 8)

The Philadelphia School 2503 Lombard St., 215-545-5323, tpschool.org (Walk 7)

Samuel S. Fleisher Art Memorial 719 Catharine St., 215-922-3456, fleisher.org (Walk 23)

Settlement Music School 416 Queen St., 215-320-2601, settlementmusic.org (Walk 22)

South Philadelphia High School 2101 S. Broad St. (Walk 10)

University of Pennsylvania 215-898-5000, upenn.edu (Walk 25)

University of Pennsylvania Fisher Fine Arts Library 220 S. 34th St., 215-898-8325, library.upenn.edu/finearts (Walk 26)

University of the Sciences 600 S. 43rd St., 215-596-8800, usciences.edu (Walk 25)

Entertainment, Nightlife, and Performing Arts

Academy of Music 240 S. Broad St., 215-893-1999, www.kimmelcenter.org (Walk 11)

Arden Theatre Company 40 N. Second St., 215-922-8900, ardentheatre.org (Walk 16)

Blue Cross RiverRink 101 S. Columbus Blvd., 215-925-7465, delawareriverwaterfront.com (Walk 15)

Bob & Barbara's Lounge 1509 South St., 215-545-4511, bobandbarbaras.com (Walk 22)

Craftsman Row Saloon 112 S. Eighth St., 215-923-0123, craftsmanrowsaloon.com (Walk 21)

Curtis Institute of Music 1726 Locust St., 215-893-5252, curtis.edu (Walk 6)

The Forrest Theatre 1114 Walnut St., 215-923-1515, forrest-theatre.com (Walk 21)

FringeArts 140 N. Columbus Blvd., 215-413-9006, fringearts.com (Walk 15)

Kimmel Center for the Performing Arts 300 S. Broad St., 215-670-2300, www.kimmelcenter.org (Walk 11)

Mann Center for the Performing Arts 5201 Parkside Ave., 215-546-7900, manncenter.org (Walk 30)

New Freedom Theatre 1346 N. Broad St., 215-765-2793, freedomtheatre.org (Walk 9)

North Bowl 909 N. Second St., 215-238-2695, northbowlphilly.com (Walk 18)

Painted Bride Art Center 230 Vine St., 215-925-9914, paintedbride.org (Walk 16)

Philadelphia Clef Club of Jazz and Performing Arts 738 S. Broad St., 215-893-9912, clefclubofjazz.org (Walk 11)

Philadelphia Metropolitan Opera House 858 N. Broad St. (Walk 8)

Plays and Players 1714 Delancey Place, 215-735-0630, playsandplayers.org (Walk 6)

Prince Theater 1412 Chestnut St., 215-422-4580, princetheater.org (Walk 13)

Quintessence Theatre Group (formerly The Sedgwick Theater) 7137 Germantown Ave., 215-987-4450, quintessencetheatre.org (Walk 29)

SugarHouse Casino 1001 N. Delaware Ave., sugarhousecasino.com (Walk 19)

Symphony House/Suzanne Roberts Theatre 440 S. Broad St., 215-985-1400, philadelphiatheatrecompany.org (Walk 11)

Temple Performing Arts Center 1837 N. Broad St., 215-204-9860, templeperformingartscenter.org (Walk 9)

Theatre of Living Arts 334 South St., 215-922-1011, venue.tlaphilly.com (Walk 22)

Uptown Theater (now closed) 2240–2248 N. Broad St. (Walk 9)

Venice Island Performing Arts and Recreation Center 7 Lock St., 215-482-9565, manayunk.com/about/dsr/veniceisland.html (Walk 27)

Walnut Street Theatre 825 Walnut St., 215-574-3550, walnuttheatre.org (Walk 21)

Wilma Theater 265 S. Broad St., 215-893-9456, wilmatheater.org (Walk 10)

The Yachtsman 1444 Frankford Ave., 267-909-8740, yachtsmanbar.com (Walk 19)

Food and Drink

9th Street Italian Market 215-278-2903, italianmarketphilly.org (Walk 23)

Bonner's Irish Pub 120 S. 23rd St., 215-567-5748 (Walk 7)

The Cambridge 1508 South St., 267-455-0647, cambridgeonsouth.com (Walk 22)

Capriccio at Café Cret N. 16th St. and Benjamin Franklin Pkwy., 215-735-9797, capricciocafe.com (Walk 5)

City Tavern 138 S. Second St., 215-413-1443, citytavern.com (Walk 17)

Claudio's Specialty Foods 924 S. Ninth St., 215-627-1873, claudiofood.com (Walk 23)

Dante & Luigi's 762 S. 10th St., 215-922-9501, danteandluigis.com (Walk 23)

David's Mai Lai Wah 1001 Race St., 215-627-2610 (Walk 2)

Di Bruno Bros. 930 S. Ninth St., 215-922-2876, dibruno.com (Walk 23)

Dim Sum Garden 1020 Race St., 215-873-0258, dimsumgardenphilly.com (Walk 2)

Earth Bread + Brewery 7136 Germantown Ave., 215-242-6666, earthbreadbrewery.com (Walk 29)

Essene Market 719 S. Fourth St., 215-922-1146, essenemarket.com (Walk 22)

Famous 4th Street Delicatessen 700 S. Fourth St., 215-922-3274, famous4thstreetdelicatessen.com (Walk 22)

Federal Donuts 701 N. Seventh St., 267-928-3893, federaldonuts.com (Walk 18)

Fiorella's Sausage 817 Christian St., 215-922-0506 (Walk 24)

Fishtown Tavern 1301 Frankford Ave., 267-687-8406, fishtowntavern.com (Walk 19)

Franklin Fountain 116 Market St., 215-627-1899, franklinfountain.com (Walk 3)

Geno's Steaks 1219 S. Ninth St., 215-389-0659, genosteaks.com (Walk 23)

Green Line Cafe 4426 Locust St., 215-822-0799, greenlinecafe.com (Walk 26)

Han Dynasty 123 Chestnut St., 215-922-1888, handynasty.net/oldcity (Walk 16)

Heffe 1431 Frankford Ave., 215-423-2309, heffetacos.com (Walk 19)

Honey's Sit 'n Eat 800 N. Fourth St., 215-925-1150, honeyssitneat.com (Walk 18)

Isgro 1009 Christian St., 215-923-3092, bestcannoli.com (Walk 23)

Jim's Steaks 400 South St., 215-928-1911, jimsouthstreet.com (Walk 22)

John Lerro Candy 2434 S. Broad St., 215-336-0411 (Walk 11)

Johnny Brenda's 1201 Frankford Ave., 215-739-9684, johnnybrendas.com (Walk 19)

John's Water Ice 701 Christian St., 215-925-6955, johnswaterice.com (Walk 23)

Liberties Walk 1040 N. American St. (Walk 18)

Lorenzo and Sons Pizza 305 South St., 215-800-1942, lorenzoandsons.com (Walk 22)

Manayunk Brewing Company 4120 Main St., 215-482-8220, manayunkbrewery.com (Walk 27)

Marchiano's Bakery 4653 Umbria St., 215-483-8585, marchianosbakery.com (Walk 27)

Marra's Italian Restaurant 1734 E. Passyunk Ave., 215-463-9249, marrasone.com (Walk 23)

McGillin's Olde Ale House 1310 Drury St., 215-735-5562, mcgillins.com (Walk 12)

Melrose Diner 1501 Snyder Ave., 215-467-6644, themelrosedinerandbakery.com (Walk 11)

Metropolitan Bakery 262 S. 19th St., 215-545-6655, metropolitanbakery.com (Walk 6)

Moshulu 401 S. Columbus Blvd., 215-923-2500, moshulu.com (Walk 15)

Old Original Bookbinder's (now The Olde Bar) 125 Walnut St., 215-253-3777, theoldebar.com (Walk 17)

Paddy's Pub Old City 228 Race St., 215-627-3532, paddyspuboldcity.com (Walk 16)

Parc 227 S. 18th St., 215-545-2262, parc-restaurant.com (Walk 6)

Pat's King of Steaks 1237 E. Passyunk Ave., 215-468-1546, patskingofsteaks.com (Walk 23)

Pizza Brain 2313 Frankford Ave., 215-291-2965, pizzabrain.org (Walk 19)

Ralph's Italian Restaurant 760 S. Ninth St., 215-627-6011, ralphsrestaurant.com (Walk 23)

Rouge 205 S. 18th St., 215-732-6622, rouge98.com (Walk 6)

Sam's Morning Glory Diner 735 S. 10th St., 215-413-3999, themorningglorydiner.com (Walk 23)

Sarcone's Deli 734 S. Ninth St., 215-922-1717, sarconesdeli.com (Walk 23)

The Schmidt's Commons 1001 N. Second St., 215-825-7552, theschmidtscommons.com (Walk 18)

Silk City Diner, Bar & Lounge 435 Spring Garden St., 215-592-8838, silkcityphilly.com (Walk 18)

Sorrentino's Deli and Grocery 4361 Cresson St., 215-487-0559 (Walk 27)

Standard Tap 901 N. Second St., 215-238-0630, standardtap.com (Walk 18)

Tavern on Camac 243 S. Camac St., 215-545-0900, tavernoncamac.com (Walk 12)

Tea Dó 132 N. 10th St., 215-923-8088, tea-do.com (Walk 2)

Tria 2227 Pine St., 215-309-2245, triaphilly.com (Walk 7)

U.S. Hotel Bar & Grill 4439 Main St., 215-483-9222 (Walk 27)

Woody's 202 S. 13th St., 215-545-1893, woodysbar.com (Walk 12)

Yakitori Boy 211 N. 11th St., 215-923-8088, yakitoriboy.com (Walk 2)

Yards Brewing Company 901 N. Delaware Ave., 215-634-2600, yardsbrewing.com (Walk 19)

Historical Landmarks, Monuments, and Memorials

23rd Street Armory 22 S. 23rd St., 215-564-1488, 23rdstreetarmory.org (Walk 7)

Battleship New Jersey 62 Battleship Place, 856-966-1652, battleshipnewjersey.org (Walk 15)

Betsy Ross House 239 Arch St., 215-686-1252, historicphiladelphia.org/betsy-ross-house /what-to-see (Walks 1 and 3)

Bishop White House 309 Walnut St., 215-965-2305, nps.gov/inde (Walk 17)

The Bourse 111 S. Independence Mall E., 215-625-0300, tinyurl.com/philadelphiabourse (Walk 16)

Carpenters' Hall 320 Chestnut St., 215-925-0167, carpentershall.org (Walk 1)

Chinatown Friendship Gate N. 10th and Arch Sts. For more information, contact the Chinatown Development Corporation, 215-922-2156, chinatown-pcdc.org. (Walk 2)

City Hall 1401 John F. Kennedy Blvd., 215-686-1776, phila.gov (Walks 8 and 13)

Cliveden 6401 Germantown Ave., 215-848-1777, cliveden.org (Walk 28)

Declaration House 599 S. Seventh St., 215-965-2305, nps.gov/inde (Walk 12)

Eastern State Penitentiary 2027 Fairmount Ave., 215-236-3300, easternstate.org (Walk 20)

Edgar Allan Poe National Historic Site 532 N. Seventh St., 215-965-2305, nps.gov/edal (Walk 18)

Elfreth's Alley Off N. Second St. between Arch and Race Sts., 215-627-8680 (museum house), elfrethsalley.org (Walks 1 and 16)

Fairmount Water Works 640 Waterworks Dr., 215-685-0723, fairmountwaterworks.org (Walk 30)

First Bank of the United States 116 S. Third St., 215-965-2305, nps.gov/inde (Walk 17)

Former headquarters of the Philadelphia Female Anti-Slavery Society (now the United States Mint) 151 N. Independence Mall E., 215-408-0112, usmint.com (Walk 3)

Former home of Cyrus Bustill 210 Arch St. (not open to the public) (Walk 3)

Former Royal Theater 1536 South St. (Walk 22)

Former site of Pennsylvania Hall (now the headquarters of WHYY) 150 N. Sixth St., 215-351-1200, whyy.org (Walk 3)

Franklin Field 235 S. 33rd St., 215-898-6151, facilities.upenn.edu/maps/locations /franklin-field (Walk 25)

German Society of Pennsylvania 611 Spring Garden St. (Walk 18)

Germantown White House (Deshler-Morris House) 5442 Germantown Ave., 215-965-2305, nps.gov/inde (Walk 28)

Grumblethorpe 5267 Germantown Ave., 215-843-4820, philalandmarks.org /grumblethorpe (Walk 28)

Headhouse Square and The Shambles Pine and S. Second Sts., southstreet.com (Walk 22)

Historic Germantown Visitor Center 5501 Germantown Ave., 215-844-0514, germantownhistory.org (Walk 28)

Independence Hall 520 Chestnut St., 215-965-2305, nps.gov/inde (Walk 1)

Integrity Trust Bank 542 N. Fourth St. (Walk 18)

The Irish Memorial 100 S. Front St., irishmemorial.org (Walk 24)

Johnson House Historic Site 6306 Germantown Ave., 215-438-1768, johnsonhouse.org (Walk 28)

Liberty Bell Center S. Sixth and Market Sts., 215-965-2305, nps.gov/inde (Walks 1 and 3)

Loudoun Mansion 4450 Germantown Ave., ushistory.org/Germantown (Walk 28)

A Man Full of Trouble Tavern 125 Spruce St. (Walk 17)

Merchants' Exchange Building 143 S. Third St., 215-965-2305, nps.gov/inde (Walk 17)

Philadelphia Fire Department's Engine Company 12 4447 Main St. (Walk 27)

Philadelphia Korean War Memorial Penn's Landing, between Dock and Spruce Sts. (Walks 3 and 24)

Philadelphia Navy Yard 4747 S. Broad St., 215-551-0251, navyyard.org (Walk 10)

Physick House 321 S. Fourth St., 215-925-7866, philalandmarks.org (Walk 17)

The Powel House 244 S. Third St., 215-627-0364, philalandmarks.org/powel-house (Walk 17)

The President's House 524–30 Market St., 800-537-7676, phlvisitorcenter.com (Walk 3)

Thaddeus Kosciuszko National Memorial 301 Pine St., 215-597-8787, nps.gov/thko (Walk 17)

The Union League of Philadelphia 140 S. Broad St., 215-563-6500, unionleague.org (Walk 11)

USS *Becuna* Columbus Blvd. and Market St., 215-928-8807, delawareriverwaterfront.com (Walk 15)

Vietnam Veterans Memorial Columbus Blvd. and Spruce St. (Walk 24)

Wyck House 6026 Germantown Ave., 215-848-1690, wyck.org (Walk 28)

Hotels

Former Bellevue-Stratford Hotel (now The Bellevue Hotel) 200 S. Broad St., 215-893-1234, bellevuephiladelphia.com (Walk 21)

Loews Philadelphia Hotel 1200 Market St., 215-627-1200, loewshotels.com (Walk 12)

The Rittenhouse 201 W. Rittenhouse Square, 800-635-1042, rittenhousehotel.com (Walk 6)

Museums

Academy of Natural Sciences of Drexel University 1900 Benjamin Franklin Pkwy., 215-299-1000, ansp.org (Walk 4)

African American Museum 701 Arch St., 215-574-0380, aampmuseum.org (Walk 3)

American Philosophical Society 104 S. Fifth St., 215-440-3400, amphilsoc.org (Walk 16)

American Swedish Historical Museum 1900 Pattison Ave., 215-389-1776, americanswedish.org (Walk 11)

Athenaeum of Philadelphia 219 S. Sixth St., 215-925-2688, philaathenaeum.org (Walk 3)

Barnes Foundation 2025 Benjamin Franklin Parkway, 215-278-7000, barnesfoundation.org (Walk 5)

Benjamin Franklin Museum and Franklin Court 317 Chestnut St., 267-514-1522, nps.gov/inde (Walk 1)

The Center for Art in Wood 141 N. Third St., 215-923-8000, centerforartinwood.org (Walk 16)

Ebenezer Maxwell Mansion 200 W. Tulpehocken St., 215-438-1861, ebenezermaxwellmansion.org (Walk 28)

The Franklin Institute 222 N. 20th St., 215-448-1200, fi.edu (Walk 4)

History of Italian Immigration Museum 1834 E. Passyunk Ave., 215-334-8882, filitaliainternational.com (Walk 23)

Independence Seaport Museum 211 S. Columbus Blvd., 215-413-8655, phillyseaport.org (Walk 15)

Mummers Museum 1100 S. Second St., 215-336-3050, mummersmuseum.com (Walk 24)

Museum of the American Revolution 101 S. Third St., 215-253-6731, amrevmuseum.org (Walk 17)

Mütter Museum of the College of Physicians of Philadelphia 19 S. 22nd St., 215-560-8564, muttermuseum.org (Walk 7)

National Constitution Center 525 Arch St., 215-409-6600, constitutioncenter.org (Walk 1)

National Museum of American Jewish History 101 S. Independence Mall E., 215-923-3811, nmajh.org (Walk 16)

The Philadelphia Contributionship 212 S. Fourth St., contributionship.com (Walk 17)

Philadelphia Doll Museum 2253 N. Broad St., 215-787-0220 (Walk 9)

Philadelphia History Museum at the Atwater Kent 15 S. Seventh St., 215-685-4830, philadelphiahistory.org (Walk 3)

Philadelphia Museum of Art 2600 Benjamin Franklin Pkwy., 215-763-8100, philamuseum.org (Walk 4)

Please Touch Museum 4231 Avenue of the Republic, 215-581-3181, pleasetouchmuseum.org (Walk 30)

Presbyterian Historical Society 425 Lombard St., 215-627-1852, history.pcusa.org (Walk 17)

Rodin Museum 2151 Benjamin Franklin Pkwy., 215-763-8100, rodinmuseum.org (Walk 5)

Rosenbach Museum and Library 2008–2010 Delancey Place, 215-732-1600, rosenbach.org (Walk 6)

Ruth and Raymond G. Perelman Building Fairmount and Pennsylvania Aves., 215-763-8100, philamuseum.org (Walk 5)

Thomas W. Evans Museum and Dental Institute 4001 Spruce St., dental.upenn.edu (Walk 26)

The University of Pennsylvania Museum of Archaeology and Anthropology (Penn Museum) 3260 South St., 215-898 4000, penn.museum (Walk 25)

Wells Fargo History Museum 123 S. Broad St., 215-670-6123, wellsfargohistory.com /museums/Philadelphia (Walk 10)

Notable Architecture

30th Street Station 2955 Market St., 800-USA-RAIL, amtrak.com (Walk 26)

Bergdoll Mansion 2201 Green St. (Walk 20)

Comcast Center 1701 John F. Kennedy Blvd., 215-496-1810, themarketandshopsatcomcastcenter.com (Walk 13)

Curtis Building 601 Walnut St., 800-627-3999, keystonepropertygroup.com (Walk 21)

Delaware Power Station 1325 Beach St. (Walk 19)

Divine Lorraine Hotel 699 N. Broad St., thedivinelorrainehotel.com (Walk 8)

English Village S. 22nd St. and St. James Place (Walk 7)

Fairmount Park Welcome Center 1599 John F. Kennedy Blvd., 215-683-0246, tinyurl.com/fairmountwelcomecenter (Walk 4)

Former home of director David Lynch 2429 Aspen St. (Walk 20)

Former Stetson Mansion 1717 Spring Garden St. (Walk 20)

Guild House 711 Spring Garden St. (Walk 18)

Horace Jayne house 320 S. 19th St. (Walk 6)

Icon 1616 Walnut St., 844-483-9141, icon1616.com (Walk 21)

The Inquirer Building 400 N. Broad St. (Walk 8)

Mount Pleasant Mansion Mount Pleasant Drive, 215-685-0274, parkcharms.org (Walk 30)

Neill and Mauran Houses 315–17 S. 22nd St. (Walk 7)

One and Two Liberty Place 1650 Market St., 215-851-9000, phillyfromthetop.com (Walk 13)

Paul Peck Alumni Center 3140–3142 Market St., 215-895-2586, drexel.edu/alumni/about/peck (Walk 26)

The Public Ledger Building 149 S. Sixth St. (Walk 21)

Rafsnyder-Welsh House 1923 Spruce St. (Walk 6)

Second Bank of the United States 420 Chestnut St. (Walk 1)

Society Hill Towers 200–220 Locust St. (Walk 17)

U.S. Custom House 211 Chestnut St., tinyurl.com/uscustomhouse (Walk 17)

Wanamaker Building (now Macy's) 1300 Market St., 215-241-9000, macys.com/philadelphia-pa (Walk 12)

The Witherspoon Building 1319–1323 Walnut St. (Walk 21)

Parks, Gardens, and Green Spaces

Aviator Park Race and N. 20th Sts. (Walk 4)

Capitolo Playground 900 Federal St., 215-685-1883 (Walk 23)

Cianfrani Park Fitzwater and South Eighth Sts. (Walk 24)

Clark Park 4300 Baltimore Ave., 215-568-0830, friendsofclarkpark.org (Walk 25)

Doughboy Park N. Second and Spring Garden Sts. (Walk 18)

Eakins Oval 2451 Benjamin Franklin Parkway, 215-607-3477, theovalphl.org (Walk 4)

Fairmount Park Horticulture Center 100 North Horticultural Drive, 215-685-0096, phila.gov (Walk 30)

Fitler Square 23rd and Pine Sts., fitlersquare.org (Walk 7)

Franklin Square 200 N. Sixth St., 215-629-4026, historicphiladelphia.org/franklin-square (Walk 15)

John F. Collins Park 1707 Chestnut St., 215-440-5500, ccdparks.org/john-f-collins-park (Walk 13)

Liberty Lands Park 913 N. Third St., 215-627-6562, nlna.org/liberty-lands (Walk 18)

Logan Square Vine Street Expressway and Benjamin Franklin Parkway, tinyurl.com/logansquarephilly (Walk 4)

Louis I. Kahn Park S. 11th and Pine Sts., kahnpark.org (Walk 21)

Love Park 15th St. and John F. Kennedy Blvd. (Walk 4)

Manayunk Wall Starting at Levering St. and Cresson St. (Walk 27)

Penn Treaty Park 1199 N. Delaware Ave., penntreatypark.org (Walk 19)

Perelman Quadrangle 215-898-5552, vpul.upenn.edu/perelmanquad (Walk 26)

The Philadelphia Zoo 3400 W. Girard Ave., 215-243-1100, philadelphiazoo.org (Walk 30)

Pretzel Park 4300 Silverwood St., manayunkcouncil.org/pretzel (Walk 27)

Race Street Pier Race St. and N. Columbus Blvd., 215-922-2386, delawareriverwaterfront.com (Walk 15)

Rittenhouse Square 18th and Walnut Sts., 267-586-5675, friendsofrittenhouse.org (Walk 6)

Roberto Clemente Park 19th and Wallace Sts., friendsofclemente.blogspot.com (Walk 20)

Schuylkill River Park 300 S. 25th St., fsrp.org (Walk 7)

Sedgley Woods Historic Disc Golf Course North 33rd and Oxford Sts., sedgleywoods.com (Walk 30)

Shofuso Japanese House and Garden Lansdowne Drive and Horticultural Drive, japanesehouse.org (Walk 30)

The Singing Fountain 11th Street and East Passyunk Avenue (Walk 23)

Sister Cities Park 218 N. 18th St., 215-440-5500, ccdparks.org/sister-cities-park (Walk 4)

Smith Memorial Playground and Playhouse 3500 Reservoir Drive, 215-765-4325, smithplayground.org (Walk 30)

Spruce Street Harbor Park Columbus Blvd. and Spruce St., 215-922-2386, delawareriverwaterfront.com (Walk 15)

Vernon Park 5800 Germantown Ave. (Walk 28)

Washington Square Walnut St. between Sixth and Seventh Sts., 215-965-2305, nps.gov/inde (Walks 3 and 21)

Weccacoe Playground 400 Catharine St. (Walk 24)

Wissahickon Valley Park McCallum Street between West Mermaid Lane and West Allens Lane, 215-247-0417, fow.org (Walk 29)

The Woodlands 4000 Woodland Ave., 215-386-2181, woodlandsphila.org (Walk 25)

Public Art

Note: Unless otherwise noted, all murals were completed by the **Philadelphia Mural Arts Program,** 215-685-0750, muralarts.org.

The Atlas of Tomorrow: A Device for Philosophical Reflection South and Juniper Sts. (Walk 22)

Billiards: A Tribute to Edward "Chick" Davis 1412 South St. (Walk 22)

Brushstroke Group 30 S. 17th St. For more information, contact the Association for Public Art, 215-546-7550, associationforpublicart.org. (Walk 13)

Building Brotherhood: Engaging Males of Color 4008 Chestnut St. (Walk 26)

Catholic Total Abstinence Union Fountain   Avenue of the Republic and States St. (Walk 30)

The Clothespin   1500 Market St. For more information, contact the Association for Public Art, 215-546-7550, associationforpublicart.org. (Walk 13)

Colors of Light: Gateway to Chinatown   247 N. 12th St. (Walk 2)

Common Threads   N. Broad and Spring Garden Sts. (Walk 8)

Communion between a Rock and a Hard Place   4129 Woodland Ave., 989-621-1934, warriorwriters.org (Walk 25)

The Evolving Face of Nursing   N. Broad and Vine Sts. (Walk 8)

Famous Franks   347 S. 13th St., wrapped around Dirty Frank's. For more information about the bar, call 215-732-5010 or visit dirtyfranksbar.com. (Walk 14)

Finding Home   21 S. 13th St., wrapped around a building managed by Project H.O.M.E. For information about the nonprofit, call 215-232-7272 or visit projecthome.org. (Walk 14)

Garden of Delight   203 S. Sartain St. (Walk 14)

Growth of a Metropolis   251 N. Third St. (Walk 16)

Harmony and the Window of Curiosities   770 S. Fourth St. (Walk 22)

Henry Ossawa Tanner: Letters of Influence   2019 N. College Ave. (Walk 20)

History of Chinatown   N. 10th and Winter Sts. (Walk 2)

How to Turn Anything into Something Else   207 N. Broad St. (Walk 8)

How We Fish   125 N. Eighth St. (Walk 2)

Independence Starts Here   216 N. Broad St. (Walk 8)

Legacy   707 Chestnut St., on the side of an apartment building (Walk 14)

Legendary   512 S. Broad St. (Walk 22)

Lotus Diamond   1228 Frankford Ave. (Walk 19)

Municipal Services Building   1401 John F. Kennedy Blvd., 215-686-8686, phila.gov (Walk 8)

Mural of Paul Robeson   4500 Chestnut St. (Walk 26)

Old City   44 S. Second St. (Walk 16)

Pathology of Devotion   1644 E. Passyunk Ave. (Walk 23)

Pedal Thru (Bikin' in the O-Zone)   200 Spring Garden St. (Walk 18)

Philadelphia Muses   1235 Locust St., on the side of a private property (Walk 14)

Philadelphia's Magic Gardens   1020 South St., 215-733-0390, phillymagicgardens.org (Walks 14 and 22)

Philos Adelphos   440 Poplar St. (Walk 18)

Pride and Progress 1315 Spruce St. (Walk 14)

Sandy's Dream 4368 Cresson Ave., tinyurl.com/sandysdream (Walk 27)

Spring 1315 Pine St. (Walk 14)

Taste of Summer 1312 Spruce St., on the side wall of Vetri Ristorante (Walk 14)

Tree of Knowledge 1301 Market St. (Walk 14)

Tribute to Jackie Robinson 2803 N. Broad St. (Walk 9)

Voa Nu, Pwisans Nu 4675 Germantown Ave. (Walk 28)

Winter: Crystal Snowscape S. 10th and Bainbridge Sts. (Walk 14)

You Can Be Stronger Than Diabetes 1706 Frankford Ave. (Walk 19)

Religious Institutions

Arch Street Meeting House 320 Arch St., 215-413-1804, archstreetmeetinghouse.org (Walk 3)

Arch Street United Methodist Church 55 N. Broad St., 215-568-6250, archstreetumc.org (Walk 8)

Berean Presbyterian Church 2101 N. Broad St., 215-769-5683, bereanpresbyterian.org (Walk 9)

Broad Street Ministry 315 S. Broad St., 215-735-4847, broadstreetministry.org (Walk 10)

Cathedral Basilica of Saints Peter & Paul 1723 Race St., 215-561-1313, cathedralphila.org (Walk 5)

Chinese Christian Church 225 N. 10th St., 215-627-2360, cccnc.org (Walk 2)

Christ Church 20 N. American St., 215-922-1695, christchurchphila.org (Walks 1, 3, and 16)

The Church of the Crucifixion 620 S. 8th St., 215-922-1128, crucifixionphiladelphia.org (Walk 24)

Church of the Holy Trinity 1904 Walnut St., 215-567-1267, htrit.org (Walk 6)

The Church of Jesus Christ of Latter-day Saints 1739 Vine St., 801-240-1000, lds.org/church/temples (Walk 5)

Circle Mission Church 764–772 S. Broad St., 215-735-3917 (Walk 11)

Congregation Mikveh Israel 44 N. Fourth St., 215-922-5446, mikvehisrael.org (Walk 16)

Congregation Rodeph Shalom 615 N. Broad St., 215-627-6747, rodephshalom.org (Walk 8)

First Presbyterian Church 410–22 Girard Ave. (Walk 19)

The First Presbyterian Church 201 S. 21st St., 215-567-0532, fpcphila.org (Walk 21)

First Unitarian Church of Philadelphia 2125 Chestnut St., 215-563-3980, philauu.org (Walk 7)

Fo Shou Temple 1015 Cherry St., 215-928-0592, phillytemple.tripod.com/index.html (Walk 2)

Free Quaker Meeting House 500 Arch St., 215-629-5801, nps.gov/inde (Walk 1)

Gloria Dei (Old Swedes' Episcopal Church) 916 S. Swanson St., 215-389-1513, old-swedes.org (Walk 24)

Greater Exodus Baptist Church 714 N. Broad St., 215-235-1394, gebch.com (Walk 8)

Highway Tabernacle 1801 Spring Garden St., 215-563-9192, highwaytabernacle.org (Walk 20)

Historic St. George's United Methodist Church 235 N. Fourth St., 215-925-7788, historicstgeorges.org (Walk 16)

Holy Spirit Adoration Sisters 2212 Green St., 215-567-0123, adorationsisters.org (Walk 20)

Kensington Methodist Church 300 Richmond St., 215-634-2495 (Walk 19)

Lutheran Church of the Holy Communion 2110 Chestnut St., 215-567-3668, lc-hc.org (Walk 7)

Masjid al-Jamia Mosque 4228 Walnut St., 267-275-8087 (Walk 26)

Masonic Temple 1 N. Broad St., 215-968-1917, pamasonictemple.org (Walk 8)

Mennonite Meeting House and Cemetery 6119 Germantown Ave., 215-843-0943, meetinghouse.info (Walk 28)

Mother Bethel African Methodist Episcopal Church 419 S. Sixth St., 215-925-0616, motherbethel.org (Walk 3)

The National Shrine of St. John Neumann 1019 N. Fifth St., 215-627-3080, stjohnneumann.org (Walk 18)

National Shrine of St. Rita of Cascia and St. Rita's Church 1166 S. Broad St., 215-546-8333, saintritashrine.org (Walk 11)

Old Pine Street Church 412 Pine St., 215-925-8051, oldpine.org (Walk 17)

Old St. Joseph's Church 321 Willings Alley, 215-923-1733, oldstjoseph.org (Walk 17)

Old St. Mary's Church 252 S. Fourth St., 215-923-7930, oldstmary.com (Walk 17)

Philadelphia Episcopal Cathedral 23 S. 38th St., 215-386-0234, philadelphiacathedral.org (Walk 26)

Philadelphia Holy Redeemer Chinese Catholic Church and School 915 Vine St., 215-922-0999, holyredeemer.cc (Walk 2)

Radha Krishna Temple 41 W. Allens Lane, 215-247-4825, iskconphiladelphia.com (Walk 29)

St. Agatha–St. James Roman Catholic Church 3728 Chestnut St., 267-787-5000, saintsaj.org (Walk 26)

Saint Andrew's Russian Orthodox Cathedral N. Fifth St. and Fairmount Ave., 215-627-3338, saintandrewscathedral.org (Walk 18)

St. Augustine Church 243 N. Lawrence St., 215-627-1838, st-augustinechurch.com (Walk 16)

St. David's Episcopal Church 150 Dupont St., 215-482-2345, stdavidsmanayunk.org (Walk 27)

St. Francis Xavier Church 2319 Green St., 215-765-4568, sfxoratory.org (Walk 20)

St. John the Baptist Roman Catholic Church 146 Rector St., 215-482-4600, stjohnmanayunk.org (Walk 27)

St. Josaphat Roman Catholic Church 124 Cotton St. (Walk 27)

St. Laurentius Roman Catholic Church 1600 E. Berks St. (Walk 19)

St. Mary Magdalen de Pazzi 712 Montrose St.; St. Paul Church, 923 Christian St.; 215-923-0355; stpaulparish.net (Walk 23)

Saint Michael the Archangel Orthodox Church 335 Fairmount Ave., 215-627-6148, saintmichaelsroc.org (Walk 18)

St. Michael's Lutheran Church 6671 Germantown Ave., 215-848-0199, stmichaelsgermantown.org (Walk 29)

St. Peter's Church 313 Pine St., 215-925-5968, stpetersphila.org (Walk 17)

St. Philip Neri Church 220–228 Queen St., 215-468-1922, stphilipneriqueenvillage.org (Walk 24)

St. Stanislaus Church 242 Fitzwater St., 215-468-1922, stphilipneriqueenvillage.org (Walk 24)

Tabernacle United Church 3700 Chestnut St., 215-386-4100, tabunited.org (Walk 26)

Temple Beth Zion–Beth Israel Synagogue 1800–1804 Spruce St. (Walk 6)

Trinity Lutheran Church 5300 Germantown Ave., 215-848-8150 (Walk 28)

Trinity Memorial Church 2200 Spruce St., trinityphiladelphia.org (Walk 7)

Ukrainian Catholic Cathedral 830 N. Franklin St., 215-922-2845, ukrcathedral.com (Walk 18)

University Lutheran Church 3637 Chestnut St., 215-387-2885, uniluphila.org (Walk 26)

Shopping

Boyd's 1818 Chestnut St., 215-564-9000, boydsphila.com (Walk 21)

Crash Bang Boom 528 S. Fourth St., 215-928-1123, crashbangboomonline.com (Walk 22)

Giovanni's Room 345 S. 12th St., 215-923-2960, queerbooks.com (Walk 12)

M. Finkel & Daughter 936 Pine St., 215-627-7797, samplings.com (Walk 21)

Maxie's Daughter 724 S. Fourth St., 215-829-2226 (Walk 24)

Reading Terminal Market 51 N. 12th St., 215-922-2317, readingterminalmarket.org (Walk 12)

The Schmidt's Commons 1001 N. Second St., 215-825-7552, theschmidtscommons.com (Walk 18)

Sullivan Progress Plaza 1501 N. Broad St., 215-232-7070, progressplaza.com (Walk 9)

Miscellaneous

12th Street Gym 204 S. 12th St., 215-985-4092, 12streetgym.com (Walk 12)

Benjamin Franklin Bridge 856-968-3300, drpa.org (Walk 15)

Boathouse Row 1 Boathouse Row, 215-685-3936, boathouserow.org (Walk 30)

Commodore Barry Club (Philadelphia Irish Center) 6815 Emlen St., 215-843-8051, theirishcenter.com (Walk 29)

Former home of Thomas Eakins 1729 Mt. Vernon St. Now the headquarters of Philadelphia Mural Arts, 215-685-0750, muralarts.org. (Walk 20)

Germantown Home 6950 Germantown Ave., 215-848-3306, germantownhome.org (Walk 29)

The Gershman Y 401 S. Broad St., 215-545-4400, gershmany.org (Walk 10)

G.J. Littlewood and Son Textile Mill 4045 Main St., 215-483-3970, littlewooddyers.com (Walk 27)

Kensington Soup Society 1036 Crease St. (Walk 19)

Lutheran Settlement House 1340 Frankford Ave., 215-426-8610, lutheransettlement.org (Walk 19)

Palumbo Playground and Recreation Center 700 S. Ninth St., 215-592-6007, palumborec.org (Walk 23)

Penn Medicine 800-789-7366, pennmedicine.org (Walk 26)

Pennsylvania Convention Center 1101 Arch St., 215-418-4700, paconvention.com (Walk 12)

Pennsylvania Hospital 800 Spruce St., 215-829-3000, pennmedicine.org (Walk 21)

Philadelphia Interfaith Hospitality Network 7047 Germantown Ave., 215-247-4663, philashelter.org (Walk 29)

The Philadelphia Sketch Club 235 S. Camac St., 215-545-9298, sketchclub.org (Walk 12)

The Plastic Club 247 S. Camac St., 215-545-9324, plasticclub.org (Walk 12)

Project Home/JBJ Soul Homes 1415 Fairmount Ave. and 1515 Fairmount Ave., 215-232-7272, projecthome.org (Walk 20)

South Philadelphia Sports Complex 3300 S. Seventh St. (Walk 10)

The University City Science Center 3711 Market St., 215-966-6000, sciencecenter.org (Walk 26)

Weavers Way Co-op 559 Carpenter Lane, 215-843-2350, weaversway.coop (Walk 29)

Wills Eye Hospital 840 Walnut St., 215-928-3000, willseye.org (Walk 21)

Appendix III: Sources of Information

Websites

Association for Public Art associationforpublicart.org

Atlas Obscura atlasobscura.com

Center City District centercityphila.org

City of Philadelphia phila.gov

Curbed Philly philly.curbed.com

The Delaware River Blog delawareriver.net

Discover Philadelphia discoverphl.com

Eater Philly philly.eater.com

The Encyclopedia of Greater Philadelphia philadelphiaencyclopedia.org

Explore Pennsylvania History, part of the Commonwealth's Department of Community and Economic Development explorepahistory.com

Fairmount Park Conservancy myphillypark.org

Free Library of Philadelphia freephilly.org

Friends of Wissahickon fow.org

Greater Philadelphia Cultural Alliance philaculture.org

Hidden City Philadelphia hiddencityphila.org

Historic Houses of Fairmount Park parkcharms.com

Historic Philadelphia historicphiladelphia.org

Independence Hall Association ushistory.org

Independence Visitor Center phlvisitorcenter.com

Kenneth W. Milano kennethwmilano.com

Naked Philly ocfrealty.com/naked-philly

Philadelphia phillymag.com

Philadelphia Business News bizjournals.com/philadelphia

Philadelphia Church Project phillychurchproject.com

The Philadelphia Gayborhood Guru thegayborhood.guru.wordpress.com

Philadelphia History Museum philadelphiahistory.org

***The Philadelphia Inquirer, The Philadelphia Daily News,* and Philly.com** philly.com

Philadelphia Mural Arts Program muralarts.org

Philadelphia Public Art philart.net

Philadelphia's Magic Gardens phillymagicgardens.org

PhilaPlace philaplace.org

Philebrity philebrity.com

PhillyMuralPics.com phillymuralpics.com

PlanPhilly planphilly.com

South Street Headhouse District southstreet.com

Southwark Historical Society southwarkhistory.org

Spirit News spiritnews.org

Visit Philadelphia visitphilly.org

Wee Wander wee-wander.com

WHYY whyy.org

Print Sources

Avery, Ron. *City of Brotherly Mayhem: Philadelphia Crimes & Criminals.* Philadelphia: Otis Books, 1997.

Cooper, George. *Poison Widows: A True Story of Witchcraft, Arsenic, and Murder.* New York: Thomas Dunne Books, 1999.

Dubin, Murray. *South Philadelphia: Mummers, Memories, and the Melrose Diner.* Philadelphia: Temple University Press, 1996.

Gallery, John Andrew. *Philadelphia Architecture: A Guide to the City.* Philadelphia: Paul Dry Books, 2016.

Graham, Kristen A. *A History of the Pennsylvania Hospital.* Charleston, SC: The History Press, 2008.

Jarvis, Elizabeth Farmer. *Images of America: Mount Airy.* Charleston, SC: Arcadia Publishing, 2008.

Kyriakodis, Harry. *Northern Liberties: The Story of a Philadelphia River Ward.* Charleston, SC: The History Press, 2012.

Litchman, Lori. *A Philadelphia Story: Founders and Famous Families from the City of Brotherly Love.* Covington, KY: Clerisy Press, 2016.

Milano, Kenneth W. *Remembering Kensington & Fishtown: Philadelphia's Riverward Neighborhoods.* Charleston, SC: The History Press, 2008.

Nickels, Thom. *Images of America: Manayunk.* Charleston, SC: Arcadia Publishing, 2001.

Northern Liberties Neighbors Association. *Guide to Northern Liberties.* Philadelphia: Northern Liberties Neighbors Association, 1982.

O'Toole, Lawrence. *Fading Ads of Philadelphia*. Charleston, SC: The History Press, 2012.

Ristine, James D. *Philadelphia's Fairmount Park*. Charleston, SC: Arcadia Publishing, 2005.

Skaler, Robert Morris. *Images of America: Philadelphia's Broad Street, South and North*. Charleston, SC: Arcadia Publishing, 2003.

Skaler, Robert Morris and Thomas H. Keels. *Images of America: Philadelphia's Rittenhouse Square*. Charleston, SC: Arcadia Publishing, 2008.

Skaler, Robert Morris. *Images of America: Society Hill and Old City*. Charleston, SC: Arcadia Publishing, 2005.

Skaler, Robert Morris. *Images of America: West Philadelphia, University City to 52nd Street*. Charleston, SC: Arcadia Publishing, 2002.

Smith, Irina and Ann Hazan. *The Original Philadelphia Neighborhood Cookbook*. Philadelphia: Camino Books, 1988.

Vance, Patricia. *Intimate Bicycle Tours of Philadelphia*. Philadelphia: University of Pennsylvania Press, 2004.

Wurman, Richard Saul and John Andrew Gallery. *Man-Made Philadelphia: A Guide to Its Physical and Cultural Environment*. Cambridge, MA: The MIT Press, 1972.

Spruce Street Harbor Park
(Walk 15, page 104)

Index

About the Author

Freelance journalist **Natalie Pompilio** lives and writes in a house on an alley off an alley in South Philadelphia. A former staff writer with *The Philadelphia Inquirer* and *The Philadelphia Daily News,* she loves hearing and telling stories. Her idea of a perfect night is sitting on her roof deck at dusk with her husband, Jordan Barnett, their two cats, and a bottle of wine while watching the chimney swifts emerge for their nightly dance.

This is her third book featuring Philadelphia. *More Philadelphia Murals and the Stories They Tell,* with coauthors Jane Golden and Robin Race, was released by Temple University Press in 2006. She partnered with New Orleans photographer Jennifer Zdon (twirlphotography.com) to self-publish the children's alphabet book *Philadelphia A to Z* in 2010. Find her work at nataliepompilio.com.

About the Photographer

Tricia Pompilio is a lifestyle and portrait photographer based in Philadelphia. After 15 years in television, she decided to focus on her children and her photography. When she's not following her husband, Vince Savarese, and their three daughters—Fiona, Luna, and Poppy—with a camera, she's probably re-reading Harry Potter 1–7 with her two black cats while Rob Thomas sings softly in the background. To see her work, visit instagram.com/triciapphotography.